Cloth in West African History

The African Archaeology Series

The African Archaeology Series offers comprehensive, up-to-date syntheses of current research on the African cultural past. Though the essence of each volume comes from archaeology, they are equally dependent upon examination of the anthropological and historical records, in order to explore the African experience and the place of the African past and lifeways in the broader world. This series permits Africanists an opportunity to transform field investigations into more general syntheses, giving context and meaning to bare bones archaeological reports, utilizing innovative methods for comprehending, as well as explaining, the past.

Series Editor: Joseph O. Vogel (University of Alabama)

Books in the Series:
· Chapurukha Kusimba, *The Rise and Fall of Swahili States* (1999)
· Michael Bisson, S. Terry Childs, Philip de Barros, Augustin F. C. Holl, *Ancient African Metallurgy: The Socio-Cultural Context* (2000)
· Innocent Pikirayi, *The Zimbabwe Culture: Origins and Decline of Southern Zambezian States* (2001)
· Sibel Barut Kusimba, *African Foragers: Environment, Technology, Interactions* (2002)
· J. D. Lewis-Williams and D. G. Pearce, *San Spirituality: Roots, Expression, and Social Consequences* (2004)
· Peter Mitchell, *African Connections: The Archaeology of Africa's External Interactions* (2005)
· Colleen E. Kriger, *Cloth in West African History* (2006)

Submission Guidelines:
Prospective authors of single or coauthored books and editors of anthologies should submit a letter of introduction, the manuscript, or a four to ten page proposal, a book outline, and a curriculum vitae. Please send your book manuscript or proposal packet to:

The African Archaeology Series
AltaMira Press
4501 Forbes Blvd., Suite 200
Lanham, MD 20706

Cloth in West African History

Colleen E. Kriger

Foreword by Graham Connah

A Division of
ROWMAN & LITTLEFIELD PUBLISHERS, INC.
Lanham • New York • Toronto • Oxford

AltaMira Press
A division of Rowman & Littlefield Publishers, Inc.
A wholly owned subsidiary of The Rowman & Littlefield Publishing Group, Inc.
4501 Forbes Boulevard, Suite 200
Lanham, MD 20706
www.altamirapress.com

PO Box 317, Oxford OX2 9RU, UK

British Library Cataloguing in Publication Information Available

Library of Congress Cataloging-in-Publication Data

Kriger, Colleen E.
    Cloth in West African history / Colleen E. Kriger.
        p.   cm.
    Includes bibliographical references and index.
    ISBN-13: 978-0-7591-0421-1 (cloth : alk. paper)
    ISBN-10: 0-7591-0421-2 (cloth : alk. paper)
    ISBN-13: 978-0-7591-0422-8 (pbk. : alk. paper)
    ISBN-10: 0-7591-0422-0 (pbk. : alk. paper)
    1. Cotton manufacture—Africa, West—History.   2. Cotton fabrics—Africa,
    West.   I. Title.
    TS1565.A4K75 2006
    677.00966—dc22

                                                              2005025535

Printed in the United States of America

♾™ The paper used in this publication meets the minimum requirements of
American National Standard for Information Sciences—Permanence of Paper for
Printed Library Materials, ANSI/NISO Z39.48-1992.

To Solange Kowert

Contents

Figures, Tables, and Maps

FIGURES

TABLES

MAPS

Foreword

It is relatively uncommon for historians to use physical evidence as a focus for their analysis of the African past. Colleen Kriger has already shown herself to be one of the exceptions in her previous book *Pride of Men: Ironworking in 19th Century West Central Africa* (1999); now she has done it again with a very different topic involving a very different part of Africa. This book is concerned with the history of cloth in West Africa, particularly in the Lower Niger region and along the Guinea Coast. It is a subject on which there is already substantial literature that reflects the important role played by textiles, both indigenous and imported, in technological, economic, social, and even religious and political matters of the region. However, Colleen Kriger starts with the cloth, rather than the history. In an unusual approach, she selects three contrasting examples of textile production and uses each of them as a starting point for her discussion of major aspects of the subject: first, vertical-loom-produced cloth with brocaded and other woven decoration; second, treadle-loom-woven strip cloth made into tailored garments with embroidered decoration; and third, the resist dyeing of cloth using indigo. In developing this discussion she draws on a wide variety of sources: the technology of the textiles themselves, using evidence from museum collections in Britain, Europe, and North America; a considerable amount of documentary evidence, including important ethnohistorical photography; oral traditions; linguistics; botany; and archaeology. Nevertheless, it is the physical evidence that remains the center of attention. As she suggests at the end of her first chapter, "This book is best seen as a translation of textiles—turning evidence gleaned from their visual and material features into written narratives—so that the history within them can be read by all."

Basically this is a work of synthesis, demonstrating yet again that our sources for understanding the history of Africa are too varied for the subject to be left to conventional historians alone. In this respect, Africanist scholarship has something to contribute to the world in general. This is a necessity for a far broader approach to understanding the African (and human) past than "history" in its strictest sense can provide; indeed, the connotations of that word, *history*, are such that perhaps we need a new umbrella term for a range of investigations that increasingly draw on any data that can throw light on the past. Certainly we need studies of the past that take their points of departure from different aspects of that data, as this book does. Museum collections of African ethnography in many parts of the world constitute archives of physical evidence about the African past that still appear to be underused. It is to be hoped that others will follow Colleen Kriger's contributions to changing this situation.

One thing that is apparent from this book is that we do need every bit of evidence that we can lay our hands on in order to pull together even the most basic account of textiles in the West African past. The author demonstrates all too clearly how little we know for certain about this important subject. It seems that there are almost more questions than answers. For instance, how old is textile production in West Africa? Why was the vertical loom used in only some parts of the region? What and when was the origin of the treadle loom that was used in other parts? At what date was cotton first used in spinning and weaving? Is it possible that wool was used at an earlier date? How did the art of dyeing reach such high standards in certain areas? Which was more significant, the influence of imported textiles on the indigenous industry or the influence of local textiles on the acceptability of imported textiles? These and other questions offer a range of challenges to future researchers.

Amongst those who certainly deserve to be challenged in this respect are members of my own profession, archaeologists who have so far contributed very little to studies of ancient textiles in West Africa and their manufacture. Apart from the indirect evidence of Nok terra-cottas, and Ife and Benin brasses, the only significant primary data available for discussion in this book has been provided by excavations at Igbo-Ukwu, Benin City, and the Bandiagara escarpment. As the excavator of the Benin textiles, in 1963, perhaps I should comment on this situation. The specimens concerned came from over forty feet below the ground surface, in a narrow well-like cistern dug into the Benin sands to a depth of fifty-seven feet, and were recovered from amongst and above a mass burial of at least forty-one young women. Although understated at the time and in subsequent publications, the conditions of excavation (done principally by Umaru Gol and myself) were dangerous and very unpleasant. However, the cloth fragments had survived because of the damp anaerobic condition of the deposit in which they were found, in spite of the quite justified reputation of the Benin sands and the humid Benin climate for destroying organic remains. In short, the recovery of these textile fragments (one of which is illustrated in this book) was something of an archaeological triumph, particularly as the only means of conserving them at the time was to seal the fragments immediately between small sheets of window glass. The disappointing thing was that subsequently nobody noticed. Colleen Kriger's use of this evidence is, to the best of my knowledge, the first time that its technical significance has been discussed, over forty years since its excavation and thirty years after its full publication—together with a specialist report from a modern textile researcher—in my book *The Archaeology of Benin* (1975).

This lack of reaction until now could explain the subsequent general failure of archaeologists working in West Africa to recover further textile remains (except for the remarkable Bandiagara evidence). If nobody is really interested in textile remains, why should archaeologists bother? The fact is that there are a number of circumstances in which textiles might survive and be excavated, provided that archaeological research plans are targeted appropriately and that excavators are adequately equipped to deal with what are usually extremely delicate fragments. The first such circumstance, as implied above, is evident in sites similar to that in Benin City, which was a site of waterlogged nonoxygenated deposits sealed deep below the present surface. The cistern in which the Benin fragments were found was only one of several excavated in the early 1960s, and cistern digging was formerly widely practiced in southern Nigeria and perhaps other parts of West Africa. There must surely be many undiscovered cisterns, some of which might contain textiles? With the aid of open-area excavation and ground-penetrating radar or magnetic survey, it should be possible to locate some of them. Furthermore, given modern radiometric dating that can now handle very small samples, any recovered textile fragments could be directly dated with an accuracy impossible four decades ago. Other waterlogged deposits, such as lake sediments and swamps, particularly if adjacent to old settlements, could also repay investigation, although the logistics of excavation are likely to need careful attention. Yet another possibility is that textile fragments might have survived in the primary silts of some of the many earthwork ditches that formerly surrounded numerous settlements, and far more of these ditches need to be sectioned than has yet been the case.

The second of the circumstances in which textiles might survive is provided by preservation due to contact with copper corrosion, as was the case at Igbo-Ukwu. It is a possibility to which archaeologists ought to give close attention when excavating artifacts of copper or copper alloy, instead of merely concentrating on art-historical matters. Admittedly, such artifacts are usually found by accident rather than systematic search, making controlled recovery unlikely, but there are ways of overcoming this problem.

In particular, the excavation of burial sites, especially in the drier savanna margins of the Sahara, has the potential to produce textile fragments, as has recently occurred at Kissi, in Burkina Faso, where both copper and iron corrosion preserved small pieces.

The third circumstance in which textile fragments can survive relies on conditions such as are found in dry cave or rockshelter deposits, as was the case on the Bandiagara escarpment. In the desert itself and on its edges, there must be sites that would present suitable conditions and would repay investigation. As with the other possibilities for finding textiles, archaeologists need to look harder. Also relevant is the recovery of indirect archaeological evidence, such as spindle whorls, dye pits or pots, and cotton pollen or phytoliths. There is indeed some discussion of spindle whorls in this book, but a comprehensive survey of excavated examples in West Africa, together with dating evidence, could prove informative.

I suspect that other sources of evidence for past West African textiles might also repay a more targeted research program, as is the case with archaeology. In particular, one wonders just how many more examples of West African textiles are tucked away in museum collections, especially in smaller collections where they might not be expected. It is to be hoped that Colleen Kriger will continue her search, which has already yielded the rich harvest discussed in this book. Artifacts *are* important sources of information about the past, and we should take note of what they have to tell us. As the author says of West African textiles at the end of her book: "They are eloquent webs of time, and they stand as a testimony to the prominent and persistent role of textiles and textile makers in the history and culture of West Africa."

Graham Connah
School of Archaeology and Anthropology
Australian National University
Canberra
5 April 2005

Preface

This is the book I was looking for in my university library over thirty years ago—though I could not have described it then and could not have written it until now. At that time I was a fine arts major with concentrations in painting and weaving. I had noticed that in contrast to the history of art (painting, drawing, sculpture, and architecture), the history of weaving or of craft in general was not formally taught and was poorly represented on the library's shelves. I particularly wanted to know more about West African textiles—how they were made, who made them, and especially why they looked the way they did. That curiosity led me first to Nigeria on a Fulbright grant, and then to many museums in Europe and North America, where I discovered treasures of textiles from all over the world whose histories had yet to be written. This particular history has been a long time in the making, but finally having the opportunity to write it has been deeply satisfying.

Doing justice to the work, the workers, their times, and their worlds has been a methodological challenge. I began developing my analytical toolkit initially as an independent scholar, reading widely and making full use of the generous help offered by individual weavers, spinners, dyers, and the curators of many museums. When I recognized that I needed scholarly training, the Interdisciplinary MA Program at York University, Toronto, provided me with the resources and structure that I needed to develop the research on which parts of this book are based. I remain indebted to the members of that first committee: Dr. Zdenka Volavka (Art History), Dr. Paul Lovejoy (History), Dr. Joan Rayfield (Anthropology), and Andy Tomcik (Graphic Art). For her responsive assistance throughout my MA project and as the external examiner of my completed thesis, I thank Dr. Lisa Golombek, West Asia Department, Royal Ontario Museum, Toronto.

While beginning an entirely new project for my PhD in History, I continued following several lines of inquiry that had arisen from the textile research. Mark Duffill was instrumental in encouraging my study of the Niger Expedition textiles in England, and he assisted me in many ways. I cannot thank him enough. The Pasold Research Fund supported my travel and the publication of my analyses of the collection in *Textile History*. Betsy Eldredge, Ann McDougall, and David Robinson were invaluable readers for the article on textile production and gender that I prepared for the *Journal of African History*, and my fellow graduate students at York, especially Martha Black, Lynn MacKay, Leslie Howsam, Susan Foote, and Sylvie Beaudreau, offered encouragement and help when it was most needed. Paul Lovejoy, Sydney Kanya-Forstner, and Jan Vansina deserve special thanks for mentoring me with good humor and being supporters of my work all along the way.

Writing this book from "inside" the technology and working processes (by focusing on several textile products) has been for me a most satisfying pleasure. For making it possible, and for his genial editorial advice and guidance, I am grateful to Joe Vogel. The four readers who generously combed and commented on the entire manuscript have improved it immensely: thank you to Graham Connah, George Dimock, Joanne Eicher, and Ann O'Hear. To them, to Kevin MacDonald for his helpful suggestions, to Shawn Murray for providing copies of her articles, to Philip Jaggar for his care and patience with my questions about linguistics, and to the many other scholars whose works are listed in the bibliography, I salute you and beg forgiveness for any errors that remain. Janet Stanley and the staff at the National Museum of African Art Library in Washington, DC, helped enormously, as did Gaylor Callahan and the interlibrary loan staff, Jackson Library, University of North Carolina at Greensboro. Thanks also to Dan Smith here at the University of North Carolina, Greensboro, for his professionalism with the photographs and images. Finally, I praise the Middlebrooks and Wilson families for their warmth and inspiration, and Adrienne, Ann, Frank, Françoise, and Oded for their unfailing friendship.

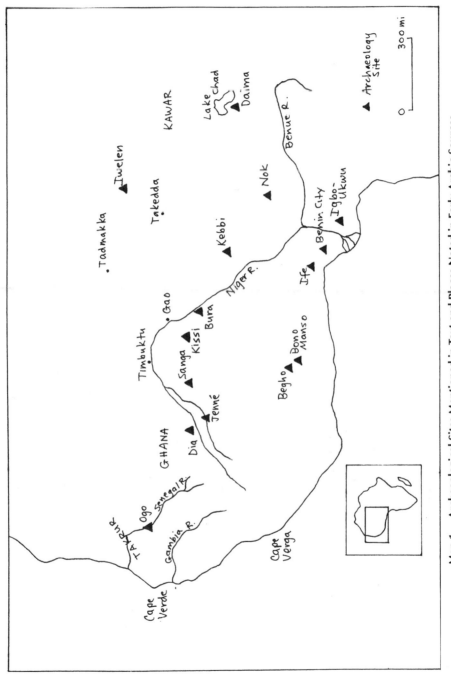

Map 1. Archaeological Sites Mentioned in Text and Places Noted in Early Arabic Sources.

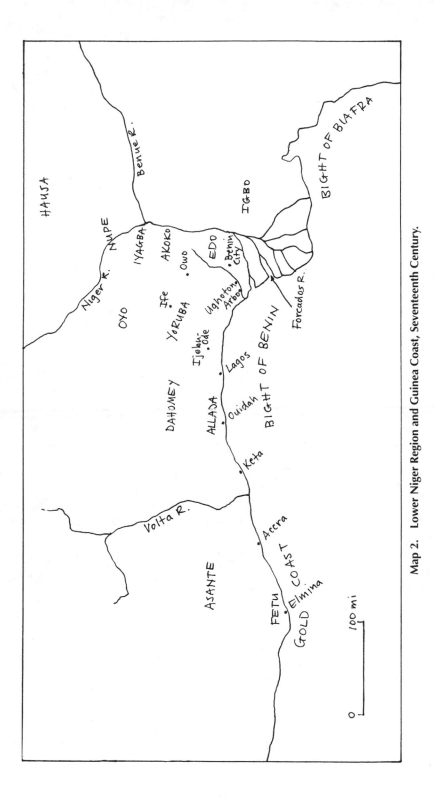

Map 2. Lower Niger Region and Guinea Coast, Seventeenth Century.

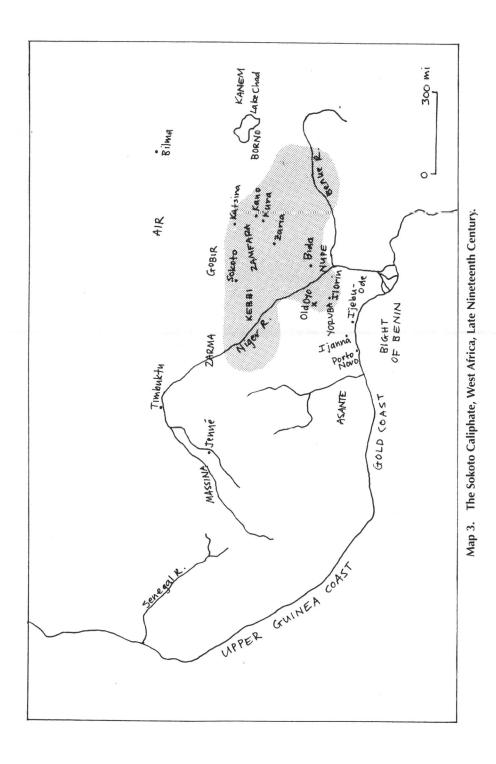

Map 3. The Sokoto Caliphate, West Africa, Late Nineteenth Century.

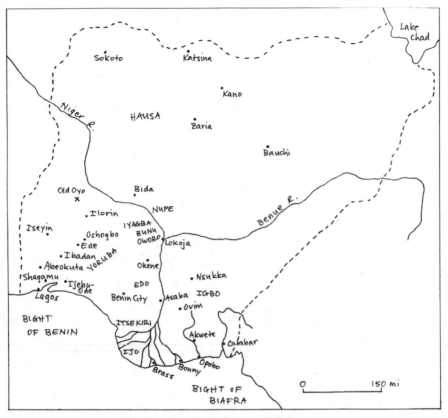

Map 4.   Nigeria, Early Twentieth Century.

1

Cloth in History

The Governors of the forts at *Whydah* are expected to attend [the "annual customs" ceremony of the Dahomey king], and make a present on the occasion; which should consist of at least one piece of Indian damask, or some other handsome silk: the vice-roy of *Whydah*, and the governors of the different towns and provinces, must be there with their presents also, and give an account of their conduct, and of every circumstance which the king wishes to be informed of. They who acquit themselves to his satisfaction, have the honor to receive some mark of his approbation; which is generally a large cotton cloth, manufactured in the *Eyo* [Oyo] country, of excellent workmanship, which they afterwards wear for an upper garment.

—R. Norris, visiting Dahomey's capital, February 1772

As various types of cloth passed through these high-level governmental channels, important relationships were being defined, reinforced, and witnessed. The Dahomey court, which paid yearly tribute to the empire of Oyo at the time this scene was observed, was at the center of the system, accepting presents of Indian silk from their governors on the coast and dispensing cotton cloth from Oyo's looms to other officials and provincial governors as a sign of official sanction and praise. On this special occasion, a political ritual was being dramatized with gifts of cloth, lending those gifts an aura that went well beyond their practical or monetary value.

Reading this late eighteenth-century account now, in the early years of the twenty-first century, it is perhaps inconceivable that a handwoven cotton cloth would be considered a prestigious reward and mark of admirable service to a king. Today we are inundated with cotton fabric, much of it relatively inexpensive, along with an astounding array of other textiles, all produced by power machinery in factories the world over. Modern industrial manufacture has not only transformed the way human labor is thought of and remunerated, but it has also changed our sense of the value of manufactured goods, especially the cloth we wear. In many places, from department stores to open-air markets, textiles are both readily available and easily affordable, and as a consequence they tend to be very much taken for granted. It is therefore instructive and worthwhile to point out, for example, that cotton—which had its beginnings in the tropics—was not always as plentiful as it is today. Indeed, it was once a rare and costly textile fiber in Europe and elsewhere. The transfer of cotton cultivation into other regions of the world, its prominent role in international trade and the rise of plantation slavery, and its central importance in the development of mechanized factory production have all been momentous events in global history.[1] We may currently take cotton for granted, but the scale and pervasiveness of its impact cannot be denied.

Textiles are one of humankind's most essential commodities, and they have much to tell us about peoples and societies worldwide, from ancient times to the present. This book traces a history of cotton cloth in one part of the world over the long term, from a time well before industrialization in Europe up to the twentieth century. Its geographical focus is the region surrounding the lower Niger River basin in West Africa, now known as Nigeria. One of the many reasons this particular place is of great historical interest is its prominent role in the trade, consumption, and manufacture of textiles. It is a place where cotton and other fibers were produced and woven and where textiles were also imported from afar, via caravans that crossed the Sahara and, later on, via merchant ships that plied the seacoast. And as the account quoted above suggests so vividly, it is a place where people's taste for cloth was well cultivated and dramatically displayed. Paying close attention to textiles—how people made, exchanged, and wore them—can offer fresh perspectives on the history of this region and also on the local, regional, and global processes that shaped it.

This book is a work of synthesis, in several respects. First, it presents a holistic approach to the study of textiles and their makers. It spans the periods mentioned above in order to chart the role of cotton in a variety of commercial networks, language communities, and labor contexts. Textiles were significant in numerous ways—socially, politically, economically, culturally, and technologically—and have been studied fruitfully from each of these vantage points. Here, the view is much wider. It has been deliberately broadened to track specific textiles and their features across space and time in order to show how cloth reached into so many realms of human activity. My aim is to demonstrate how multifaceted and multidimensional the significance of cloth has been in this part of West Africa for centuries. Second, the source material for this work includes many different types of historical evidence. Given the prominence of orality in the region's societies prior to the twentieth century, the written documentary record, especially for social and economic matters, is relatively superficial and uneven. Luckily there are other sources. In this case, the evidential base has been expanded to include types of data that may be unfamiliar to some historians, such data types as technical analyses and detailed descriptions of textiles, the names for these textiles and their features, archaeological fragments of cloth, ceramic spindle whorls, other manufacturing tools and raw materials, and so on. As convincing records of people's specific and deliberate acts, discrete remnants such as these from the past can be surprisingly eloquent, especially when gathered together and assessed alongside one another. Moreover, this kind of visual and material evidence can be used not only to fill gaps in the written and oral records, but also to correct information in them that may be erroneous or anachronistic.[2] As a third element of this study's synthetic approach, I have combined some of my own original research with the findings of many other scholars. This study draws on an especially heterogeneous published literature, and one that represents a number of academic specialties, each with its own particular set of intellectual approaches, scholarly debates, and central issues. To represent them all in a comprehensive manner would turn this book into a multivolume encyclopedia.[3] Here, for the sake of accessibility to a broad audience, my intent is to provide an overview of and introduction to the topic at hand and to open up new research questions and lines of inquiry for the future.

COTTON AND WEST AFRICAN HISTORY

Much more is known about textile production and trade in West Africa in the nineteenth and twentieth centuries than in earlier periods. A major stumbling block has been the relative lack of reliable description and documentation of textiles, textile workers, and their workshops, especially before the onset of European colonial expansion in Africa in the mid- to late nineteenth century. Moreover, those writings on the topic that do exist range enormously, being the products of individuals with varied perspectives and occupations. Important observations were made by some of Europe's more exceptional geographical explorers, such as Heinrich Barth and Gustav Nachtigal,[4] but it was not until the period of formal colonial rule in the twentieth century that serious studies devoted specifically to West African textiles began to appear. Major early milestones were *Le coton chez les noirs* by Charles Monteil, who served as a colonial administrator in French West Africa, and the chapters on Asante cloth in *Religion and Art in Ashanti* by Robert Rattray, a captain in the Royal Navy.[5] Accounts describing textile production in Nigeria appeared somewhat later, and they too were usually written by colonial officials.[6] All of these sources remain useful to some degree, though most of them followed the rather static ethnographic models that were influential at the time. They described textiles and their manufacture as they were currently observed and paid little attention to questions about historical change. Monteil, who surveyed the Arabic-language literature, was an exception on this point.

Of course it was cotton's potential as a cash crop for export that interested European merchants and officials the most. Turning Africa into a source of raw cotton for European textile industries was an ongoing imperial desire, starting with promising nineteenth-century reports of cotton growing in abundance in the lower Niger region and elsewhere in West Africa, and continuing with the strategies developed for promoting cotton cultivation during the colonial era. A number of recent historical studies have focused on this important issue, contributing substantially to our knowledge about colonial labor exploitation and coercive taxation policies as well as major transformations in the agricultural sector of African economies during the twentieth century.[7] But as these studies have shown, intensifying the production of cotton and capturing the market for it was far from easy, and it proved to be especially difficult in regions where there was an active indigenous textile industry already in place. At times there was even talk of trying to destroy local textile manufacture, especially in Nigeria, so as to be able to export the entire cotton harvest to Britain, an idea that Marion Johnson dubbed "cotton imperialism."[8] Such plans were hardly more than fleeting fantasies, though, as artisans in Nigeria and other parts of West Africa continued to produce considerable quantities of their own cotton cloth during colonial rule and after.

Seen in this light, as an example of colonial conflict and struggle, the persistence of cotton textile production in West Africa, even in the face of overseas imports and colonial marketing policies, takes on significant political overtones. In the 1970s, Marion Johnson addressed the question of competition in the marketplace between European and African manufactured goods, suggesting that there were several factors that worked to the benefit of local artisan producers. One was the protection offered to inland markets by the high cost of transport, at least until the first decades of colonial rule. Thereafter, some workers might still rely on another factor, which was the comparative advantage they could enjoy because of relatively low wages and other production costs. Diversifying their economic activity helped to create this advantage. As examples, Johnson cited the combination of textile work with farming, where basic subsistence needs would be taken care of, or with trading, which offered other kinds of subsidies. Only when there were alternative occupations with potentially higher profits did significant numbers of men and women leave their textile workshops behind. Yet another factor, only briefly mentioned by Johnson, had to do with the strength of consumer demand for certain products such as special luxury textiles. Working for the luxury markets was an attractive strategy because the textiles produced for those markets offered wider profit margins and could not be successfully imitated by overseas companies.[9]

More recently, Richard Roberts has studied the case of French West Africa and colonial cotton policies from the nineteenth century through the first half of the twentieth century. He confronts colonial politics much more directly than Johnson did. His work offers painstakingly detailed analyses of the continuing efforts on the part of the French to turn their West African colonies into producers of cotton for the factories back home, efforts that failed for the most part, especially in the Senegambia and upper Niger regions. Among the reasons cited by Roberts for this failure were the actions and reactions of West African consumers and producers. Consumer demand and the purchasing power of West African elites and middle classes proved to be remarkably elastic and, when combined with the resiliency and dynamism of domestic cotton production and textile manufacture, served to stymie the French and prevent them from dominating the market for raw cotton.[10] The story of this struggle, between what Roberts calls the "two worlds of cotton," is most effectively documented and conveyed on the colonial side, the one that is more fully represented in the official archives.

Documentation about the other world of cotton, the one in which so many West African men and women worked, is woefully thin and incomplete by comparison. We are, in fact, still a long way from understanding in sufficient detail how and why particular groups of artisans in West Africa continued to produce cotton textiles in the face of competition from overseas products and markets. Before we can begin to make better assessments on this score, we need a more richly developed picture of just what the work was, what skills it entailed, what the most important products and centers of production were, and how they changed. In other words, the general explanations noted above need to be tested, fleshed out, and illustrated with concrete examples in order to counter an archival record that privileges colonial interests and attitudes. This book seeks to make a contribution toward that end. Among other things, my study identifies some of the more salient changes in textile production as the region took part in centuries of commerce. The time covered includes the eras of Muslim trade and Atlantic trade, and the importation of textiles from India as well as from Europe. Combining these major commercial periods brings home the point that textile workers in West Africa had been contending with foreign competition much earlier than the twentieth century. Along the way, technologies were transferred to new locales, centers of manufacture arose and declined, specific textile products were imitated or revised, and prices were affected by a variety of production and transport costs.

This study also includes examples of how the production and consumption of cloth interacted, and it shows the relationships between economic activity and cultural values.[11] More specifically, I am interested in the ways visual preferences shaped consumer markets for textiles, be they locally made or imported, and also how exchanging cloth, through gift and trading networks, led to innovations and revisions in the manufacture of standard, well-established products. In other words, what things looked like often mattered a great deal, especially in the predominantly oral societies of Africa where objects were deployed as tangible vehicles for finalizing contracts, diplomatic and trade agreements, and other such legal compacts. One illustration of this point is an episode from oral traditions about the early kings of Lagos and the beginnings of European commerce. As the story goes, the king of Lagos at the time of the first Atlantic slave traders was Oba Akinsemoyin, and it was while he was engaged in dealings with these traders that he received a gift of gorgeous velvet cloth. Exotic textiles, of course, were often coveted as powerful measures of royal magnificence. So, in a gesture both shrewd and deferential, he immediately sent the cloth to his superior, the Oba of Benin, saying that only his majesty was worthy of possessing it. The Benin king enthusiastically welcomed the gift, and urged Oba Akinsemoyin to continue his relations with the slave traders. As Titilola Euba so aptly summed up, "And so for a piece of cloth the slave trade became entrenched in Lagos."[12]

Although this episode cannot be verified, it nevertheless does have the ring of truth. As will be seen in the following chapters, there is reliable evidence testifying to the weight such gifts carried in the cross-cultural exchanges of diplomats, rulers, merchants, and travelers in Africa's past. Attending to visual issues, that is, what certain textiles looked like, can call attention to possible underlying motivations behind the particular choices made by consumers, the actions taken by traders, and the production and training strategies adopted by artisan producers. In short, homing in closely on the features of various major textile products can expose continuities and changes in production and consumption, and can do so in greater detail than the available written record allows.

MATERIAL CULTURE AND HISTORICAL ARCHAEOLOGY

Textiles are at the center of this book's exegesis—as a focus for posing this study's research questions and as the major primary sources on which the study is based. Museum objects and archaeological remains are relatively unconventional sources for historians.[13] The history presented here may therefore seem rather unusual, because it relies so heavily on material and visual evidence, and because it also borrows analytical tools and methodologies from the disciplines of archaeology, art history, and anthropology. Some readers might call it a work in *material culture*, others might see it as *historical archaeology*. The former designation refers to the analysis of objects, especially manufactured ones, as primary sources for pursuing questions having to do with technology, social organization, consumption patterns, ideology, or cultural practices. It is such a catchall term, in fact, that it defics clear definition.[14] The latter designation refers to an approach in archaeology that entails, for example, a readiness to scrutinize written documents and other archival sources alongside material remains and to excavate sites that may date back only a few centuries. Again, there are wide-ranging differences among scholars attempting to define the term more precisely.[15] In both cases, there is a recognition that certain areas and topics of research can be strengthened substantially by the addition of other categories of evidence, leading to convergences and overlappings of academic disciplines.

Interdisciplinary cross-fertilization and borrowing have, of course, long been a hallmark of both Africanist scholarship and textile history in general. Textiles, even though they are of major importance in history, including Africa's, are especially difficult to trace, and the study of them tends to fall between the disciplinary cracks. Conventional research in any single one of the disciplines mentioned above would have failed to uncover very much about the long-term contributions textile workers have made to West African societies. For example, most of the case studies cited in the following chapters focus on the twentieth century. To broaden our understanding of cloth manufacture, taking it further back in time than anthropological research can go, examination of the archaeological evidence is essential. However, the archaeological record is skewed in favor of those materials that are least likely to decompose. Textiles, and most of the tools that were used to produce them, were made primarily of ephemeral materials that rarely survived or left traces in the archaeological record.[16] As a result, the scant but precious archaeological remains there are for textile manufacture in West Africa, while crucial to the chapters in this book, are supplemented here with a variety of other sources. These include textiles from museum and private collections, vocabulary items from major languages in the region, botanical data, explorers' and merchants' accounts, and tools and techniques used in textile manufacture.

A work of synthesis, especially when it is aimed at a general readership, is most useful and effective when presented in narrative form. Given the complexity of this topic, it was obvious to me that designing a coherent structure and clear parameters for the text was vitally important. Early on in the planning, I decided that my goals might best be realized by constructing several independent but interrelated historical narratives, hence my choice to examine very intently and precisely the features of three individual textile products from one specific region in West Africa. All made in twentieth-century Nigeria, these three textile products are a brocaded cotton wrapper, a pair of embroidered cotton trousers, and a resist-patterned indigo-dyed cotton wrapper. Each product serves as the centerpiece for one of the three main chapters that follow.[17] Telling the story of three selected textile products presents different facets of this region's history by leading us into the particular set of people, trends, and events of the past that gave each product its own very specific visual and material qualities. In all cases, the storyline reaches across language boundaries, cultural and religious divisions, and a variety of political landscapes. And it crosses our own intellectual boundaries as well, by looking at workers who are often analyzed in isolation from one another, such as male and female, slave and free, rural and urban. Only by bringing them together is it possible to portray the social complexity of textile manufacture and the dynamics of how it changed.

PUTTING TEXTILES INTO WORDS

This book is a history of textile production and trade in the Nigerian region as viewed through the textiles themselves. Much of my evidence comes from analyses of textile specimens that are in museum collections and also from descriptions of others that can be found in the published literature. Manufacturing these textiles involved workers of many kinds, all of them employing labor-intensive technologies. Acknowledging and elucidating the enormous investment of time, skill, knowledge, and effort they made adds a large piece that has heretofore been missing from the general history of West Africa and the lower Niger basin. But it is by no means an easy or straightforward task to glean historical evidence from textiles. Analyzing and interpreting them—putting into words what can still be seen of the evidence of the skilled hands that made them—can seem arbitrary or perhaps even mystifying. To help and encourage the reader, I include below some general vocabulary items, descriptions of technical processes, examples of analyses, and illustrations that will be useful in understanding the text.

Cloth is made of fiber, but not all fibers are spun into thread, and not all threads are woven into textiles. In many parts of Africa's rainforests, for example, fibers from young leaves of the raphia palm (*Raphia vinifera*) were selected and carefully processed (but not spun), and woven into textiles that served many uses, including that of a form of currency.[18] Then there is *bark cloth*, a category of nonwoven fabrics that can have structures ranging from very sturdy to thin and delicate. Such cloths were made in West and Central Africa by carefully removing sections of the inner bark of certain selected trees and then pounding those sections with a mallet to make them wider, softer, and more flexible.[19] In other cases, various types of fiber were spun and then twisted together into heavier threads or cordage that would then be knotted, twined, or plaited by hand into clothing and other useful articles.[20] Most of the cloth discussed in this book was of another type, that is, it was woven on a loom using continuous threads that were produced by spinning or knotting fibers together.

Identification of the fiber content of a fabric can be very informative. Not only do different fibers affect the fabric's qualities and characteristics, but the presence of certain kinds of fibers in a particular textile can open up issues having to do with production and trade. Natural fibers come from many different sources, primarily plants and animals, and they are very much conditioned by a variety of ecological factors. It matters a great deal, for instance, whether a particular animal or plant was domesticated or not, and how well it could thrive in a temperate or tropical climate. Knowing where and when a textile was made, from what kind of fibers, and whether those fibers were made locally can shed light on economic linkages between textile workers, agricultural or pastoral production systems, and merchant groups. Moreover, there can be substantial variation in type, length, and quality of specific plant and animal fibers, and even between varieties of the same plant or animal species, which will have an impact on how textile manufacture must be carried out and what the final product will be like. Specialized methods of cleaning and processing have been developed for different types of fibers in order to prepare them for spinning, and how carefully these methods were followed would result in cloths of varying quality. Much of this information is available by direct observation. When examining a textile with a magnifier, an experienced researcher can identify its fibers and make assessments of their quality and, by extension, the skill of the workers who produced and processed them.

Threads too, and the tools used to make them, can also yield useful information. Consider the qualitative features that can suggest the degree of skill of a particular thread's manufacturer, with the smoothest and finest yarns exhibiting the exceptional skills of a master spinner and the relatively lumpy, uneven, and weak yarns indicating perhaps a novice, or a hurried, careless worker. Spinning, which turns separate fibers into a long and continuous thread, is an exacting task. It was especially so in West Africa, where spinning cotton was done with a handheld spindle. This tool was a thin stick with a baked clay *whorl* placed at the lower end. The whorl was usually round or trapezoidal in form and specially made for the purpose of adding weight.[21] Spinners gathered a mass of prepared fibers together and, while gradually drawing some of them out with one hand, would rotate or twirl the spindle with the other hand to give the fibers a twist.[22] How much twist had been imparted to the fibers resulted in very different kinds of thread that would be suited for specific purposes. Given a choice in materials, a well-trained and conscientious weaver will select the strongest yarns for the *warp*, or lengthwise threads, of the loom, since they can better withstand tension of the loom. These yarns will have extra twist, whereas the *weft*, or crosswise threads, can be thicker and fluffier, with lighter twist. Once we have observed in many examples of textiles that fine, tightly twisted threads were consistently used as warps, and that softer threads with less twist were consistently used as wefts, we can reasonably infer that spinners' work was specialized. Hence, measurement of the average diameter of yarns and their degree of twist can suggest aspects of both production organization and the spinners' skills. Unfortunately, however, descriptions at this level of detail are not always available in catalogues and other publications, especially for African textiles.

Spinning direction is another important feature of thread. Spinners learn to spin by turning the spindle in one direction or the other, clockwise or counterclockwise, and this spinning direction can be clearly seen in the thread itself. Detailed descriptions of textiles often include this information, and the convention is to use the letter *s* or *z* as a reference to which way the fibers are oriented (fig. 1.1). When a single element of thread is being described, the notation is straightforward: it is either s-spun or z-spun. Complications arise, however, when heavier yarns are made with multiple elements. This process is called *plying*, and the numbers of elements in any such yarn are given in the terminology 2-ply, 3-ply, and so on. Plying can be in either direction as well, and a useful convention for showing that information is to use an upper case *S* or *Z*.[23] Both of these conventions are followed in the descriptive sections of the text.

Sometimes observed differences in the direction of spin can prompt questions that have important historical implications. However, interpreting this kind of evidence is difficult, especially when yarn descriptions are incomplete and the precise method of spinning is not known. The Nile valley, which has been relatively well explored archaeologically, and where textile finds have been well documented, provides an illustration of the kinds

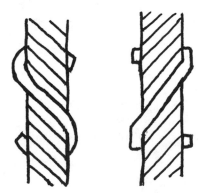

Figure 1.1. Spinning Direction, *s*-twist and *z*-twist. Drawing by the Author.

of questions that can be generated. For example, scholars have noted that flax fibers have a natural tendency to rotate slightly in the s-direction when drying, and so it comes as no surprise that most linen thread in ancient Egypt was spun while damp in the s-direction.[24] Linen textiles woven up-river in Nubia before AD 550 exhibit the same feature, as do other Nubian textiles made from cotton and from animal fibers such as camel and goat hair. However, textiles from Nubian sites dating to the Muslim period (AD 900 onward) were woven of cotton thread spun in the z-direction.[25] The reason for this difference is unclear. One interpretation would be that the techniques of cotton spinning changed, but that explanation could be challenged by early twentieth-century evidence of a continuity in the tools and techniques of Nubian spinning practice, whether the fibers involved were flax, wool, or cotton.[26] The spindle, held in the right hand with the whorl placed at the top, would produce thread with an s-twist, the opposite of how West African spinners held their spindles and made their z-spun yarns. Why there was a shift then in the spin-type of cotton yarns used by weavers in at least some parts of Nubia after the tenth century must therefore remain an unresolved question.

Textiles, strictly speaking, are fabrics that are woven on a loom. Weaving is a particular process by which two independent sets of threads are interlaced together: the lengthwise, or warp, threads are held under tension in the loom; and the crosswise, or weft, thread is passed between sets of raised and lowered warp threads. When the weft is beaten into place, it intersects each warp thread at a right angle. Then the orientation of the warp threads is reversed—the ones that had been raised are now lowered, and the ones that had been lowered are raised. The weft thread is passed back through this opening in the threads and is beaten in against the previous weft. And so on.[27] A continuous weft thread passed back and forth will result in a firm, bound edge at each side of the warp—a self-edge, or *selvage*. This feature confirms that a fabric has been woven on a loom and that it is indeed a textile.

Weaving has been done for millennia, the world over, using many types of looms.[28] Their basic operating principles are, however, remarkably similar. Anni Albers puts it very well:

> During the 4,500 years or, in some estimates, even 8,000 years that we believe mankind has been weaving, the process itself has been unaffected by the various devices that contributed to greater speed of execution. We still deal in weaving, as at the time of its beginning, with a rigid set of parallel threads in tension and a mobile one that transverses it at right angles.[29]

Nevertheless, the type of loom available to a weaver does matter. To people living in a modern, industrialized society, the most important issue will be time savings, and highly efficient and productive power looms will be considered superior to so-called primitive handlooms. Gross output and volume production will be paramount. Different criteria, however, might place more value on the particular features and qualities of textile products, and also on their potential variety, with the result being a reliance on looms not designed for high-speed, high-volume production. A *simple* loom, for example, is a flexible loom, capable of making all sorts of cloth. And the relatively laborious, slow-operating *backstrap* loom of ancient Peru allowed its weavers the scope to create almost all the fabric structures known today, and some that are no longer made at all.[30] This point is often overlooked when comparisons are made between industrial and preindustrial manufacture. In fact, an increase in mechanization comes at a cost, as it diminishes the range of design possibilities for looms and other machines.[31] A telling example is the attempt by some European textile manufacturers to imitate popular textiles made on West African handlooms. One company had to invest in a highly complex reengineering of its machinery in order to replicate certain types of brocade patterns and other distinctive features of African weaving carried out on those simple handlooms. Even so, after all this effort, a practiced eye can easily see the difference between the original and the imitation.[32]

This example also illustrates another important point, which is that textile structures show traces of the type of loom that produced them. In the case of West African textiles, regular spacing of the warp threads can be an indicator that the textile in question was woven with a reed, or combed beater, as opposed to a batten, or weaving sword. And a repeated error in warp manipulation indicates that brocading or openwork was done with a supplementary *harness* or *shed stick*, rather than by handpicking the warp threads each time. Once the type of loom is identified, additional evidence from written accounts or replication experiments can help in estimating labor inputs and inferring other useful information such as the gender of the weaver. These issues will be discussed more fully in chapters 2 and 3.

Weaving is a craft based on calculation and counting. In order to set up a loom, the weaver must estimate how much thread is needed for the warp, which depends on the type of thread, its thickness or fineness, and the intended dimensions and density of the fabric. Then the warp threads have to be measured out to the correct length, placed in sequential order, and arranged on the loom. How the warps are arranged and manipulated creates different types of fabric structures. The most common, elementary textile structure is a *plain weave*, with single alternating warp threads raised or lowered and single weft threads passed through and beaten in (fig. 1.2). Using pairs of thread rather than single threads for the warp and weft creates what is then called a *basket weave*. Other types of structures are made by changing the proportion of warps to wefts. Many more warp than weft threads per square inch, such that the wefts can hardly be seen in the fabric,

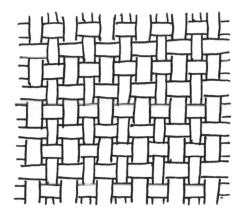

Figure 1.2. Plain-Weave Fabric, Single-Yarn Elements, One Weft over One Warp. Drawing by the Author.

creates a *warp-face weave*. Having more weft than warp threads per square inch creates a *weft-face weave*. Tapestries are weft-face textiles, their imagery made with different colors of weft threads completely covering the warps.

Textiles that are intended to be used as clothing are often woven as plain-weave structures with both the warp and weft visible. Such fabrics can be embellished by adding other yarn elements into the plain-weave structure, by including different colors among the warp and weft threads, or both. These are examples of *loom-patterning*, since the embellishments are produced within the structure of the textile as it is woven. The two major forms of loom-patterning that are discussed in this book are brocading with supplementary weft threads and the creation of striped or checkered patterns with colored warps and/or wefts. In brocading, an additional thread is woven in so that it "floats" over the plain-weave ground and is held down at intervals by one of the plain-weave threads (fig. 1.3). All sorts of colored patterns

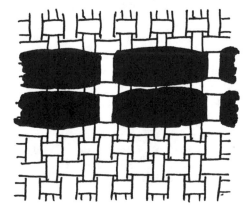

Figure 1.3. Loom-Patterning: Supplementary Weft Element, Floating over Five Warps and Held in Place by the Sixth. Also Called Brocading. Drawing by the Author.

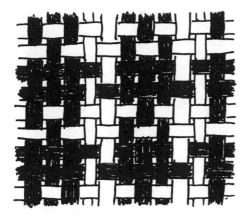

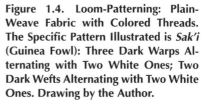

Figure 1.4. Loom-Patterning: Plain-Weave Fabric with Colored Threads. The Specific Pattern Illustrated is *Sak'i* (Guinea Fowl): Three Dark Warps Alternating with Two White Ones; Two Dark Wefts Alternating with Two White Ones. Drawing by the Author.

can be made within plain-weave structures simply by alternating the color of threads. This can be done by sight, or it can be done in a systematic way by counting. Very regular patterns are made with *pattern repeats*, thread counts that are repeated over and over (fig. 1.4). Examining a textile and counting its threads can reveal the system used by the weaver in arranging a pattern.

To sum up, examining and comparing textiles, along with their documentation, can take us inside the work process to reveal much about the textiles' makers and others associated with the process. Identifying the tools that were used allows us to understand the technological parameters within which the artisans worked. Differences in technical conventions can prompt historical questions about technology transfer, market orientation, and innovation. Describing the fibers, how they were processed, and what dye was used to color them, can reveal information about raw-material production, technology, and trade. Carefully noting thread measurements, fabric densities, tailoring methods, and embroidery stitches (fig. 1.5) can suggest the skills of the artisans, whether the artisans were specialized, and if they had adopted laborsaving strategies. Analyzing the patterns or imagery of certain textiles can even provide evidence of political or religious ideology and cultural values. All of these things and more make textiles invaluable historical sources. But in order to gain access to this information, one must know the specific technology as well as the historical circumstances and conditions that give a textile its particular character.

On occasion, colleagues have suggested that textiles are "texts" and that I am "reading" textiles when I use them as historical sources. That is not so, but the confusion interests me. The material and visual features of textiles

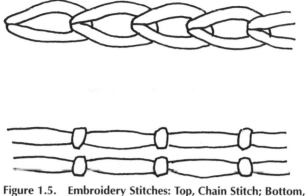

Figure 1.5. Embroidery Stitches: Top, Chain Stitch; Bottom, Couching (Threads "Floating" on Surface, Held Down by Small Tie-Down Stitches). Drawing by the Author.

that I analyze are not at all the same as the sign systems and morphemes of written language. Textiles are not readable in the way a text is, even though, interestingly enough, the words *textile* and *text* do share the same Latin root meaning "that which is woven." I would suggest that this etymological relationship may be rooted in orality and spoken practice rather than writing or literacy. Weaving and spinning, the ancient processes of making textiles and continuous threads, are often employed as tropes representing time and the passing of time. These specific processes are entirely and relentlessly sequential, as is oral narrative. We implicitly recognize this when we use certain metaphors: the warp and woof of history; the thread of an argument; and to tell a story is to "spin a yarn." The thing itself, however, the thread or the textile or the garment, is created by any number of working processes, with the result that textiles are complex in multiple and changing ways. Breaking them apart into elements to see their complexities requires careful and systematic documentation, examination, and description, and an equally careful and systematic analysis of their technical qualities. They must be viewed alongside other textiles and connected to their own special social and cultural contexts. This effort is worthwhile, for the historical object itself can often be more reliable than a contemporary written account or description of that history might be. It is firsthand evidence of what certain people actually did do at some time in the past. For that reason I have chosen to include charts of technical information and other data to bring readers closer to the objects themselves. This book is best seen as a translation of textiles—turning evidence gleaned from their visual and material features into written narratives—so that the history within them can be read by all.

NOTES

The epigraph for this chapter is taken from Robert Norris, *Memoirs of the Reign of Bossa Ahadee* (1789; repr., London: Frank Cass, 1968), 87.

1. See for example, Joseph Inikori, "Slavery and the Revolution in Cotton Textile Production in England," in *The Atlantic Slave Trade: Effects on Economies, Societies, and Peoples in Africa, the Americas, and Europe*, ed. J. E. Inikori and S. Engerman (Durham, N.C.: Duke University Press, 1992).

2. Colleen Kriger, "Textile Production in the Lower Niger Basin: New Evidence from the 1841 Niger Expedition Collection," *Textile History* 21, no. 1 (1990).

3. It should also be noted that almost all of the archaeological evidence cited here is from the published literature, and does not include references to studies currently underway or in press.

4. Heinrich Barth, *Travels and Discoveries in North and Central Africa*, 3 vols. (1857; repr., London: Frank Cass, 1965); Gustav Nachtigal, *Sahara and Sudan*, trans. and ed. Allan G. B. Fisher and Humphrey J. Fisher, with Rex S. O'Fahey, 4 vols. (1879; New York: Barnes and Noble, 1971–1984).

5. Charles Monteil, *Le coton chez les noirs* (Paris: Librairie Emile Larose, 1927); R. S. Rattray, *Religion and Art in Ashanti* (Oxford: Clarendon Press, 1927).

6. Examples are K. C. Murray, "Women's Weaving among the Yorubas at Omuaran in Ilorin Province," *Nigerian Field* 5 (1936); J. D. Clarke, "Ilorin Weaving," *Nigeria Magazine* 14 (1938); and A. E. Southern, "Cloth Making in Nigeria," *Nigeria Magazine* 32 (1949).

7. Allen Isaacman and Richard Roberts, eds., *Cotton, Colonialism, and Social History in Sub-Saharan Africa* (Portsmouth, N.H.: Heinemann, 1995); Allen Isaacman, *Cotton is the Mother of Poverty: Peasants, Work, and Rural Struggle in Colonial Mozambique, 1938–1961* (Portsmouth, N.H.: Heinemann, 1996); Richard Roberts, *Two Worlds of Cotton: Colonialism and the Regional Economy in the French Soudan, 1800–1946* (Stanford, Calif.: Stanford University Press, 1996); Osumaka Likaka, *Rural Society and Cotton in Colonial Zaire* (Madison: University of Wisconsin Press, 1997); and Thomas Bassett, *The Peasant Cotton Revolution in West Africa: Côte d'Ivoire, 1880–1995* (Cambridge: Cambridge University Press, 2001).

8. Marion Johnson, "Cotton Imperialism in West Africa," *African Affairs* 73, no. 291 (April 1974).

9. Johnson, "Cotton Imperialism," 185–86; and Johnson, "Technology, Competition, and African Crafts," in *The Imperial Impact: Studies in the Economic History of Africa and India*, ed. Clive Dewey and A. G. Hopkins (London: Athlone Press, 1978).

10. Roberts, *Two Worlds of Cotton*, 283–92.

11. General studies of consumption patterns include David Richardson, "West African Consumption Patterns and Their Influence on the Eighteenth-century English Slave Trade," in *The Uncommon Market: Essays in the Economic History of the Atlantic Slave Trade*, ed. Henry Gemery and Jan Hogendorn (New York: Academic Press, 1979); George Metcalf, "A Microcosm of Why Africans Sold Slaves: Akan Consumption Patterns in the 1770s," *Journal of African History* 28, no. 3 (1987); and

Stanley Alpern, "What Africans Got for Their Slaves: A Master List of European Trade Goods," *History in Africa* 22 (1995).

12. Titilola Euba, "Dress and Status in 19th Century Lagos," in *History of the Peoples of Lagos State*, ed. Ade Adefuye et al. (Lagos: Lantern Books, 1987), 144; John B. Losi, trans. and ed., *History of Lagos* (1914; Lagos: African Education Press, 1967), 13.

13. This situation is changing, however, as some historians are beginning to recognize the potential of artifacts and imagery for writing social and cultural histories. See Victoria E. Bonnell and Lynn Hunt, eds., *Beyond the Cultural Turn* (Berkeley, Calif.: University of California Press, 1999), 11. See also the invited review essays by Ronald Grigor Suny et al., in *American Historical Review* 107, no. 5 (December 2002).

14. See my review of *African Material Culture*, ed. Mary Jo Arnoldi, Christraud Geary, and Kris Hardin, *Technology and Culture* (January 1998):142–44.

15. For an excellent introduction, see Kit W. Wesler, "Historical Archaeology in West Africa," in *Historical Archaeology in Nigeria*, ed. Wesler (Trenton, N.J.: Africa World Press, 1998).

16. Graham Connah wrote a succinct and useful discussion of the limitations of archaeological evidence in *African Civilizations: An Archaeological Perspective*, 2nd ed. (Cambridge: Cambridge University Press, 2001), 2–3, 11–12. Timothy Insoll also addressed this problem, noting that although the fundamental importance of cloth and clothing in the Muslim world is generally recognized, it is underrepresented in the literature because of its relative absence from the archaeological record. Insoll, *The Archaeology of Islam* (Oxford: Blackwell, 1999), 158–59.

17. Since I began writing this book, I have been introduced to other works similarly organized. My thanks go to my colleague, Dr. Lisa Tolbert, for telling me about: Sarah Hill, *Weaving New Worlds: Southeastern Cherokee Women and Their Basketry* (Chapel Hill: University of North Carolina Press, 1997); and Laurel Thatcher Ulrich, *The Age of Homespun: Objects and Stories in the Creation of an American Myth* (New York: Knopf, 2001).

18. Jan Vansina, "Raffia Cloth in West Central Africa, 1500–1800," in *Textiles: Production, Trade, and Demand*, ed. Maureen Mazzaoui (Aldershot, UK: Ashgate, 1998); and Phyllis Martin, "Power, Cloth and Currency on the Loango Coast," *African Economic History* 15 (1986).

19. John Picton and John Mack, *African Textiles* (London: British Museum, 1979), 42–47.

20. See for example, Rogier Bedaux and Rita Bolland, "Vêtements féminins médiévaux du Mali: Les cache-sexe de fibre des Tellem," in *Man Does Not Go Naked*, ed. Beate Engelbrecht and Bernhard Gardi (Basel: Museum für Völkerkunde, 1989). For a survey of non-loom fabrics, see Irene Emery, *The Primary Structures of Fabrics* (Washington, D.C.: The Textile Museum, 1980), 19–70.

21. Different weights of whorl would be used, depending on the fiber, its length, and the type of thread, heavy or fine, that was desired. For a discussion of whorls, their features, and their placement on the spindle shaft in antiquity, see E. J. W. Barber, *Prehistoric Textiles: The Development of Cloth in the Neolithic and Bronze Ages* (Princeton, N.J.: Princeton University Press, 1991), 51–65.

22. This procedure is not as simple as it sounds. For a remarkable survey of the variety of techniques and tools in early twentieth-century Egypt and Sudan, see Grace

Crowfoot, *Methods of Handspinning in Egypt and the Sudan* (Halifax: King and Sons, 1931).

23. Emery, *Primary Structures of Fabrics*, 10–14.

24. Rosalind Hall, *Egyptian Textiles* (Princes Risborough, UK: Shire, 2001), 12; Barber, *Prehistoric Textiles*, 65–68.

25. Ingrid Bergman, *Late Nubian Textiles* (Stockholm: Scandinavian University Press, 1975), 12–14; Christa C. M. Thurman and Bruce Williams, *Ancient Textiles from Nubia* (Chicago: Art Institute of Chicago, 1979), 36–38, 49–51.

26. See Crowfoot, *Methods of Handspinning*.

27. See Anni Albers, *On Weaving* (Middletown, Conn.: Wesleyan University Press, 1965), 19–21.

28. Albers, *On Weaving*, 22–37.

29. Albers, *On Weaving*, 22.

30. Albers, *On Weaving*, 21.

31. Albers, *On Weaving*, 25.

32. Bea Brommer, ed. *Bontjes voor de Tropen: De export van imitatieweefsels naar de Tropen* (Helmond: Gemeentemuseum, 1991).

2

From Kings and Priests to Brides

A mainstay of dress for men and women throughout the history of the lower Niger River region has been the rectangular cloth called the *wrup-per*, which is worn draped around the body and secured under the arm, over the shoulder, or at the waist. This chapter begins with a particularly beautiful one—a dazzling arrangement of pure color and layers of linear and geometric pattern. Bands of yellow intersected by subtle shadings of red and blocks of multicolored patterning and openwork are superimposed upon white stripes; other bands of red, yellow, and white stripes cross a field vibrating with tonal changes and punctuated by multicolored motifs and zigzags. The wrapper's interlocking webs of luminosity shimmer and energize the eye: it is a truly resplendent textile.

All of this visual richness was achieved in a single process of weaving, with three intersecting planes of pattern playing off against each other within the structure of the fabric itself (fig. 2.1). Technically, this textile would be classified as a *compound-weave* fabric, meaning that in addition to the basic plain-weave structure of warp and weft—a simple network of two intersecting elements—there is an added set of woven threads. In this case, they are an example of what are called *supplementary* wefts, or crosswise threads, woven in such a way as to create individual motifs and patterns that appear to float on only one side or face of the cloth.[1] This type of woven patterning, also called brocading, is often confused with embroidery, though they are entirely different techniques. Unlike brocading, which is integral to the weaving process, embroidery is a separate, postloom process done by sewing threads onto an already woven textile. Brocading is much more difficult and challenging for it requires careful planning beforehand, and then throughout the process it asks for a high degree of skill and patient

19

Figure 2.1. Brocaded Women's Wrapper, Made in Bida, Nigeria, ca. 1975, 72^1/$_4$ Inches Long by 50 Inches Wide (See Also Detail in Fig. 2.9). UCLA Fowler Museum of Cultural History, Colleen E. Kriger Collection of Nigerian Textiles, X2005.24.15.

technical control on the part of the weaver. In addition to brocaded patterns, the weaver of this textile employed another very unusual technique that appears at intervals in the fabric. Referred to technically as *openwork*,[2] it is a method of patterning that involves interrupting and modifying the fabric's structure. In this case, rows of holes or slits were deliberately woven into the fabric by means of separate, discontinuous wefts. So to sum up: in all respects—color, composition, technique—the maker of this textile was clearly a master of the craft of weaving.

Apart from its visual features, this cloth is interesting also in the way it combines handwork with mechanized processes. It is made of two separate handwoven pieces sewn together by machine—one piece about 24½ inches wide, the other about 25½ inches wide. Altogether, it measures about 50 inches wide by 72¼ inches long. Rather than having a folded-over hem, the edges were machine stitched to secure the fabric structure, while the fringed ends were left showing. Twisting, plying, and knotting by hand then carefully reinforced these ends. All of the warp and weft threads were made by industrial spinning machines, and all were colored with synthetic, industrially produced dyes. Pairs of fine z-spun cotton yarns formed the single warp (lengthwise) element, and they were used in fours as the single weft (crosswise) element. The brocading was done with heavier, glossy rayon yarns. A practiced eye can see that although the materials are all the products of modern factories, the textile itself was woven on a very basic, preindustrial handloom—two apparently conflicting facts that raise questions about the history of this particular type of textile. It would be tempting to assume that the designs were invented rather recently for Western tourists or Westernized Nigerians, since the designs rely so completely on imported materials. Following that assumption, this textile might be considered a new cultural form that lacks historical significance. In this chapter I will demonstrate that such assumptions could not be more mistaken, and that tracing this textile's features—material, technical, and visual—takes us very far back in time. Starting with the ecosystem and natural resources of this textile's region of manufacture, the story of how this cloth came to be created winds along the arteries of commercial and political alliances, back and forth across language boundaries, and through centuries of trade and economic change. Certain cultural values and practices, by conditioning what was traded and how, and by serving as vehicles for societies to assimilate selected novelties, are central to this history. And these many variables, as we will see, coalesced in such a way that in the end, a female weaver had a type of loom at her disposal, as well as the special technical and design skills needed, for weaving this particular cloth in just this way.

MATERIALS: FIBER AND THREAD

This vibrantly colored, intricately striped and brocaded cloth, woven in the 1970s by a woman in the Nupe city of Bida,[3] is the product of a specific kind of loom with an ancient history. Sometimes called the *vertical* loom, or the *continuous warp* loom, it was used early on in settlements of the tropical rainforest belt along the Bights of Benin and Biafra and their hinterlands (fig. 2.2). It is not known precisely how far back in time this loom was invented, though its many structural variations suggest that specific groups of weavers made adaptations and modifications to it gradually over time and in different locales—a process attesting to its antiquity. The vertical loom is

Figure 2.2. Woman Weaving on a Vertical Loom, Ovim, SE Nigeria, 1928. Photograph by A. W. Banfield. Copyright the Estate of Frank Banfield, Canada.

most likely a close relative of the *raphia* loom, the tool used by weavers of raphia cloth in the equatorial rainforests that stretch southeastward into the Congo basin. In the region of the lower Niger River, which saw the development of two major textile technology complexes, the earliest weaving was done with indigenous materials, probably on a variant of the vertical loom. With the vertical loom as a centerpiece, weavers in Igbo, Edo, Yoruba, and other forest communities created a textile technology that was distinctly different from the one that other weavers created in the Hausa-speaking areas of the northern savannas (see chapter 3).

The forests of the lower Niger region have been home to settled populations for several thousand years. Supported by a diet based on yam cultivation, oil-palm products, and fish from its many interior rivers and streams as well as the sea, people there created a sylviculture out of the resources of their tropical environment. All parts of trees and bushes—fruit, leaves, roots, bark—were exploited. Among the most important tree products were palm oil, gum, beeswax, a host of medicines, dyestuffs, rope and twine, potash, charcoal, ashes for soap, carved implements, canoes and paddles, gourds, kola, building materials, furniture, and firewood.[4] Certain trees also yielded what were probably some of the first materials that were used for making cloth. For example, table 2.1 below shows several species of trees that were known in the Edo language as *ighwian* or *okwen*. The bark of these trees was gathered in the wild and then processed in different ways to produce cordage, fishing gear, or a fiber that could be either pounded or plaited by hand into fabric or spun into thread and woven on a loom. In the absence of more complete and concrete historical evidence, we are left to speculate about how cloth making might have developed long ago in forest communities—from the pounding out of bark cloth to the making

Table 2.1. *Ighwian/Okwen* Trees and Their Products

Apocynaceae *Conopharyngia pachysiphon*
   (= *Tabernaemontana pachysiphon*)
   Ewe: *dai*
   Yoruba: *dodo, abo*
   Edo: *ibbu, ubu, ighwian*
   Igbo: *pete-pete, ivuru* (Achi)
The bark yields a fiber used for making "lifa cloths" (Asaba, in Igboland), "dodo cloth" (Lagos, in Yorubaland). Wood used for making combs; bark, fruit, and roots used for medicinal purposes.

Apocynaceae *Conopharyngia penduliflora*
   (= *Tabernaemontana penduliflora*)
   Edo: *ibbu, ovimbu, igbo, ighwian*
   Efik: *agwagwani*
Bark, fruit, and roots used for medicinal purposes. All names sometimes used for other species and probably other genera.

Mimosaceae *Acacia pennata*
   (= Leguminosae)
   Edo: *okwenkwen*
A long strong fiber from the stems is made into fishing gear, cordage, and so forth.

Caesalpiniaceae *Brachystegia eurycoma*
   (= Leguminosae)
   Edo: *okwen, okwein, okhuen*
The bark is used in southern Nigeria to make a sort of cloth. This is worn, carried under the chin, as a protection from rain or as a shield against arrows. Native to Cameroon.

Euphorbiaceae *Ricinodendron africanum*
   Edo: *okhuen*
Okhuen = a tree; a cloth woven from the fibers of raphia [*sic*] leaves.
   Yoruba: *erimado*
   Igbo: *okwe*
   Efik: *nsa-sanga*
Tree used for carving and for making musical instruments; seeds used as rattles and as counters in games; bark used for medicinal purposes.

Note: Updated botanical terminology is in parentheses.
Sources: Dalziel 1937, 159, 176–77, 207, 370–71; *Index Kewensis* 1908, supp. 3, p. 47; 1921, supp. 5, p. 35; 1959, supp. 12, p. 24; Melzian 1937, 80, 155, 172. Spellings adapted to Roman alphabet.

of fibrous cords and nets, then from this to the plaiting of mats, baskets, and belts, and finally to the spinning of thread and weaving. Just this small selection of trees offers up the materials that would have made it possible for people in the forest belt to advance through the technological stages leading from nonwoven fabrics to loom-woven textiles.

Weavers working with the vertical loom have employed a variety of fibers, either gathered in the wild or cultivated, processed locally or imported from elsewhere, and some of them spun into thread and others not. The earliest forest textiles made were most likely woven of unspun fibers, such as young palm leaflets, which required soaking, beating, and combing before being dressed and woven on the loom. Of the various different palm trees that have been used to make textiles in Africa, the most important ones in the lower Niger region were several species of *Raphia vinifera*, some of which were valuable also as a source of palm wine. So far, no evidence has come to light that raphia palms were deliberately cultivated for the specific purpose of producing textiles on a large scale, as they were in parts of central Africa, though some Igbo communities reportedly established palm-tree plantations west of the Niger for wine tapping. These locales could easily have become sources of supply for raphia fiber as well, since the gathering of it does not endanger the life of the tree.[5]

Unspun fibers such as raphia were sturdy and resilient but also presented some important technical disadvantages. A major one, often noted in the literature, was that the cloths made of raphia were limited in their dimensions to the length of the individual raphia fibers, which grow to a maximum of four feet. That weavers easily got around this problem is hardly ever noted in the literature, and so it is uncertain exactly when weavers began to do so. For example, raphia cloths were among the textiles exported from the Benin kingdom and resold by Europeans elsewhere on the Guinea Coast, but a 1591 reference to "cloth made of the barke of palm trees" did not specify dimensions. It is not until we come upon an observation made in 1778 that we have more precise information about the lengths and widths of textiles worn as wrappers. Raphia wrappers made in Benin were described by a French trader at that time as pale buff in color, woven almost as finely as silk, and eight or nine feet in length.[6] In other words, they were roughly the same size as cloths woven from handspun cotton yarns. It is likely that by this time, if not before, weavers were splicing or knotting raphia fibers together to make a continuous thread. One can see further evidence of this by examining the technical features of cloths now in museum collections. Various examples from different locales, made of either raphia or raphia and cotton in the nineteenth century, were woven to lengths of five or six feet using knotted raphia threads.[7] What is most interesting about these raphia and cotton cloths is the technical evidence they provide that cotton had not completely displaced other fibers. Raphia cloth continued to be made alongside cotton—and in the face of centuries of textile imports from overseas—which suggests that consumers in the region continued to prefer it for certain purposes and considered it necessary for special ceremonial occasions. Indeed, cloths woven entirely of raphia fiber were deemed significant enough in Yorubaland to be designated by their own specific vernacular name: *òdùn*, meaning a "grass" cloth made from "bamboo" fibers; and *odon,* or *odun,* meaning a "cloth of palm-leaf fibers."[8]

Nevertheless, the advent of spinning did bring some notable improvements in cloth making. Above all, unrestricted lengths of continuous thread offered weavers much more flexibility in making longer, wider, and more densely woven cloths. Several types of strong linen-like fibers, often grouped together and referred to generically in the literature as *bast,* may have been spun into thread from very early times. One such fiber (see table 2.1 above)—made from Apocynaceae *Tabernaemontana pachysiphon*—was used in the twentieth century for weaving treasured cloths reserved for funerals in the Kabba area, and for sacred rituals performed by the Oba of Benin.[9] Both of these religious contexts suggest that the processing, spinning, and weaving of this tree fiber bore significant and widely held cultural value. It is quite possible that the ritual use of such cloths was, at least in part, a metonymic gesture reflecting the tree's well-known importance as a source of various medicinal substances. Other tree and plant species have also been spun into thread, although precise identification of them is difficult because the vernacular terminology is applied very generally and dictionary definitions do not always include botanical references. Some examples of dictionary definitions are the Nupe word, *yifuru,* meaning "hemp," and the Yoruba word, *ògbò,* meaning "linen, flax."[10]

Wild silk fibers were also regularly available throughout the region. Unlike the more familiar, glossy filament silk produced in Asia from cultivated silkworms, this kind of silk consisted of relatively coarse brown or white fibers that had to undergo laborious processing in order to be spun into thread. The fiber itself was created by several varieties of caterpillar, which nested in and fed on particular trees and bushes according to the locale (see table 2.2 below). Living together in dense clusters that could number in the hundreds, these fiber-producing larvae, when they reached maturity, would spin a communal nest around themselves. Several weeks later, each one would then spin its own individual cocoon. It was primarily the stronger, outer fiber of the communal nest that was collected in the wild for making textiles. Nests might be found in either trunks or branches, depending on the type of tree, and after being gathered they would be degummed in a boiling alkaline solution, then dried, carded, and spun. In Yorubaland and in Nupe country, wild silk yarns were woven into very elegant and costly cloths,

Table 2.2.   Wild Silk: Moth Varieties, Species of Host Plants, and Lexical Terms for Silk Fiber

Moth	Host Tree/Bush	Lexical Term
Anaphe vuilleti	Caesalpiniaceae (= Leguminosae) Tamarindus indica Moraceae Ficus platyphylla	**Hausa:** tsamiyar tsamiya, rimin tsamiya **Nupe:** tsamiya
Anaphe moloneyi	Caesalpiniaceae (= Leguminosae) Isoberlinia doka Moraceae Ficus platyphylla	**Hausa:** tsamiyar doka, tsamiya fakale **Yoruba:** sãnyán
Anaphe ambrizia, Anaphe moloneyi	Papilionaceae (=Leguminosae) Afrormosia laxiflora	**Hausa:** tsamiyar makarfo
Anaphe infracta	Euphorbiaceae Bridelia micrantha	**Yoruba:** sãnyán
Anaphe venata	Sterculiaceae (= Malvaceae) Triplochiton scleroxylon	

Note: Updated botanical terminology is in parentheses.
Sources: Dalziel 1937, 111, 137–38, 195, 200–202, 226–27, 281; Banfield 1969, 441; Golding 1942, 40; Index Kewensis 1953, supp. 11, p. 126; 1970, supp. 14, p. 4.

sometimes blended with handspun cotton or imported silk. In Hausaland, wild silk was spun by Quranic scholars for embroidering imagery on trousers and robes.[11] It is not known how long ago this fiber began to be used in local textile manufacture.

Even more intriguing is the question of when cotton began to be cultivated in the lower Niger region. This important question is complicated by the existence of a northern textile technology complex that was characterized by its use of a narrow treadle loom, which probably originated in India and has long been associated with Muslim trading networks in the savanna and Sahel (a semidesert southern fringe of the Sahara). The earliest evidence for this particular loom in the vicinity of the lower Niger is indirect, coming from a compilation of observations and descriptions of the Kanem region that was written in Arabic by Al-'Umari in the 1330s. Already by that time the treadle loom was being used to produce a cloth strip currency in Kanem, presumably made of cotton and called *dandi*.[12] Given its association with Islam, it is reasonable to assume that cotton spinning and weaving on the treadle loom was well established in the Hausa kingdoms by at least the fourteenth century. The development of high-volume textile production in this area in later years, especially during the nineteenth century, and the extensive trading networks that distributed cotton strip-woven cloth throughout much of West Africa, have left an impression in the literature that this was the older, more dynamic textile complex.[13] Following on from this, one might then presume that cotton was introduced into the lower Niger region from the north.

Lexical terminology and botanical evidence suggest that the answer to the question of the origin of early cotton cultivation is much more complex than a single north–south transfer. Indications are that there were interactions in both directions between cotton growers in textile complexes in both north and south. Lexical terminology in the south, for example, shows no clear evidence of borrowing from Hausaland in the north. The words for cotton in Hausa, a Chadic language, are *abduga* and *ka'da*, while in the Kwa languages they were, in Yoruba, *òwú, efewu*; in Edo (Benin), *owu, oru, oruru*; in Igbo, *olulu, owulu*; and in Nupe, *lulu, kece*.[14] Moreover, the varieties of cotton grown before the introduction of Allen's long-staple in the colonial period do not present a simple pattern either. There were Old World and New World cottons grown in both textile complexes, and the terminology for them also suggests transfers in more than one direction (see table 2.3 below).[15]

Table 2.3. Cotton Species and Lexical Terms

Family Malvaceae	
Genus, Species	*Language, Lexical Term*
*Gossypium arboreum Linn.	**Hausa:** *ba-kanuwa; kanawa; matanka nawa.* **Yoruba:** *akeshe; òwú yanwure*
*Gossypium Simpsonii Watt [a variety of *G. arboreum*?]	**Hausa:** *gwandi, gwandai, ba-gwandara* (Katsina); *'yar k'arfi* (Kano), *'yar tsauri* (Sokoto—*k'arfi* and *tsauri* = strength or hardness)
**Gossypium vitifolium Lamk. (= *G. barbadense*)	**Hausa:** *buke* (Gando area, but said to be from Nupe) **Yoruba:** *òwú Ishan* (*Ishan:* a place name in [colonial] Benin district); *Kabba* **Ibo:** *owulu Isa*
**Gossypium hirsutum L.	**Hausa:** *chukwi; la'bai* (Kano, Daura, Kazaure); *lutua; mai laushi; 'yar tabshi* (Kano, Sokoto, and western Hausa) "the boll of *la'bai* is loose and fleecy" *laushi* and *tabshi* both = soft
**Gossypium peruvianum Cav. (= *Gossypium barbadense*)	**Hausa:** *ba tuka; ba ka tuka* (Sokoto and Katsina); *gwandi* (Daura); *gundi, gwundi* (Zaria "indigenous") **Yoruba:** *òwú* (original *òwú* of Oyo); *agbede* (place name in [colonial] Benin district); Ilorin: *òwú ogodo* (*ogodo* = yaws; capsules resemble yaws)

Note: Updated botanical terminology is in parentheses.
*Old World cottons.
**New World cottons.
Sources: Dalziel 1937, 123–24; Watson 1980, 363; Usher 1974, 281; Porcher, et al. 2004.

Most of these fibers—raphia, bast, and cotton—were used to produce the oldest existing examples of cloths that have been unearthed in this part of West Africa. Since buried textiles tend to decompose rather quickly, they usually do not appear in the archaeological record unless some sort of special condition ensures their survival. Contact with copper or copper alloys, for example, preserved some very early textiles at the archaeological site of Igbo-Ukwu.[16] Dating from the ninth century, Igbo-Ukwu provides us with the earliest direct evidence we have for weaving in the region. Over twenty cloth fragments were excavated, all of them woven on a loom in plain weave of various densities from coarse to fine. Several had open, gauze-like structures. The threads were varied in terms of their material makeup, but despite microscopic analyses they have not yet been botanically identified. They are therefore described generically as "grass" and "bast." The structures of the threads were also varied. The "bast" fiber was spun in the s-direction, perhaps as a result of the fiber's natural twist (as is the case with linen).[17] Two of these elements were then plied together in the Z-direction. One of the "grass" threads was substantial, consisting of three 2-ply elements, each made of twisted "grass" fibers.[18] The types of fibers used indicate indigenous manufacture, and the heaviness of some of the yarns along with the openwork structures of some of the cloths point to the vertical loom as the probable tool that was used to weave them.

Other archaeological evidence comes from the capital of the Benin Kingdom on the western side of the Niger River. A deep shaft containing female remains from what appears to have been a human sacrifice also included some fragments of cloth, located at levels dating to the thirteenth century. In other words, this cloth, like the Igbo-Ukwu examples above, dates to a period prior to the arrival of Europeans on the coast. The materials and structures of the threads have been microscopically analyzed, though here again, the fibers could not be identified precisely. The fabrics are similar to one another, and are made up of several types of yarn elements. Flat, raphia-like fibers have been woven together with insertions of finer yarns placed at intervals, a strategy devised most probably for strengthening the fabric structure. Threads in other fabrics, tentatively identified as cotton, were used singly or plied together. They were spun in the opposite direction from the so-called bast fibers from Igbo-Ukwu, that is, in the z-direction, which is consistent with cotton-spinning practice elsewhere in West Africa at this time. Some single elements were paired and plied together in the S-direction, while still other, heavier threads consisted of as many as seven elements plied together. These latter *cabled* threads were woven into the cloths at intervals in order to create a ribbed pattern. The woven structures of the fabrics were also varied, including plain weave, network and openwork, and supplementary wefts that were applied to show patterning on one side of the cloth.[19] Here again, the use of raphia, the variety of types and weights of yarns, the unusual structures of the fabrics, and the mixing of raphia with other (possibly cotton) elements all indicate that the fabrics were locally made on a vertical loom.

What these rare archaeological fragments illustrate is something that tends to be underappreciated in the historical literature: the spinning of various fibers into threads and then the use of these threads for weaving on vertical looms preceded the European coastal trade. Such a claim is not particularly outlandish, for it is also consistent with written accounts of observations made by Portuguese mariners and traders and the others who followed their lead in exploring the Guinea Coast. Although the earliest of these mariners probably first sailed into the Bight of Benin in the early 1470s, direct contact between Europeans and the inland Benin Kingdom did not take place until 1485 or 1486. A description by Pacheco Pereira, who made four visits to Benin in the 1490s, mentioned that there was a market center on the Forcados River, and that the goods available there included cotton cloths. By 1505, the factor at the newly established Portuguese trading post at Ughoton, north of the Forcados and about thirty miles inland, was purchasing local textiles regularly in order to clothe slaves and make ships' awnings, and also to send to Costa da Mina to be exchanged for gold. In that year alone he reported buying a total number of 1,816 locally woven cotton cloths.[20]

These transactions marked a new era for societies on the west coast of Africa, and one that brought their merchants, artisans, and other workers more directly than ever before into international commercial networks. But this change was not an immediate or dramatic one, for during the first two hundred years of Atlantic trade, European merchants had to adapt to regional markets and trading patterns that already existed in West Africa. Along the Bight of Benin, for example, there was a regional system of exchange that was handled by canoe men plying the river systems and the coastal lagoons.[21] What was new was the intercontinental scale of these commercial operations. Portuguese caravels built for ocean winds and currents opened up the waterborne trade and were able to connect regional West African markets with each other and with the Indian Ocean and Atlantic systems. Integral to all of these commercial networks, regional and global, old and new, were production centers and markets for textiles: cotton cloth was a major import and export product in Indian Ocean commerce; linen and woolen textiles were important European trade items; Indian textiles and cotton production were crucial to the development of Atlantic commerce and plantation economies in the New World; and textile imports and exports played a pivotal role in the development of the Guinea trade on Africa's western coast. Over the next three and a half centuries of the trans-Atlantic slave trade, demand for all sorts of textiles—from Europe, Asia, and Africa—facilitated the commercial transactions that brought African captives onto European ships to be transported as slaves to the New World. And among those demanded textiles were cloths produced on the vertical loom in the lower Niger region.

CLOTH AND EARLY DRESS

Preferences and values of consumers are the key to understanding markets and trade. In his description of the Guinea Coast, Pacheco Pereira was concerned above all with charting the coastline and providing navigational information to future mariners. Nevertheless, he does offer as well some brief glimpses of textile consumption there in the late fifteenth century.[22] Valuable though they are, his views are limited in important ways. He does not usually indicate whether the cloth people were wearing was made in Africa or elsewhere; moreover, his references to cloth imports are confined mainly to the goods marketed by Europeans. There is no explicit reference to trading operations carried out solely by African merchants. In matters of dress, his standards are conditioned by the long sleeves, fitted jackets, stockings, and trousers current in Europe at that time. It is therefore not clear what he means by the term *naked*, that is, whether he is describing total nudity or only partial covering of the body.[23] Far more useful are his references to cotton cloth, which was still relatively rare in most of Europe at the time. Describing peoples living in upper Guinea, around Cape Verga and Sierra Leone, he writes that some of them went naked while others were dressed in cotton. In these same places, there was a demand for imports of linen and red cloth. Similarly, on the Gold Coast, he describes the people there as naked except for loin cloths or striped cloths that were considered an elegant form of dress for the nobility. Textile imports there were linens, red and blue cloth, and striped woolen cloth from North Africa (*lanbens* or *hambels*). Although he mentions a trade in cotton cloth on the Forcados River in the Niger delta, he does not describe the dress of people living in the area. But he does state that products from the Forcados River market, especially cotton cloth and slaves, were much in demand on the Gold Coast, and that Portuguese merchants clever enough to take advantage of this market were profiting handsomely in gold. This particular trading relationship—one that linked the Bight of Benin with the Gold Coast—would prove to be an especially important and long-lasting one for West African textile producers.

The patterns of textile consumption, exchange, and production before the advent of the Guinea trade cannot be traced with precision, but once again the archaeological record provides some important early clues. Evidence from Igbo-Ukwu establishes the antiquity of weaving and ceremonial regalia, but it tells us next to nothing about the kinds of textiles that were worn in the ninth century. The three excavation sites, and Igbo Isaiah, Igbo Richard, and Igbo Jonah,[24] yielded very different kinds of evidence: Igbo Isaiah is believed to have been a regalia storehouse where beautifully embellished bronze vessels and other valuables were kept; Igbo Richard represented burial and grave goods; and Igbo Jonah consisted of disposal pits of some kind. The most plausible explanation so far as to who the important person buried at Igbo-Ukwu might have been centers on the institution of the *Eze Nri*, a position that combined sacred and secular leadership authority. But if this was a priest and the storehouse goods were the paraphernalia of his shrine, questions arise as to how he was able to amass such considerable wealth and from where. What is certain is that there were wide-ranging trade contacts of some sort already in place by the ninth century, networks that were extensive enough to have brought thousands of trade beads from far-off continents to the rainforests of the lower Niger. It has been suggested that other goods from overseas found their way to forest communities around this time as well, including foreign textiles.[25] We will never know this for sure, and unfortunately we will also never know what kind of garb this priest (if priest indeed he was) wore on ceremonial occasions, aside from the beaded and copper ornaments that were buried with him. The surviving textile fragments from Igbo-Ukwu all came from the storehouse site, where they were used simply as coverings to protect some of the more precious bronze containers.

It is not until the thirteenth century that we have clearer evidence of particular types of textiles being used as clothing. The burial site excavated near the king's palace in Benin City was no ordinary grave. That this was a ritual sacrifice is apparent: as many as forty young women were thrown together into a pit or cistern, along with decorated bronze jewelry and beads made of glass and agate. Their clothing or burial shrouds, too, were impressive. Some of the textile fragments were densely woven in plain weave, while others included more complex structural embellishments such as network and openwork. Another fragment showed evidence of supplementary threads woven in to make brocaded patterns on one side of the cloth (fig. 2.3).[26] All were probably early products of the vertical loom; and the intricacies of design and pattern-making techniques are convincing evidence that their makers had achieved a high degree of skilled craftsmanship. These were exceptional cloths, perhaps made specifically for this occasion.

Much less is known about early dress and weaving in the Yoruba kingdoms.[27] But given the likely historical links between Ife and Benin— as suggested by oral traditions and linguistics—it is reasonable to suggest that in Yorubaland too, royal and ceremonial dress included certain types of fancy, locally woven textiles. One eloquent example of visual evidence comes from a figural sculpture portraying a Yoruba king, the Oni of Ife, cast in brass and dated by thermoluminescence to the early fourteenth or early

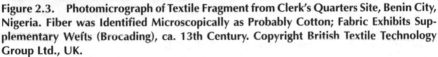

Figure 2.3.   Photomicrograph of Textile Fragment from Clerk's Quarters Site, Benin City, Nigeria. Fiber was Identified Microscopically as Probably Cotton; Fabric Exhibits Supplementary Wefts (Brocading), ca. 13th Century. Copyright British Textile Technology Group Ltd., UK.

fifteenth century. It is a rarity—of all the castings found at Ife, it is the only full-length figure to have survived intact. Standing in an erect and frontal position, the figure is extravagantly bedecked in items of regalia. Beads adorn his crown, wrap his arms, and encircle his legs. Ropes and strands of beads cover his torso, topped off by a heavy beaded collar and his badge of office. He wears a cloth wrapper folded at the waist and cinched by what appears to be a cloth belt trimmed with beads. Other emblems of his authority are a ram's horn held in his left hand, and a scepter of beads and cloth in his right.[28] He displays the power and splendor of his office, an office held during the period of Ife's cultural florescence, when protective walls surrounded the town and the floors of some buildings were paved with potsherds carefully laid down in striking patterns. Ife, having been a site of bead production from the early fourteenth century, was probably also the source of the original beaded crowns that conferred legitimacy to Yoruba kings.[29] It would not be surprising if special textiles were woven there too, but it cannot be said for certain whether the cloth worn by this figure was complex or simple in its design or whether it was made locally or imported.

Placed in a regional context, oral evidence claiming that official patronage of weavers was institutionalized prior to the Guinea trade becomes highly plausible. One such claim has been made for the Benin Kingdom. Oba Ohen, believed to have ruled in the first half of the fifteenth century, is cited by oral historians as the founder of the royal weavers' guild, *owina n'ido*, the establishment of which was an event that initiated a new stage in the history of textile manufacture in the kingdom. Of the importance of textiles to Benin court rituals and official dress there is no doubt, since it has been well documented that intricately patterned cloths produced by the guild were commissioned for the use of chiefs, priests, and the king himself.[30] The guild could indeed date back to the fifteenth century or earlier, as suggested by the antiquity of the special techniques for which its members were well known. One of these techniques, the creation of patterns with supplementary weft threads, is a feature of some of the burial fragments dating to the thirteenth century, evidence that lends credibility to the claim that the royal weavers' guild had very early origins.

A similar situation can be seen in the Yoruba kingdom of Ijebu-Ode, where oral traditions and technical evidence from ceremonial textiles also suggest a long history of official patronage of weavers. Ijebu-Ode was another of the earliest textile producing and bulking (distribution) centers noted specifically by European traders along the Bight of Benin. Competing claims about how it came to be so must be viewed in relation to the kingdom's political history. Ijebu-Ode's past can be divided into two main periods: a predynastic time of earliest settlement that included the emergence of numerous "mini-states," and a subsequent age of kings that is believed to have begun around the fourteenth century. Waves of immigration from Ife, Benin, and other locales during both periods resulted in a population composed of many local identities.[31] This complex demographic and social history is reflected in oral traditions recounting the origins of the vertical loom and weaving in the kingdom. Some villages, claiming to be descended from the predynastic population, insist that their ancestors established the vertical-loom technology in Ijebu-Ode, while a majority of the kingdom's peoples believe that it was brought from Ife by a culture hero named Afin.[32] Technical evidence suggests that there is good reason to accept both versions. That is because here too, weavers used supplementary weft threads on one side of the cloth—the same technique used in Benin—to make complex imagery on textiles that were worn exclusively by chiefs, titleholders, and priests. People, ideas, and items of regalia all circulated among the kingdoms in the region, as did craftsworkers and their skills. It is likely then that predynastic weavers were later joined by specially trained weavers brought to Ijebu-Ode from other kingdoms for the precise reason that they could make patterned ceremonial cloths for the new regime. What is certain is that in these two (and probably other) forest locales, weaving was well established by the fifteenth century, with workshops stratified and differentiated by their marketing strategies. Some workshops made cloth for the everyday needs of ordinary folk while others specialized in making fancy textiles designed specifically for an elite of political officials, religious leaders, and the wealthy.

In short, the market for textiles was already well developed when international commerce opened up on the Bight of Benin, and foreign merchants had to adapt to this existent market. Cloth was imported not simply because of scarcity. Nor did Edo and Yoruba merchants import foreign textiles simply because they were cheaper or fancier than the locally made varieties. Quite the opposite was true. Local weavers produced a variety of textiles for fancy or everyday dress, and, as we shall see in the next section, many of these local textiles sold at prices that were competitive with overseas imports. Consumers here were already familiar with an impressive array of cloth types—plain and patterned, small and large—made of different kinds of threads, structures, and fibers. They had specific tastes and were careful to inspect merchandise thoroughly before striking a deal. Hence the cultural preferences and acuity of African buyers were to play an important role in trade and had to be taken into account by European suppliers, as contemporary merchant records amply show.

WEAVING, WRAPPERS, AND TRADE IN THE SEVENTEENTH AND EIGHTEENTH CENTURIES

Trade along the Guinea Coast defies neat and succinct description, and it would be quite misleading to characterize it in general terms. It was carried out through a complex exchange system called *assortment bargaining*,[33] with traders having to come to agreement on the amounts, types, and values of merchandise to be transferred in each direction. The assortment of goods on either side of a transaction included commodities of many kinds, from processed materials and finished manufactures to human captives, all of which were subject to shifting patterns of supply and demand that kept merchants scrambling to market and update their stores. Correspondence and accounts from company records are filled with complaints about the vagaries and vicissitudes of trade relations and the logistical intricacies of commerce on the Guinea Coast. Minor conflicts and attempts at deception, among Europeans and Africans alike, could easily escalate into violent reprisals, disrupting what tenuous security there might be and making trade more costly and fraught with risk. Personal relationships and some degree of trust between trading partners, however intermittent, were therefore key. And how one fared in the cutthroat competition for establishing and maintaining such relations depended a lot on the quality of goods one could offer, from the special gifts that had to be given to attract and seal partnership agreements to the actual supplies of more ordinary merchandise that would make up the deal. Hence there were two interrelated commercial networks that operated in international trade, the first being the exchange between prominent merchants and officials of rarities and other exotic goods among themselves, which then served as the necessary prelude to a second network represented by the more substantial exchanges of basic import and export goods. Textiles were major products in each of these networks, however, setting the stage for the transfer of textile technology, materials, and visual imagery into new communities.

What written sources there are from this period are somewhat misleading in that they contain more numerous and detailed references to cloth imported from overseas than for the local export cloths they were receiving in exchange. European merchants had to be constantly aware of how well or how poorly their own products were competing against those of their rivals, and also of what sorts of gifts might have the greatest leverage with particular West African kings and officials. What their accounts and descriptions reveal is how selective the import process was. Reading between the lines, we can discern from them what some of the cultural values were that mediated assessments and selections of foreign products. From outright requests for certain specific presents to general references stating what would "sell well," it was by and large the choices and desires of well-positioned men that determined which new colors, designs, and materials would make the most impressive additions to West African wardrobes.[34] On the Gold Coast in 1701, for example, gifts offered by the Dutch West India Company to an official trader from Asante were carefully noted for future reference, and included a red velvet cloth with gold-lace border, a large gilded mirror, a crested helmet, a fancy umbrella, and four sheets of gold leather. Several decades later, Dutch company officials on a trade mission to the King of Dahomey witnessed some of the more elaborate examples of the king's imported garments. While hosting a formal dinner for his guests at court, the king engaged in a fashion parade, performing three complete costume changes, from his European-style coat of gold-embroidered red velvet to another tailored black dress-coat, also embroidered in gold, to a voluminous wrapper or robe of silver brocade or embroidery.[35] This public display certainly must have conveyed a strong message to all in the audience, not only about the king's personal preferences and tastes, but above all about his important position in international trade and his skill in capitalizing on it.

There were also some special cases where imported novelties were universally admired, appropriated, and quickly assimilated into the paraphernalia of some of the region's cultural institutions. One prominent example can be identified by examining the persistent demand for scarlet wool cloth

woven in Europe. This specific type of fabric was coveted in many West
African locales, though for different uses and purposes. In some Yoruba areas, for example, scarlet cloth was imported to be unraveled, the bright red
thread then rewoven into ceremonial cloths—some for display at funerals,
others to be worn as masquerade costumes representing ancestors.[36] Scarlet
wool cloth, called *ododo* in the Edo language, was particularly important in
the Benin Kingdom. The reign of Oba Ewuare, during the second half of
the fifteenth century, is remembered not only as the beginning of a century
of military expansion but also as the time when red flannel began to be
imported. Named after the Yoruba term for scarlet, *ododo* may have initially
entered the kingdom through Yoruba intermediaries before the Dutch and
others became direct suppliers of it on the coast.[37]

Imported red wool was quickly absorbed into Benin culture, where the
court closely monitored its use. A German merchant observed in the early
seventeenth century that gold and silver were not valued highly in Benin
and Lagos, but brass was, and so was anything that was red. The Benin king
reputedly restricted the wearing of red coral beads and red scarlet cloth to
only those who had his official permission to do so.[38] Another description
from 1668 described the uniforms of the kingdom's military officers as made
of imported scarlet cloth.[39] And as was the case in Yorubaland, some woolen
cloths were unraveled so that local weavers could use the thread. Members
of Benin's royal weavers' guild recounted that in the past it was their prerogative to weave a cloth reserved exclusively for the king—a complex fabric
woven with bast threads, spun from the processed bark of the *ighwian* tree,
and embellished with brocaded imagery in multicolored wool. Other bast
cloths made for chiefs had their patterns rendered somewhat less gloriously
with cotton threads.[40]

How to explain this admiration for wool, especially red wool? It wasn't
because these colors were not already available to weavers in the tropical
rainforests, since local dyers were able to produce many of them, including
red.[41] Most likely it was the intensity and saturated quality of the color: compared to cotton and other cellulose fibers, wool absorbs natural dyes much
more easily and deeply. Hence dyed wool, especially wool dyed scarlet,
would have been immediately appreciated for its exceptional luminosity—a
visual power that was evidently seized upon by political and religious elites
and deployed in their service. What is most noteworthy about this case is
that it shows how some specially chosen imported materials could be readily
integrated with indigenous ones to transform significant ceremonial clothing
traditions.

For the majority of the population, however, conventions of dress were
revised, not revolutionized, by the international trade in textiles. Initially,
imported cloth was adapted to already well-established conventions and

styles of dress that were based on the wrapper. In Benin, and most likely in neighboring kingdoms as well, seventeenth- and eighteenth-century clothing reflected a variety of social divisions that were defined by age, gender, and class. Contemporary descriptions are corroborated by portrayals of dress in Benin sculptural figures and the famous cast brass plaques that once adorned the king's palace. These we know to be remarkably veristic and therefore reliable visual sources, especially in matters of dress, thanks to painstaking research by art historians.[42] Youths—male and female—apparently went unclothed until they married. Then, upon reaching adulthood, they adopted gendered modes of dress. Adult men wore plain and patterned wrappers cinched at the waist, very much in contrast to the tailored jackets, trousers, and pleated kilts that characterized their European visitors.[43] Adult women— at least in this part of the Guinea Coast—were for the most part restricted from wearing the linens imported from Europe and the cotton *kannekins* from India that were favored by the most fashionable men, and wore instead plain or dyed-blue *Benin cloth* wrapped around their torso and folded over at the waist, sometimes with a smaller cloth over their breasts. Their counterparts to the west in Fetu country along the Gold Coast wore cloth from overseas—a simple linen or woolen cloth if they were poor or more voluminous, elegant, and expensive imports if they were among the wealthy. Social position was also evident in the number of cloths worn at a time: ordinary people wore a single wrapper while the rich might wear as many as four, draped and layered in such a way as to show all of them off. This mode of dress, based on layers of cloth and noted in general for Benin, was described also and in greater detail by observers in the port of Allada and on the Gold Coast, where overseas imports were worn by most of the population. While poor men in Fetu wore a small loincloth of low-quality linen, their betters in Allada dressed in three or four small cloth wrappers, artfully arranged so that all could be seen. In both places, the wealthiest men wore several silk cloths topped off by an exotic silk gown or a luxuriously woven cloth worn toga-like over one shoulder.[44] For the most part, yardage straight from the loom was much preferred over sewn, seamed, and fitted garments. Long lengths of fabric were cut down to the proper size for making the wrappers, shawls, and underclothes that continued to serve as customary dress on the Guinea Coast (see table 2.4 below).

Dutch and English company accounts specify by name the seemingly innumerable types of yardage their ships carried to ports on the Bight of Benin during this time, most of it coming from Indian and European manufacturers (see table 2.5 below). But that variety is merely a first impression, based solely on the nomenclature. Textile imports were subjected to selection, and a relatively coherent set of consumer preferences can be revealed if we identify the visual and material features of those overseas cloths that were

Table 2.4.   General Vocabulary for Cloth

Yoruba	Edo
abòra = a garment, a mantle	emobo = dress of the Oba's; not the most elaborate one
agò = a shroud; dress of the egúngún	
aso = cloth, garment, apparel	egbele = small piece of embroidered [sic] cloth worn around the waist by people attending Oba's ceremonies
awe, ayé = breadth of cloth	
elegodo = coarse calico	
gele or gèlè = head-tie, handkerchief	ekun okhuo = women's big cloth (ekun = waist; okhuo = cloth)
gogowú = a large country cloth	
ibante = an apron	ogbu = a big covering cloth for men; bigger than ekun okhuo
iborùn = shawl	
ìgbàjá = girdle, narrow strip of cloth tied around the loins	ododo = scarlet cloth (Yoruba ododo = scarlet color)
ìpelé = small outer cloth worn by women	okhuen = a cloth woven from the fibers of raphia [sic?] leaves; a species of tree
ìtélèdí = common cloth, underclothing	
kidzikpa, kíjìpá = coarse country cloth woven by women	oseba = a cloth worn by women when working at home: it goes from the waist to the knees (not identical with ovi ukpon, which is only an undercloth)
odon, òdùn = cloth of palm leaf fibers	
ògbon = gauze	
sányan = raw silk, coarse woven silk	ovi ukpon = undercloth
	oza = strip of cloth used to fasten ovi ukpon by women; men either wrap it tightly, or wear ugbekun (belt)
	ugbekun = belt
	ukpon = cloth

Sources: Bowen 1858; Crowther and Sowande 1950; Melzian 1937. Edo spellings adapted to Roman alphabet.

consistently favored. Some of them were undoubtedly singled out and appreciated as unusual products that were not available in nearby workshops, such as the woolen *kerseys, perpetuanas,* and *says* that came from European looms. Others, however, were very much like the textiles woven locally on the vertical loom. Many were closely related in terms of their fiber content; most of the imported cloth fell into the category of cottons and linens, using fibers that were the same or similar to those used by local weavers. A number of the imports also closely resembled vertical-loom cloth in color and pattern. Imported linens were often the natural beige color of the fiber, much as raphia, bast, and wild silk textiles were. And cottons from overseas were usually plain (muslins, undyed calicos, or *salempors*), dyed (*baft* or kannekins), or loom-patterned stripes and checks (such as ginghams and *nicanees*), as were the standard varieties of locally woven country cloth. Only the painted and printed calicos, chintzes, and *Haarlems* were true novelties in the cotton and linen category. Indeed, *Guinea cloth* became a generic term for the cotton cloths woven in India and preferred by many consumers on the Guinea Coast. In other words, far from being dramatic

Table 2.5. Textile Imports to Benin from Europe and India (Pre-1900)

Cotton*	Linen	Wool	Silk	Mixed
baft [dyed]	cambric	kerseys	damask	annebaas (wool
calico	canvas	perpetuanas	velvet	on linen,
Cambay	damask	says		wool on
chintz [printed or	Haarlem			cotton)
painted]	plathilios			fustian
Coromandel	sheets			(cotton/linen)
gingham [loom	Silesian			gingham
patterned	tickings			(cotton/silk)
stripes and checks]	Ypres			gold/silver
kannekins [dyed]				brocade
muslin [undyed				
cotton]				
nicanees [loom				
patterned				
stripes]				
Salempor [staple				
cotton cloth]				
tickings				

*Bracketed descriptions from Irwin and Schwartz.
Sources: Alpern 1995, 6–10; Irwin and Schwartz 1966, 57–72; Jones 1995, 311–25; Law 1997, xviii–xix; Reikat 1997, 218–42; Ryder 1969, index; Schneider, in Weiner and Schneider 1989, 177–213.

new trendsetters that offered long-overdue variety to a dreary local market, imported textiles were for the most part preselected to conform to established tastes and cultural values. European merchants quickly learned that adherence to such matters of taste were crucial if there was to be any successful trading. For example, attempts by England's Royal African Company to have English weavers copy certain types of these Indian-made Guinea cloths met with failure, since consumers in West Africa could easily spot the difference and consistently refused to buy the European imitations.[45] Here again we see the important role of culture in shaping markets and mediating economic transactions.

The textile trade on the Bight of Benin was exceptionally complex because this was one of several areas along the coast where cloth was imported *and* where West African weavers produced cloth for export. References to this export trade in the written sources are sketchy and very difficult to interpret. What records there are mention exports numbering in the thousands of pieces of cloth at certain times, but it is hard to determine what they looked like and how they were made. For example, some foreigners in the early period of the Guinea trade only mentioned what they considered to be the unusual features of certain types of cloth, leaving it open to question how many other types there were and the availability of each. "Very curiously woven" Benin cloths struck the eye of one merchant in 1591, much as another admired the attractive, multicolored and patterned cloths sold in Lagos in 1603, probably the product of inland Yoruba looms.[46] These tantalizing references indicate that not all patterned cloth was reserved for local political elites, but it is not clear exactly what the patterns were.

Plain or patterned, the West African cloth exported along the Bight of Benin was undoubtedly produced on the vertical loom. A common feature of vertical-loom textiles was woven breadth: they were wider than West African strip-woven cloth, narrower than most overseas cloth, and narrower than a finished wrapper. Hence several separate cloth units had to be sewn together, and depending on how many of these units there were, the finished wrapper size varied. Vertical-loom wrappers came to be known and named by this feature. When merchants began to handle large numbers of them in the seventeenth century, that is, when cotton textile exports from Benin and surrounding areas were regularly being bulked and shipped to other ports on the Guinea Coast, wrappers were classified according to the number of individual woven breadths that were included per entire cloth. For example, a description of Benin in the mid-seventeenth century mentions two major products of Benin looms, each a wrapper of different size: one made up of three breadths of cloth, the other made up of four breadths of cotton dyed indigo blue or patterned with blue-and-white stripes. The latter, called *mouponoqua* (*ukpon nokhua*, or big cloth)[47] in the original Dutch account, was approximately 5 to 6 feet long by 4½ feet wide.[48] The popular three-breadth unit served as a term of accounting—*dreibants*—used by the Dutch to calculate their cloth purchases.[49] If we combine these midcentury descriptions of Benin cloth with later reports about cotton cloth exports from Ijebu-Ode, we see indications of uniformity in the production methods of weavers who were making trade cloth. Textiles manufactured on the vertical loom in the hinterlands of Allada, Lagos, and Benin reportedly came off the looms in standard widths of about twelve to fourteen inches.[50]

What evidence we have for making comparisons suggests that some West African textiles competed very well against foreign cloth in the coastal trade. One factor was cost. During this period, the seventeenth and eighteenth centuries, when all textiles were produced in preindustrial workshops and transport costs were relatively high, certain types of cloth exported from entrepôts along the Guinea Coast could be sold at lower prices there than cloth coming from overseas. To cite one example, if we compare the estimated values of a wrapper made from the highest-priced Benin cloth and one made out of imported linen, the latter could be at least 30 percent more costly than the former (see table 2.6 below). Moreover, African-made cloth could be much more profitable for the merchant. Whereas European textiles sold on the Guinea Coast for just under twice their cost, merchants sold native cloths from Benin and the Cape Verde Islands for up to three or

Table 2.6.　Comparative Prices for Cloth on the Gold Coast, Mid-Seventeenth Century

Linen versus Cotton

1660: European linen sold on the Gold Coast at 128 ells per large benda (2 oz., 8 engels gold). Wrapper dimensions for Benin "big cloths" were given in 1668 as 2 ells wide by about 2$1/2$ ells long; therefore, a wrapper of European linen would require two lengths of 2$1/2$ ells. This means that about 15 wrappers of linen could be had per large benda. 1664: "Calde" cloths (from Benin) sold on the Gold Coast at 22 per benda (2 oz. gold).

Sources: Jones 1998, 18; Jones 1995, 141, 315; Makepeace 1991, 147; Jones 1983, 331.

Misc. imported cloth, 1680s

Second hand sheets (linen)	3 s. 6 d. each
Indian cottons	5 s.–10 s. per piece (each 10–20 yards)
Woolens	40 s. each
Benin cloth	5 s. each
Allada cloth	40 s. each
Mandinga cloth	120 s. each

Source: Public Record Office, London, T 70 230, quoted in M. Johnson 1978, 263.

four times what they had paid for them.[51] In short, a canny merchant could realize very high profits if he understood what kinds of textiles to purchase in which ports, and where on the coast particular textiles were most in demand. One set of market prices from the Gold Coast illustrates how several types of Benin cloth fared in competition with exports from Allada and the Ivory Coast:[52]

Allada cloth	5 brass bracelets
Benin cloth, 3-breadth	3 brass bracelets
Benin *calde* cloth	12 brass bracelets
Benin cloth, 5-breadth, dyed blue	7 brass bracelets
Quaqua cloth from Ivory Coast	5 brass bracelets

All of these textiles, in varying numbers and at different times, were sold to Gold Coast merchants who then resold many of them to their contacts upcountry. For merchants dealing in Benin cloth, a category that surely included Yoruba exports, the Gold Coast was only one of a number of possible markets. Textiles coming into the ports of Arbo and Lagos were bulked and sorted to be shipped to ready markets on the Gold Coast, the Gabon estuary, Angola, the island of São Tomé, and as far away as the West Indies and Brazil. A few of the written sources describe the specific regional market preferences that structured this trade: striped cloths were exchanged for gold on the Gold Coast, while indigo-blue cloths were most desired in Gabon and Angola in exchange for ivory and slaves.[53]

Available figures for the volume of textile exports during the seventeenth and eighteenth centuries give only fleeting glimpses, but they are impressive (see table 2.7 below). For some years at least, the numbers are comparable to those for Cape Verde textiles exported by the Pará-Maranhão Company in the second half of the seventeenth century, which were produced under direct merchant supervision and with more labor-efficient looms.[54] How weavers in the Bight of Benin hinterland achieved these levels of production is undocumented, but it can be safely assumed that such market expansion had a significant impact on the textile workshops in Benin, Ijebu-Ode, and their environs. While weaving on the vertical loom might well have been already practiced to some degree in many parts of the region, surely more workers were brought into textile production as the pace and volume of output intensified. Unfortunately, the precise vehicles for and avenues of technology transfer are obscure. Oral traditions in the region corroborate a late seventeenth-century account estimating that Benin cloths came from far inland, perhaps beyond the forest fringes. In the far inland area of northeast Yorubaland especially, varying degrees of Benin influence can be discerned in certain cultural practices, institutions, and dynastic traditions. Akintoye has described an early trade route running northward from Benin to Owo and on through Akoko and Iyagba to Nupeland. Another branch veered to the northwest and led through Ekiti to a market center near Ife. Throughout this area, cloths were woven on vertical looms, and most commonly in

Table 2.7.   Reported Exports of Benin Cloth on Guinea Coast

1505	1,816 cloths	Purchased by Portuguese factor B. Fernandez.
1633	6,461 cloths	Dutch ship arrived on Gold Coast with Benin cloths (reportedly left behind another 6,000 for lack of cargo space).
1644–1646	16,000 cloths	Dutch purchased cloths at Arbo (probably supplied by Ijebu-Ode); claimed that the English purchased even more.
1698	285 cloths	Dutch ships carrying fewer cloths; decline in
1699	200 cloths	trading value and Portuguese competition cited as the reason.
1708	2,016 cloths	Dutch ship carried Benin cloths to Gold Coast (in demand again).
1717	samples of cloth and 6,000 lbs. locally spun cotton yarns	Sent to Europe by Dutch West India Company for marketing information.
1736	1,798 cloths	Dutch ship arrived in Elmina with Benin cloth.
1789	1,000 cloths	Unidentified ship carried cargo of Benin cloth.
1816	10,000 cloths	São Tomé merchant carried cargo of Benin cloth.

Source: Ryder 1969.

three varieties: two-, three-, and four-breadth wrappers. The four-breadth type was still being referred to in the 1960s as *aso-Adó*, or "cloth for Benin." During the seventeenth and eighteenth centuries, export merchants took European goods on credit and then traveled to inland workshops to have Benin cloths made over the next five or six months. In other words, the textiles were not ready-made for export, though there is no evidence so far that merchants were able to establish a *putting out* system of production.[55] Weaving undoubtedly remained an independent occupation, and the technology remained much the same. Hence higher levels of production had to have been achieved by technology transfer and expansion of the workforce.

Very few descriptions of the labor process exist, but it appears that most of the weavers and spinners were women, probably aided by child labor. A French merchant who made several extended visits to Benin between 1769 and 1783 observed weaving and indigo dyeing first hand. He stated that women did both, and that the loom used was a vertical one. Cloths were of either cotton or raphia, the former made with three breadths, the latter four breadths. Both types of wrapper were described as being eight feet long, though that figure may well have been an exaggeration. He also remarked on the volume of textile manufacture and that looms could be found in most houses.[56] Other early observers also report that women were the major weavers throughout the Benin Kingdom, and oral testimonies from nearby Owo claim that weaving was an ancient female occupation.[57] Cultivation of cotton and "grass" for the purpose of producing textiles, noted in an eighteenth-century account, suggests that workshops of women weavers were well established also in the northern Yoruba kingdom of Oyo at that time.[58] Where there were exceptions to this gendered labor pattern, it was in workshops producing special types of ceremonial cloth for political leaders and titleholders. Both men and women were observed at different times weaving in Benin's royal palace, and cloths for titleholders in Ijebu-Ode, as well as Bunu funeral cloths, were reportedly woven by men and women.[59]

There are no reports on spinning save for oral testimonies purporting to recount what was believed to have been done in the past. Historians of Benin's royal weavers' guild state that long ago, women were weavers and men were spinners, the reverse of how labor was organized in recent times.[60] In all likelihood, however, most spinning was done by women with a small handheld spindle, a skill that took years to master.[61] Hand spinning always presented a considerable drag on production, being a laborious process that involved preparing the fiber and carefully spinning a consistently strong and even thread. Before widespread mechanization, spinning required the exploitation of labor no matter where in the world it was done. In Europe, women and children produced linen thread under harsh working conditions, much as cotton spinning depended on low caste (pariah) and female labor on India's Coromandel Coast.[62] Female and child labor produced almost all of the handspun thread in West Africa.[63] Hence the production of textiles, especially when it was intensified for export markets, placed enormous pressures on women's labor especially, and it was probably because of that bottleneck that very high volumes of exports from the lower Niger region were difficult to sustain for any length of time. This situation did not improve until the late 1800s when machine-spun cotton began to be imported into West Africa from England and France.[64]

To sum up, over the period of the seventeenth and eighteenth centuries, at the height of the trans-Atlantic slave trade, production of textiles on the vertical loom became more widespread in response to demand from regional and international trade. If the net effect of this expansion was not a volume of exports rivaling that of India, there nevertheless must have been important economic consequences for the lower Niger region, especially regarding women's incomes and labor patterns. Although we lack precise information about what those consequences were, changes in the nineteenth and twentieth centuries offer some suggestions. Weaving continued to be a viable occupation for some women in the nineteenth and twentieth centuries, even in the face of competition from the lower-cost products of industrialized looms. Additional centers of cotton cloth manufacturing arose, relying on the tools and techniques of this ancient weaving technology while incorporating new imported materials and adopting different production strategies. No longer able to undercut the prices of overseas textiles, which had become much cheaper than ever before by the late nineteenth century, women weavers drew inspiration from the region's past history of embellished ceremonial cloth and designed novel forms of fancy textiles that were aimed at the luxury market. At the same time, however, there were other women who chose to abandon their looms.[65] The gradual decline of weaving in former major production centers such as Benin and Ijebu-Ode raises some fundamental questions about women's work in these centers, such as to what degree women were able to exercise control over their own labor, how much their earnings were, and what alternative occupations were open to them. Weaving could be a viable and even lucrative occupation for women, but only given the right circumstances and well-chosen production strategies.

WEAVING, WRAPPERS, AND TRADE IN THE NINETEENTH AND TWENTIETH CENTURIES

Women's work was much affected by changes in the region's trading patterns in the nineteenth and twentieth centuries. One distinct set of changes centered on the coast and its hinterland. The legal abolition and decline of the Atlantic slave trade and the subsequent rise of palm oil trade and production for export along the coast meant that merchants had to reorient their operations and adapt to new economic conditions. Scholars have debated whether these changes might be considered revolutionary or if they signaled an economic crisis—the consensus now being that, important though it was, the transition to palm oil production did not bring about a major restructuring of society.[66] What it did do was attract more people into the export sector. Women were the major processors of palm products and therefore the key to production, but how much they themselves were able to earn from this work varied from place to place in the region. In parts of Yorubaland, women were involved in the production and trade of palm oil on a significant scale, and some women, brokers especially, became quite wealthy. Elsewhere, it was not the women but their husbands who amassed wealth from the palm trade. In Igboland, for example, palm oil production was especially intense, and over time men were able to gain control over most of the trade and most of the profits by marrying many women and exploiting their wives' labor. The processing of palm kernels was, however, another story, and in that domain women's control was not eroded. The net result was that when palm kernel exports rose in the late nineteenth century, women finally did begin to benefit directly from this export trade and to see an improvement in their incomes.[67]

Fortunately for some women there was a promising alternative. The case of Akwete, a town in Igbo country that became an important textile-producing center starting in the second half of the nineteenth century, demonstrates how enterprising and well-positioned weavers could tap into the wealth generated by the export trade in palm products. The weavers of Akwete capitalized on their geographical location and longstanding trading relations with their Ijo neighbors in the Niger delta who had become wealthy export merchants with a taste for certain kinds of luxury cloth, both from overseas and from closer to home. Akwete weavers began to imitate these imports for sale to the Ijo, who were known to pay very high prices for just the right kinds and colors of cloth. The vertical loom, which had been formerly used by Akwete weavers to make simple cloths of plain weave, was adapted slightly to enable them to make a very different type of cloth. This cloth was characterized by elaborate brocaded patterns that formerly had been restricted to ceremonial textiles in the Benin and Yoruba kingdoms. In other words, Akwete women modified their looms and developed new skills to engage in import replacement for rich and fashionable Ijo consumers. And in doing so, they reversed the export strategy followed by women weavers in former times, who produced low-cost goods to undercut the prices of simple plain-weave cotton imports. In this case they did the opposite: they wove complex *compound structure* textiles aimed specifically at a group of consumers known to have major purchasing power.

One reason this change took place in Akwete had to do with ecological factors and the town's strategic role in the palm oil trade. It was in an area where, primarily because of the soil conditions, oil palms did not do well. Just to the north, however, in the communities of the Ngwa Igbo, the situation was the reverse and oil palms flourished, turning Ngwa into a major supplier of palm oil. Akwete, situated on the Imo River between Ngwa and the coastal ports of Opobo and Bonny, was therefore well placed to establish a middleman role in trade, and it became an important bulking and marketing town in the export trade. When production volume increased and the port of Bonny became a major exporter of palm oil in the 1820s, prosperity in the region rose significantly and continued to do so until prices fell in the 1870s and 1880s. It was during this period of economic expansion that *Akwete cloth* was first created and marketed as a fancy textile product.[68]

Oral traditions recounting the genesis of Akwete cloth make claims to Igbo origins for textile-patterning techniques that had already been integrated into the region's cultural history for centuries. The "invention" of Akwete cloth is conveyed by way of a cliché, or mnemonic stereotype, which takes the guise of a legendary weaver known as Dada Nwakata or Dada Nwakwata. Several versions of the tradition have been published.[69] Common elements in these versions suggest how and approximately when the invention occurred, though it is unlikely that Dada Nwakata did it single-handedly. Consistent with the ways in which we know that accounts of origin are formed, where historical processes involving groups of people become compressed and reduced over time into one single historical cliché, it is probable that this individual weaver represents many others.[70] And if there ever truly was a Dada Nwakata, she was probably one of the most famous and successful of Akwete cloth makers, but not necessarily the first. The tradition credits this woman with inventing new weaving designs sometime in the mid-nineteenth century, designs in some cases woven with thread unraveled from foreign cloth. By recounting that she envisioned these innovations in her dreams or was inspired by spirits, the tradition employs the trope of supernatural sanction, a device that sets its bearer apart from others. Dada Nwakata's superior skill and success are then amplified by an emphasis on her secrecy and control, for she is described as having kept people from seeing her practice her craft. It is said that only after her death did other women weavers then follow her lead. Incorporated into some variants of the tradition is a song composed and sung by traders in her honor: *egerebite nwada erenkpota*, or *egerebite nwada eregh mkpota*, which translates as "it's very difficult to purchase Nwada's cloth (it's very expensive)."[71]

Other evidence corroborates the general message of the oral tradition and provides some specific details as to how and when this historical change took place. Aronson has shown very convincingly that there is a core of truth to this oral tradition, and that the wealthy palm oil traders of coastal Ijo ports such as Bonny, Brass, New Calabar, and Okrika were the targeted consumers. Oral testimonies gathered in those towns consistently state that the Ijo never had a history of weaving textiles for themselves, but that they depended on imports. Moreover, testimonies gathered in Akwete and other communities in the Ndoki Igbo area describe totally different types of textiles woven before the invention of Akwete cloth. These textiles were also made on the vertical loom but were very narrow in width, and came in two main forms: a plain-weave cotton cloth known as *akwa mirri*; and a plain-weave cloth of raphia, or raphia and cotton, called *okuru*. These same types of textiles were also woven in other Igbo communities into the twentieth century, especially in Asaba, Abakaliki, Nsukka, and Ovim (fig. 2.2). Examples of the much wider, more heavily patterned Akwete cloths began appearing in European museum collections in the late nineteenth century, having been acquired by British merchants during the 1880s and 1890s, indicating that the new textile form was established around midcentury or perhaps earlier. Akwete cloths were also kept in the treasure chests of prominent coastal Ijo families, along with other valuable textiles and precious objects that had been handed down over generations.[72] Clearly a major change had occurred in weaving practice, and Ijo consumers played a central role.

Further clues to this history come from visual, technical, and linguistic evidence, and they center on one distinctive type of ceremonial cloth from Ijebu-Ode in Yorubaland. Known there as *aso olona*, or "cloth with patterns," it was heavily embellished with brocaded patterns and worn either draped on the shoulder of chiefs and titleholders in the Oshugbo society, or as a large wrapper of several breadths sewn together and again as a prerogative of chiefs, titleholders, priests, and other members of the ruling elite. The most important motifs woven into these cloths were schematic representations of water-dwelling creatures—crocodiles, frogs, fish, snakes—that symbolized deities and forces of the spiritual domain (fig. 2.4).[73] Some of these same motifs were woven into the oldest type of Akwete cloth known in Ijo communities, a type of cloth these communities revered the most. It was called by the Ijo name *ikakibite*, or "tortoise cloth." That the borrowing of these motifs and the brocading technique for making them occurred through trade is strongly suggested by different ways of dressing the loom and preparing the patterning stick as practiced by Ijebu-Ode weavers and weavers in Akwete. A more direct borrowing process, such as itinerant Yoruba teachers coming to Igboland, or Igbo apprentices being sent to learn from Yoruba teachers, would have resulted in technological continuity, not these slight but important differences.[74] Aronson has pointed out that these types of fancy textiles were not like the trade cloths designed and woven for export from Ijebu-Ode, but were instead woven for special use within the kingdom by its rulers and religious leaders. As an explanation of how such valuable and prestigious textiles reached the Ijo, she suggests that they might have made their way to the Niger delta along with certain religious and political institutions, since there had been historical connections between Ijebu-Ode and the Itsekiri, neighbors of the Ijo. Another very plausible vehicle of transfer could have been the high-level gift-giving networks that were so necessary for arranging, sealing, and maintaining trade relationships. One can easily imagine Ijo and Itsekiri palm oil brokers amassing

Figure 2.4. Ijebu-Ode Cloth with Brocaded Imagery, Including Mudfish Motif. Collected Late 18th Century, Accession no. 716.29. Copyright the Trustees of the National Museums of Scotland.

stunning collections of textile treasures received from their suppliers in the delta hinterland and also from foreign exporters along the coast. Trading networks marked the parameters within which small numbers of precious and highly priced ceremonial cloths could also be exchanged. An earlier example would be the so-called Benin rugs—possibly signifying the impressive, elaborately brocaded and cut-pile ceremonial shoulder cloths of the Ijebu-Ode, or their Benin counterparts—that were worn by high officials on the seventeenth-century Gold Coast and were called a "king's garment."[75]

In certain respects, Akwete cloth can be seen as a new form of textile tradition reflecting a more rapid pace of change. It is overtly and transparently a multiethnic product, relying heavily on borrowing and innovation. Originally modeled on a clearly defined and distinctive Edo/Yoruba prototype worn by political elites, it was transformed by Igbo weavers into a general and more accessible type of prestige cloth for the wealthy. And although men and women in Igbo communities wore it on important social occasions, the primary consumers of it were their neighbors in eastern Ijo country. Over time, Akwete cloth came to include many more variants, as Ijo patrons brought treasured heirlooms or rare textiles from overseas to be copied by the women weavers of Akwete. The female masters of this craft, to display their individual skill and imagination, invented additional new designs. Cloth made in Akwete thus came to incorporate many more design compositions and pattern elements relative to textiles woven by other women in the region.[76] Akwete cloth was quickly seized upon as a tradition in both Igbo and Ijo societies. Igbo-speakers naturalized it by recounting the oral traditions of Dada Nwakata and via lexical terminology, with particular cloths and design motifs, whatever their origin, all having names in the Igbo language.[77] At the same time, Ijo-speakers naturalized it by coining their own names and also through their ritual practices, for Akwete cloth served, along with other highly esteemed imported cloths, as special dress for the most significant personal and communal occasions of a lifetime, such as funeral processions and display, and ceremonies surrounding marriage. One example, recorded in a late nineteenth-century wedding photograph, shows *ikakibite* (tortoise cloth) used as a formal backdrop and also as the bride's costume (fig. 2.5).

As Akwete weavers replicated, recontextualized, and transformed this older textile prototype, they adopted several useful laborsaving strategies having to do with weaving techniques and the labor process. One of these was to work only with imported threads. By the beginning of the twentieth century, Akwete cloths were being made entirely of factory-spun yarns imported from Europe: cotton, some silk, and later, as a cheaper substitute for silk, rayon. Handspinning became a skill of the past, leaving more women able to devote their time entirely to weaving. Another change was in the weaving width. These new fancy cloths were most often woven at widths

Figure 2.5. *Ikakibite* (Tortoise Cloth). Chief William Brown and His Two Wives and Daughter. Bonny, N.C.P. Photographer Unknown, ca. 1897. Himburg Photographic Album, no. 1995-240052. Eliot Elisofon Photographic Archives, National Museum of African Art, Smithsonian Institution, USA.

much wider than ever before—an average of forty-five inches—which meant that a single breadth was sufficient to make an entire wrapper. This change alone cut the weaving time at least in half. Finally, the weavers made adjustments to the labor process, though in complex ways that have not yet been fully spelled out. Weaving went from being a part-time seasonal activity carried out by some women to a full-time occupation for most women in the town. But this restructuring was not without its costs. Women had to cover their other labor obligations by buying slaves with their sales profits. A standard Akwete cloth reportedly sold for enough to buy one slave while the more elaborate cloths brought in enough profit to purchase two slaves. Women still needed control over the labor of others in order to devote themselves full time to weaving and marketing their cloth. After the trade in palm oil declined and slavery finally came to an end during colonial rule, women became traders and brokers of Akwete cloth, presumably by exploiting family labor in textile manufacture and other work.[78]

The case of Akwete is perhaps the best-documented example of a transformation of weaving on the vertical loom in the Niger basin region, but it is not an isolated one. Similar changes took place further inland, within another quite different set of economic conditions that arose from the creation of a major polity to the north in the early 1800s. With the founding of the Sokoto Caliphate in the northern savannas, textile workers were drawn into a powerful new trading system. This Islamic state, created initially by jihads of the sword in the first decade of the nineteenth century, expanded to become by the century's end one of the largest countries in West Africa. Its economy impressed foreign visitors who remarked upon the thriving agricultural sector and the flourishing production and trade of manufactures, especially that of cotton textiles. Trade routes crisscrossed the lower Niger basin along north–south and east–west axes, linking up with international networks on the coast and at the Sahara's edge. Long-distance routes traversing the savanna grew in importance over the nineteenth century, due in large part to the success of the caliphate's well-organized traders and their large, profitable caravans. The huge quantities of textiles traded in these interior networks were not only products from within the caliphate itself, but they also included reexports from around the region. They were carried into the caliphate from all directions—imports from Europe, for example, along with cloth produced in Yoruba country, were traded from the south (fig. 2.6). Cloth was exported and traded out of the caliphate in other directions as well: east to Borno, north across the Sahara, south to the coast, and westward along the kola routes to Asante. Much of this cloth was produced by women on the vertical loom.[79] In other words, merchants in the Sokoto Caliphate capitalized on preexisting workshops and markets— the textile trade to Asante, for example, was in many ways an overland manifestation of the centuries-old maritime commercial relationship between the Bight of Benin and the Gold Coast.

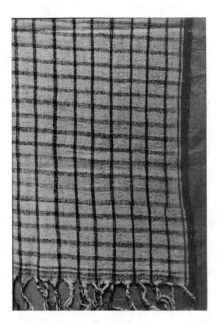

Figure 2.6. Cotton Wrapper, White and Indigo, Woven on a Vertical Loom in Yorubaland and Traded Northward, 63 Inches Long
by 38 Inches Wide. Collected in 1841. Stanger
Collection, Accession no. 1.xii.1856. Photograph by the Author. Copyright the Wisbech
and Fenland Museum, UK.

Vertical-loom technology, which had already been carried northward with
the coastal export trading frontier, was transferred to communities north of
the Niger via slave raids in the nineteenth century. Women and girls skilled
in spinning and weaving were undoubtedly among the many captives taken
from towns and villages in northeast Yorubaland, first by mounted raiders
from the Nupe kingdom, and then by caliphate armies.[80] We know the
loom was being used in Nupe communities before midcentury, based on
the evidence from a major collection of textiles brought back to England
by members of the 1841 Niger Expedition. They purchased the cloths in
markets near the Niger-Benue confluence, making careful notations as to
price, where the cloths were made, and, in some cases, what they would be
used for. Weavers using the vertical loom, presumably women, produced
the majority of these textiles, and they offer an unusual and valuable window onto trade between Yorubaland and the caliphate. In these textiles we
see confirmation that vertical-loom weaving technology was established at
least as far north as Nupeland by 1841, over a generation earlier than scholars had previously thought. And we also see some indications of weavers'
production strategies, which emerge when we compare the material and
technical features of the cloths in relation to how much they cost in the
market.[81]

Women in Nupe and Yorubaland followed some marketing and laborsaving strategies that were similar to those adopted by the women weavers

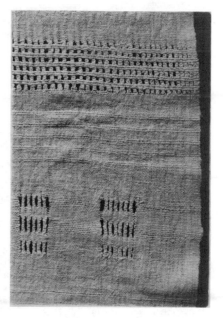

Figure 2.7. Cotton Wrapper, Woven on a Vertical Loom, with Openwork Techniques, 57 Inches Long by 45 Inches Wide. Collected in 1841. Stanger Collection, Accession no. 1.xii.1856. Photograph by the Author. Copyright the Wisbech and Fenland Museum, UK.

in Akwete. One strategy was to aim at the higher-priced sector of the market by producing cloth with complex patterning as either openwork (fig. 2.7) or brocaded stripes and motifs. An example from the 1841 Niger Expedition collection has cotton supplementary wefts traversing the woven breadth and several horizontal rows of individual pattern motifs rendered in red wool (fig. 2.8). It was the second most costly of the wrappers from this collection that had been made in workshops south of the Niger-Benue confluence. Some women also ensured higher prices for their textile products by working with finer-quality yarns and weaving denser fabric, features that could easily be recognized by discerning consumers. Using silk yarns in the weaving also added greater value to their products, a strategy followed by weavers of the several Nupe cloths in the collection. Women also reduced their labor costs by weaving breadths of cloth that were 50 percent wider than the earlier standard widths of twelve to fourteen inches. Using widths of twenty to twenty-eight inches, their wrappers could be made with two vertical loom cloths rather than three or four, which cut the weaving time considerably. Out of all the vertical-loom cloths in this sample, Nupe women produced the most expensive ones: narrow, striped headcloths made of fine silk and cotton that would have been worn by the wives or concubines of prominent Muslim men.[82]

Weavers in this area also took up elaborate brocaded patterning and factory-spun yarns, though it happened slightly later than in Akwete and

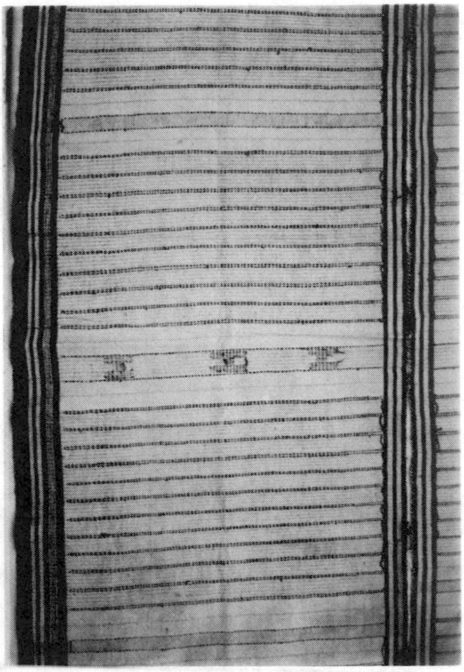

Figure 2.8. Cotton Wrapper, Woven on a Vertical Loom, with Brocading in Indigo-Dyed Cotton and Red Wool, 66 Inches Long by 33 Inches Wide. Purchased at Eggan, 1841. Niger Expedition Collection, Accession no. 43.3-11.42. Photograph by the Author. Copyright the Trustees of the British Museum, UK.

was prompted by a different set of circumstances. Okene, an Ebira market town just south of the Niger-Benue confluence, became a prominent center for this kind of women's weaving in the early twentieth century. It was known for two main types of vertical-loom cloths: cotton *country cloths* made with handspun yarns; and fancy brocaded textiles woven with factory-spun yarns. The former, wrappers made up of three or four woven units, are usually considered to be the genuinely traditional cloths of Okene, while the latter are relatively recent additions to the repertoire of Ebira weavers. When asked about the antiquity of their craft, Ebira weavers state that it is something Ebira women have done from the beginning of time, adding that the oldest types of cloth they wove were made of cotton and bast, and the oldest methods of making patterns were stripes and openwork.[83] The weavers' claims are certainly plausible, given that the *Ishan* variety of cotton was well established in their area,[84] and the specific bast fiber they mention is the same variety that was used by the royal weavers of Benin. Similarly, the patterning techniques mentioned in the weavers' accounts could easily be accepted as very old ones. Openwork techniques were present in the archaeological fragments from the palace at Benin City and from Igbo-Ukwu, and the early trade cloths exported along the coast were often patterned in stripes made with dyed cotton yarns. In short, textiles with these particular features do indeed have a long history in the region.

However, the assertion that this is an ancient Ebira tradition is questionable. The technology was probably very old in this geographical locale but not necessarily so among Ebira-speakers. They are relative newcomers to areas south of the confluence, in contrast to neighboring groups such as the Yagba, Bunu, and Oworo, who are thought to be among the indigenous inhabitants of these areas. The Ebira are said to have originated in the Benue valley, with groups of them setting out in the eighteenth century on a series of migrations that took them southwestward into Igala territory and eventually to their present locations.[85] Sorting out the question of how and when they began to practice weaving on the vertical loom thus poses a major challenge. The confluence area has had a long history of trade, immigration, slave raiding, overlordships, returning migration of slaves, and intermarriage, making for a very complex social and cultural landscape.[86] The twentieth-century distribution of the vertical loom includes northern Ebira as well as Igala and Idah, though this might be the result of the loom's general transfer northward into Hausaland during colonial rule.[87] Alternatively, it can be suggested that weaving on the vertical loom would have been easily subject to Ebira influence as immigrant Ebira men married local wives and brought female slaves into their new households. As I have argued elsewhere, marriage and slavery were used very effectively as vehicles for transferring technology from one language group to another and also for asserting some degree of control over women's labor, knowledge, and skill in textile production.[88]

A patriarchal workshop model provides the core image in Okene oral traditions explaining the relatively recent "invention" of fancy patterned textiles. Credit for introducing imported thread and establishing the technique of brocading is routinely given to Alhaji Ibrahim, a prominent Muslim businessman appointed in 1917 to serve as *Atta*, or paramount chief, of the Ebira under Britain's colonial administration. Testimonies all portray his household as a weaving workshop run by his wives, whom he supplied with multicolored silk, cotton, and wool yarns imported from Britain. Some claim that in 1922 he opened a store in Okene to make these yarns available to other weavers outside his palace, though at first the yarns, the silk yarns especially, were too costly for most women to buy. Less clear is the explanation for the "invention" of brocading. Wives of the Atta, so the tradition goes, began at this same time to weave brocaded patterns into their cloth. To do this, they modified the loom by adding multiple shed sticks, an innovation they claimed originated in Ilorin.[89] Just how this so-called Ilorin technique was brought to Okene, and by whom, is not mentioned.

Obviously this legend streamlines and condenses a much more uneven, protracted, and multilayered historical process. Picton offers technical evidence suggesting as much, for the variety of techniques for making brocaded patterns in *Okene cloth* directly challenges the oral tradition's single reference to Ilorin.[90] Also, the timing of the legend is rather late. Already in 1841, women in this general locale were weaving brocaded imagery mechanically, with a supplementary shed stick, including both isolated motifs and colored bands spanning the entire breadth of the fabric.[91] O'Hear has attempted to trace the history of brocading in Ilorin, and concludes that there were undoubtedly many avenues by which this textile technique was transmitted among workshops and across language boundaries.[92] Missing from the Alhaji Ibrahim legend, tellingly, is any mention of concubinage or slavery. However, Alhaji Ibrahim, as a wealthy Muslim official, was very likely to have had in his household a large population of women—slave and free—most likely from disparate communities. Hence variations in brocade techniques could reflect their differing backgrounds and learned weaving practices. Future research may bring us closer to understanding the history of textile technology and manufacture in northern Yorubaland and the Niger-Benue area, though it will necessarily involve an interdisciplinary approach combining evidence from archaeology, linguistics, textile technology, iconography, and oral history.

Both types of Okene textiles—the older country cloths made of handspun yarns and the newer fancy cloths made of factory-spun yarns—were worn as wrappers and were also used for ceremonial display. In the scholarly literature they are sometimes placed in separate categories and in opposition to each other—as "traditional" cloths versus cloths "produced for export." This type of categorization is misleading, however, and has the unfortunate effect of foreclosing useful historical questions. The so-called traditional country cloths were of several distinct types, with three or four woven breadths and with varying stripe patterns, each cloth and pattern having its own name. Certain ones were designated as cloth to be used as burial shrouds or as the cloth of ancestor costumes in masquerade performances. But how long these rather austere textiles have been deemed the proper ones for burial is uncertain. Ebira weavers and their counterparts in neighboring Bunu recall that Alhaji Ibrahim banned in Okene the use of *aso-ipo* cloth, which was a funeral cloth woven with red-wool patterning.[93] Certainly the plain cotton and bast *ita-ogede* cloth he prescribed instead was much more in line with Muslim preferences. But other questions arise. Were *ita-ogede* cloths already used for burials? Or was this a new tradition invented by Alhaji Ibrahim? Moreover, country cloths were not restricted to ritual use, at least in the twentieth century, for they were all available for sale in the market and many were worn as clothing in Okene and beyond. Calling country cloths "traditional" is therefore problematic, as is categorizing brocaded textiles solely as export products. Many fancy cloths were indeed produced for sale, and large numbers of wrappers were exported to markets all over Nigeria. But they were not solely commercial products without any cultural significance. Scholars have documented how they were used in ceremonial displays—as burial shrouds and in masquerade costumes—and how specific cloth designs and motifs were given Ebira names.[94] Other scholars

describe how these cloths were used in Ebira communities for other important ceremonies—by age-grade groups and by families' public celebrations
of marriage.[95] All of these practices served to naturalize fancy cloth as an
important component of Ebira culture.

Perhaps the legend of Atta Alhaji Ibrahim is best understood as a metaphor
for the colonial period and as a mnemonic device for remembering important events during that time. His reign, a long one from 1917 to 1954,
coincides with the height of formal colonial rule, when Okene weaving
underwent major transformations. Young girls in Okene during this time
gradually ceased to take up spinning, and lighter-weight factory-spun yarns
became the norm, purchased by weavers to produce the new type of fancy
cloths with brocaded patterns. The prices of factory-produced yarns had
finally come within the reach of large numbers of weavers, and women in
market towns like Okene, taking advantage of their direct access, eagerly
bought them up. By the 1950s, the handloom weavers of Nigeria were using several million pounds of imported cotton yarns per year.[96] The reign
of Atta Ibrahim might also represent the contradictory era of cotton imperialism: those colonial policies aimed at undermining the production of
cotton textiles in Nigeria in order to turn it into a market for British-made
cloth. The plan was also intended to encourage cotton cultivation in order to supply the spinning machines and looms of Lancashire.[97] The effort
failed. Instead, raw cotton continued to be spun in some rural areas and
in the north, and weavers all over Nigeria, including women, continued to
practice their craft. There may be good reason to revere Atta Alhaji Ibrahim
and other cotton-yarn brokers like him, for they did much to safeguard and
support the manufacture of cloth on the vertical loom. This work, which had
for centuries provided women with a marketable skill and viable occupation, now guaranteed them their own independent income under a colonial
administration that was intent on relegating them to the informal economy.

MARRIAGE CLOTHS IN BIDA

Tailored garments, whether modeled after Muslim attire or westernized dress, became everyday clothing for most Nigerians by the 1960s.
Nevertheless, wrappers continued to be woven and worn, sometimes along
with shirts and blouses, mostly by women. Certain kinds of wrappers also
remained valuable as cultural products that were charged with meaning.
The special fancy cloth described at the beginning of this chapter, which
was woven in the Nupe town of Bida, is one of the most highly valued
kinds of vertical loom cloth produced there. It is an essential component of
the bride's dowry in marriage ceremonies both in Bida and in surrounding
rural areas.[98]

The cloth's weaver, whose name could not be tracked down, was most likely a member of a relatively wealthy Muslim household. Weaving one of these elaborately brocaded textiles is painstaking and labor-intensive work, involving at least a month or more of time at the loom. For that reason, plus the fact that the cost of imported materials is so high, the skills and practice of weaving in Nupeland are confined almost entirely to women of the upper classes. Described as a "leisure time" activity, it is heavily subsidized by the labor of others. Only those fortunate women who have access to servants, or, in the past, who had access to slaves, can or could set aside the time needed to weave this kind of brocaded cloth. Their profits are theirs, and they are comparable to the profits made by male artisans.[99] In this particular case, the superior quality of the cloth and its complex design is a testament to the weaver's mastery.

This textile must also be acknowledged and appreciated as a collective achievement. It can be viewed as a summation of major textile techniques and production strategies that developed regionally over time. We have seen how the vertical loom came to Nupeland and other locales north of the Niger-Benue confluence, and why the cloth was woven at twenty-five inches—wider than the older Ijebu-Ode and Benin textiles, but narrower than Akwete cloths. We have also learned why this weaver chose to use imported yarns, and why it is not surprising that her special arrangement of stripe patterning is reminiscent of the work of Ilorin women weavers. Similarly, it is understandable why she would rely on two important patterning devices, openwork and brocading, and why cloths with this patterning would be so coveted by Nigerian consumers. One interesting and distinctive feature of this cloth is the weaver's method of brocading, which in its counting system (see table 2.8 below) differs from most other brocading methods

Table 2.8. Brocading Techniques and Counting Systems

Cloth, Geographical Location, Date	Brocading "Tie-Down" Threads	Counting System (Thread Count Repeat)
Figs. 2.1 and 2.9, Bida, 1970s	oooooXoXoooooXoX	$5+1+1+1=8$
Fig. 2.8, Seluk (Yagba?), 1841	oooooXoXoooooXoX	$5+1+1+1=8$
Akwete cloth, 1970s	oooooooXoooooooX	$7+1=8$
Ijebu-Ode cloth, 1970s	oooooooXoooooooX	$7+1=8$
Okene cloth, 1970s	oooooooooooXoooooooooooX	$11+1=12$
	oooooooooXoooooooooX	$9+1=10$
	oooooooXoooooooX	$7+1=8$
Fig. 2.10, Bida, 1970s	oooooooooooXoooooooooooX	$11+1=12$

o = warp threads covered by brocade
X = warp thread that holds brocade in place

Sources: Aronson 1980, 104–5; Aronson 1982, 171; Chogudo 1987, 31; and data from the 1841 Niger Expedition Collection and private collections.

Figure 2.9. Detail of Brocading and Openwork Techniques, Woman's Wrapper, Bida, Nigeria (See Entire Cloth, Fig. 2.1). UCLA Fowler Museum of Cultural History, Colleen E. Kriger Collection of Nigerian Textiles, X2005.24.15.

discussed in this chapter (figs. 2.9 and 2.10). But very much like her fellow weavers in Akwete and Okene, she employed a varied and imaginative vocabulary of motifs, from zigzags and lozenges running lengthwise along the strips and bands of color, to geometric and zoomorphic patterns resembling birds, lizards, and frogs sitting horizontally in twos and threes across the web.

The history of how this textile came to be is a facet of the history of the Niger basin region, a story that follows a particular loom, certain special fibers, and especially, unusual techniques of embellishment. Throughout this story, we have seen that imported ideas, techniques, and materials were embraced while at the same time certain cultural preferences and values persisted. There was the basic continuity of the wrapper form, a preference for certain fibers such as cotton and silk, and a love of indigo and natural fiber colors, as well as an interest in the luminosity offered by red-wool threads, multicolored wool, dyed silks and rayons, and the metallic sheen of Lurex.[100] Textiles such as this one have played a major role in West African trade and in the workings of that region's social and political relations. In the process, they were marked and transformed by historical changes of many kinds: technical adaptation, cultural borrowing, import substitution, pursuit of novelty, deliberate innovation, and choices of production and marketing strategies. Brocade and openwork began as features that distinguished the

Figure 2.10. Detail of Brocading Technique, Woman's "Duna" Cloth, Bida, Nigeria. UCLA Fowler Museum of Cultural History, Colleen E. Kriger Collection of Nigerian Textiles, X2005.24.16.

precious ceremonial cloths that were the prerogative of kings and priests. With the passage of time, they came to grace the precious wedding cloths of wealthy Nupe brides.

NOTES

1. Irene Emery, *The Primary Structures of Textiles* (Washington, D.C.: The Textile Museum, 1980), 140–43.

2. Emery, *Primary Structures of Textiles*, 84–85.

3. Nupe is a language spoken in what is known as the "middle belt" of Nigeria, an area between the northern savannas and the southern rainforests. The history of Nupe kingdoms is thought to go back as far as the fifteenth or sixteenth century. Nupeland was incorporated into the nineteenth-century Sokoto Caliphate. See Ade Obayemi, "The Yoruba and Edo-Speaking Peoples and Their Neighbors before 1600," in *History of West Africa*, ed. J. F. A. Ajayi and Michael Crowder (New York: Columbia University Press, 1976), 1:196–263; Michael Mason, *Foundations of the Bida Kingdom* (Zaria, Nigeria: Ahmadu Bello University Press, 1981).

4. Graham Connah, *African Civilizations: An Archaeological Perspective*, 2nd ed. (Cambridge: Cambridge University Press, 2001), 145–50; Hans Melzian, *A Concise Dictionary of the Bini Language of Southern Nigeria* (London: Kegan Paul, 1937). The language spoken in the Benin Kingdom is now more commonly referred to as Edo, not Bini.

5. J. M. Dalziel, *The Useful Plants of Western Tropical Africa* (London: Crown Agents, 1937), 499–500, 506, 511–12.

6. J. F. Landolphe, *Mémoires du Capitaine Landolphe contenant l'histoire de ses voyages pendant 36 ans, au côtes d'Afrique et aux deux Amériques* (Paris: J.S. Quesne, 1823), 1:121.

7. Colleen Kriger, "Textile Production in the Lower Niger Basin: New Evidence from the 1841 Niger Expedition Collection," *Textile History* 21, no. 1 (1990): 49–51.

8. Samuel Crowther and E. J. Sowande, *A Dictionary of the Yoruba Language* (1937; repr., London: Oxford University Press, 1950), 182; T. J. Bowen, *Grammar and Dictionary of the Yoruba Language* (Washington, D.C.: Smithsonian Institution, 1858), 64.

9. Kriger, "Textile Production in the Lower Niger Basin," 56n56.

10. Samuel Crowther, *A Grammar and Vocabulary of the Nupe Language* (London: Church Missionary House, 1864), 204; Crowther and Sowande, *Dictionary of the Yoruba Language*, 183.

11. Paul Küller, *Wilde Seiden Afrikas* (Berlin: Radetzki, 1913); J. C. Ene, "Indigenous Silk Weaving in Nigeria," *Nigeria Magazine* 81 (1964); F. D. Golding, "The Wild Silkworms of Nigeria," *Farm and Forest* 3 (1942).

12. Nehemia Levtzion and J. F. P. Hopkins, eds., *Corpus of Early Arabic Sources for West African History* (Cambridge: Cambridge University Press, 1981), 260. For the early history of Kanem and the greater Lake Chad area, see Abdullahi Smith, "The Early States of the Central Sudan," in *History of West Africa*, Ajayi and Crowder, vol. 1.

13. See for example, Peggy Stoltz Gilfoy, *Patterns of Life: West African Strip-Weaving Traditions* (Washington, D.C.: National Museum of African Art, 1987); and National Museum of African Art, *History, Design, and Craft in West African Strip-Woven Cloth* (Washington, D.C.: National Museum of African Art, 1992).

14. Dalziel, *Useful Plants of Western Tropical Africa*, 122–23; A. W. Banfield, *Dictionary of the Nupe Language* (1914; repr., Farnborough, UK: Gregg International, 1969), 1:253, 329. Yoruba, Edo, Igbo, Nupe, Igala, Ebira, Idoma, and Gbari are all Kwa languages that have been spoken in the area around the confluence of the Niger and Benue rivers for centuries. They are part of a much larger language family,

Niger-Congo, which differs markedly in speech from the Chadic languages. See Obayemi, "The Yoruba and Edo-Speaking Peoples"; and Smith, "Early States of the Central Sudan."

15. As Donna Maier points out, however, cotton plants cross-pollinate rather easily, making it difficult to confidently infer agricultural experimentation from botanical evidence. See Maier, "Persistence of Precolonial Patterns of Production: Cotton in German Togoland, 1800–1914," in *Cotton, Colonialism, and Social History in Sub-Saharan Africa*, ed. Allen Isaacman and Richard Roberts (Portsmouth, N.H.: Heinemann, 1995), 77.

16. Igbo-Ukwu is the general term for excavations that were done at three separate sites in the town of Igbo-Ukwu, in southeastern Nigeria. They are most famous for spectacular finds of copperworking and cast leaded bronzes.

17. See E. J. W. Barber, *Prehistoric Textiles: The Development of Cloth in the Neolithic and Bronze Ages* (Princeton, N.J.: Princeton University Press, 1991), 66–67.

18. Thurstan Shaw, *Igbo-Ukwu: An Account of Archaeological Discoveries in Eastern Nigeria* (Evanston, Ill.: Northwestern University Press, 1970), 1:240–44; vol. 2, plates 495–503.

19. Graham Connah, *The Archaeology of Benin* (Oxford: Oxford University Press, 1975), 236–37, 251, and plates 45–48.

20. A. F. C. Ryder, *Benin and the Europeans, 1485–1897* (New York: Humanities Press, 1969), 24, 27n3, 33, 37; R. E. Bradbury, *Benin Studies* (London: Oxford University Press, 1973), 33.

21. Robin Law, "Trade and Politics behind the Slave coast: The Lagoon Traffic and the Rise of Lagos, 1500–1800," *Journal of African History* 24 (1983).

22. Duarte Pacheco Pereira, *Esmeraldo de situ orbis*, trans. and ed. George H. T. Kimble. (London: Hakluyt Society, 1937).

23. For a useful discussion of the cultural meanings of *clothing* and *nakedness*, see Esther Goody and Jack Goody, "The Naked and the Clothed," in *The Cloth of Many Colored Silks: Papers on History and Society Ghanaian and Islamic in Honor of Ivor Wilks*, ed. John Hunwick and Nancy Lawler (Evanston, Ill.: Northwestern University Press, 1996).

24. Named for three male members of the Anozie family who owned the compounds where the excavations took place.

25. Shaw, *Igbo-Ukwu: An Account of Archaeological Discoveries*, 1:285; E. J. Alagoa, "The Niger Delta States and Their Neighbors, to 1800, " in Ajayi and Crowder, *History of West Africa*, 1:362–64.

26. Connah, *Archaeology of Benin*, 62–66, 236–37.

27. Yoruba-speakers make up much of the population of southwestern Nigeria and parts of the modern nation of Benin. They established a number of ancient kingdoms in the region and also developed a complex system of religious beliefs and philosophical principles, accompanied by an extraordinarily rich corpus of visual arts and oral traditions. The Ile-Ife kingdom, which is often credited as the first kingdom in the region, grew to prominence by the tenth century and flourished especially in the twelfth to fifteenth centuries. See Obayemi, "The Yoruba and Edo-Speaking Peoples," in Ajayi and Crowder, *History of West Africa*, vol. 1.

28. Ekpo Eyo and Frank Willett, *Treasures of Ancient Nigeria* (New York: Alfred A. Knopf, 1980), 96–97.

29. Obayemi, "The Yoruba and Edo-Speaking Peoples," 212–15.

30. Paula Ben-Amos, "Owina n'ido: Royal Weavers of Benin," *African Arts* 11 (1978).

31. Obayemi, "The Yoruba and Edo-Speaking Peoples," 220–24.

32. Lisa Aronson, "Ijebu Yoruba Aso Olona: A Contextual and Historical Overview," *African Arts* 25, no. 3 (1992): 53.

33. For a discussion of assortment bargaining, see Philip Curtin, *Economic Change in Precolonial Africa: Senegambia in the Era of the Slave Trade* (Madison: University of Wisconsin Press, 1975), 247–53.

34. Robin Law, ed., *The English in West Africa, 1681–1683: The Local Correspondence of the Royal African Company of England, 1681–1699, Part I* (Oxford: Oxford University Press, 1997); Margaret Makepeace, ed., *Trade on the Guinea Coast, 1657–1666* (Madison: University of Wisconsin Press, 1991).

35. Albert Van Danzig, *The Dutch and the Guinea Coast 1674–1742: A Collection of Documents from the General State Archive at The Hague* (Accra: Ghana Academy of Arts and Sciences, 1978), 79, 296–97.

36. Obayemi, "The Yoruba and Edo-Speaking Peoples," 262.

37. Bradbury, *Benin Studies*, 34; Melzian, *A Concise Dictionary of the Bini Language*, 134.

38. Adam Jones, trans. and ed., *German Sources for West African History, 1599–1669* (Wiesbaden: Franz Steiner, 1983), 41.

39. Adam Jones, trans. and ed., *Olfert Dapper's Description of Benin* (Atlanta, Ga.: African Studies Association Press, 1998), 19.

40. Philip Dark, *An Introduction to Benin Art and Technology* (Oxford: Clarendon Press, 1973), 66–67; Ben-Amos, "Owina n'ido: Royal Weavers of Benin."

41. Melzian, *A Concise Dictionary of the Bini Language*, 206.

42. Paula Ben-Amos, "Who Is the Man in the Bowler Hat? Emblems of Identity in Benin Royal Art," *Baessler-Archiv*, N.F. 31 (1983); Ezio Bassani and William Fagg, *Africa and the Renaissance: Art in Ivory* (New York: Center for African Art, 1988).

43. Augustus Pitt-Rivers, *Antique Works of Art from Benin* (New York: Dover, 1976); Philip Dark, *An Illustrated Catalogue of Benin Art* (Boston: G.K. Hall, 1982).

44. Jones, *Olfert Dapper's Description*, 13–14; Jones, *West Africa in the Mid-Seventeenth Century: An Anonymous Dutch Manuscript* (Atlanta, Ga.: African Studies Association Press, 1995), 53; Jones, *German Sources for West African History*, 203–4.

45. John Irwin and P. R. Schwartz, *Studies in Indo-European Textile History* (Ahmedabad: Calico Museum of Textiles, 1966), 26, 65.

46. Ryder, *Benin and the Europeans*, 84; Jones, *German Sources for West African History*, 41.

47. P. E. H. Hair, "An Ethnolinguistic Inventory of the Lower Guinea Coast, Part II," *African Language Review* 8 (1969): 256.

48. Jones, *Olfert Dapper's Description*, 18; Jones, *West Africa in the Mid-Seventeenth Century*, 309.

49. Ryder, *Benin and the Europeans*, 94; Jones, *West Africa in the Mid-Seventeenth Century*.

50. G. A. Robertson, *Notes on Africa, Particularly Those Parts Which Are Situated between Cape Verd and the River Congo* (London: Sherwood, Neely, and Jones, 1819),

301–2; Hugh Clapperton, *Journal of a Second Expedition into the Interior of Africa* (1829; repr., London: Cass, 1966), 136–37.

51. On the Gold Coast, the ratio of cost to sale price of overseas imports was quoted as 1/1.75 in 1645 and 1/1.95 in 1819. For Benin cloth in 1698, the ratio was 1/3, and for Cape Verde cloth in the mid-eighteenth century it was 1/3.3 to 1/4. See Lars Sundström, *The Exchange Economy of Pre-colonial Tropical Africa* (original title, *The Trade of Guinea*, 1965; repr., New York: St. Martin's Press, 1974), 173.

52. Jones, *West Africa in the Mid-Seventeenth Century*, 141.

53. Ryder, *Benin and the Europeans*, 94; John Adams, *Sketches Taken during Ten Voyages to Africa between the Years 1786 and 1800* (1822; repr., New York: Johnson Reprint, 1970), 24–25, 27; Marion Johnson, *Anglo-African Trade in the Eighteenth Century*, ed. J. Thomas Lindblad and Robert Ross (Leiden: Centre for the History of European Expansion, 1990), 10.

54. António Carreira, *Panaria Cabo-Verdiano-Guineense* (Lisboa: Museu de Etnologia Ultramar, 1968).

55. S. A. Akintoye, "The Northeastern Districts of the Yoruba Country and the Benin Kingdom," *Journal of the Historical Society of Nigeria* 4 (1969): 544–46; Ryder, *Benin and the Europeans*, 131.

56. Landolphe, *Mémoires du Capitaine Landolphe*, 1:121; 2:49.

57. Ben-Amos, "Owina n'ido," 51; Robin Poynor, "Traditional Textiles in Owo, Nigeria," *African Arts* 14, no. 1 (1980): 47.

58. Robert Norris, *Memoirs of the Reign of Bossa Ahadee* (1789; repr., London: Cass, 1968), 138.

59. Ben-Amos, "Owina n'ido," 51; Aronson, "Ijebu Yoruba Aso Olona," 53; Elisha Renne, "Aso Ipo, Red Cloth from Bunu," *African Arts* 25, no. 3 (1992): 64, 69.

60. Ben-Amos, "Owina n'ido," 51–52.

61. Colleen Kriger, "Textile Production and Gender in the Sokoto Caliphate," *Journal of African History* 34 (1993).

62. Jane Schneider, "Rumpelstiltskin's Bargain: Folklore and Merchant Capitalist Intensification of Linen Manufacture in Early Modern Europe," in *Cloth and Human Experience*, ed. Annette Weiner and Jane Schneider (Washington, D.C.: Smithsonian Institution, 1991), 190–92; Joseph Brennig, "Textile Producers and Production in Late Seventeenth-century Coromandel," in *Textiles: Production, Trade, and Demand*, ed. Maureen Mazzaoui (Aldershot, UK: Ashgate, 1998), 171.

63. Kriger, "Textile Production and Gender."

64. Marion Johnson, "Technology, Competition, and African Crafts," in *The Imperial Impact: Studies in the Economic History of Africa and India*, ed. C. Dewey and A. G. Hopkins (London: Athlone Press, 1978), 265.

65. See for example, Elisha Renne, "The Decline of Women's Weaving among the Northeast Yoruba," paper presented at the annual meeting of the African Studies Association, Chicago, 28–31 October 1988; and Renne, *Cloth That Does Not Die: The Meaning of Cloth in Bùnú Social Life* (Seattle: University of Washington Press, 1995), 143–49.

66. Robin Law, *From Slave Trade to "Legitimate" Commerce: The Commercial Transition in Nineteenth-century West Africa* (Cambridge: Cambridge University Press, 1995); Martin Lynn, *Commerce and Economic Change in West Africa: The Palm Oil Trade in the Nineteenth Century* (Cambridge: Cambridge University Press, 1997).

67. Susan Martin, *Palm Oil and Protest: An Economic History of the Ngwaa Region, Southeastern Nigeria, 1800–1980* (Cambridge: Cambridge University Press, 1988).

68. Lynn, *Commerce and Economic Change*, 37; Lisa Aronson, *Akwete Weaving: A Study of Change in Response to the Palm Oil Trade in the Nineteenth Century* (PhD diss., Indiana University, 1982), 14, 16, 86. See also Lisa Aronson, "Tricks of the Trade: A Study of Ikakibite (Cloth of the Tortoise) among the Eastern Ijo," in *Ways of the Rivers: Arts and Environment of the Niger Delta*, ed. Martha Anderson and Philip Peek (Los Angeles: UCLA Fowler Museum of Cultural History, 2002).

69. Aronson, *Akwete Weaving*, 26–27; Richard Nwewueze Ikegwuonu, *Akwete Traditional Weaving* (BA thesis, University of Nigeria, Nsukka, 1971), 6–8.

70. Jan Vansina, *Oral Tradition as History* (Madison: University of Wisconsin Press, 1985).

71. Ikegwuonu, *Akwete Traditional Weaving*, 6; A. E. Kamalu, *Akwete Cloth* (BA thesis, Ahmadu Bello University, Zaria, 1965), 4–5.

72. Lisa Aronson, "History of the Cloth Trade in the Niger Delta: A Study of Diffusion," in *Textiles of Africa*, ed. D. Idiens and K. G. Ponting (Bath, UK: Pasold Research Fund, 1980); Aronson, *Akwete Weaving*.

73. The cloth illustrated in figure 2.4 was accessioned by the museum in 1860, with descriptive notes stating that it was collected in 1790. See Aronson, "History of the Cloth Trade," 96, 106n26.

74. Aronson, "History of the Cloth Trade"; Aronson, "Ijebu Yoruba Aso Alona."

75. Jones, *German Sources for West African History*, 186.

76. Aronson, "History of the Cloth Trade"; Aronson, *Akwete Weaving*; Adebukola Alawode, "Akwete Weaving Complex in Ndoki Tribe of Ukwa Local Government, Aba, Imo State," *Humanitas: Man's Past and Present* 3 (1985/1986).

77. Aronson refers to this process by another term, *cultural authentication*, citing Eicher and Erekosima. Aronson, "Ijebu Yoruba Aso Olona," 60; Joanne Eicher and Tonye Erekosima, "Kalabari Cut Thread and Pulled Thread Cloth: An Example of Cultural Authentication," *African Arts* 14, no. 2 (1981).

78. Aronson, *Akwete Weaving*; Ikegwuonu, *Akwete Traditional Weaving*.

79. Kriger, "Textile Production in the Lower Niger Basin."

80. S. Nadel, *A Black Byzantium: The Kingdom of Nupe in Nigeria* (London: Oxford University Press, 1951); Renne, *Cloth That Does Not Die*.

81. Kriger, "Textile Production in the Lower Niger Basin."

82. Kriger, "Textile Production in the Lower Niger Basin."

83. J. A. Ohiare, "Textile Production in the Ebira-Speaking Region: An Aspect of Its Technological Development from the 19th Century to Date," in *Archaeology and Society: Proceedings of the 8th Annual Conference of the Archaeological Association of Nigeria, Minna, June 25–July 1, 1989*, ed. J. F. Jemkur and A. D. Igirgi (Zaria, Nigeria: Archaeological Association of Nigeria, 1989).

84. Aliyu Sule Ododo Chogudo, *Traditional Textile Industry among the Ebira Tao since 1920s: A Case Study of Okene Local Government Area, in Kwara State, Nigeria* (BA thesis, University of Ilorin, Nigeria, 1987).

85. Chogudo, *Traditional Textile Industry*, 4–5.

86. See for example, Ann O'Hear, "The Yoruba and the Peoples of the Niger-Benue Confluence," in *Yoruba Frontiers*, ed. F. Afolayan and T. Falola, forthcoming.

87. Venice Lamb and Judy Holmes, *Nigerian Weaving* (Hertingfordbury, UK: Roxford Books, 1980), 175.

88. Kriger, "Textile Production and Gender."

89. John Picton, "Women's Weaving: The Manufacture and Use of Textiles among the Igbirra people of Nigeria," in *Textiles of Africa*, ed. D. Idiens and K. G. Ponting (Bath, UK: Pasold Research Fund, 1980), 77–79; Ohiare, "Textile Production in the Ebira-Speaking Region," 52–54.

90. Picton, "Women's Weaving," 78–80.

91. Kriger, "Textile Production in the Lower Niger Basin."

92. Ann O'Hear, "The Introduction of Weft Float Motifs to Strip Weaving in Ilorin," in *West African Economic and Social History: Studies in Memory of Marion Johnson*, ed. David Henige and T. C. McCaskie (Madison: University of Wisconsin, African Studies Program, 1990).

93. Renne, *Cloth That Does Not Die*, 146.

94. Picton, "Women's Weaving"; Ohiare, "Textile Production in the Ebira-Speaking Region."

95. Chogudo, *Traditional Textile Industry*; Renne, *Cloth That Does Not Die*.

96. Marion Johnson, "Technology, Competition, and African Crafts," 265.

97. Johnson, "Cotton Imperialism in West Africa," *African Affairs* 73 (1974).

98. Lamb and Holmes, *Nigerian Weaving*, 213–15.

99. Nadel, *Black Byzantium*, 297; Judith Perani, *Nupe Crafts: The Dynamics of Change in Nineteenth and Twentieth Century Weaving and Brasscasting* (PhD diss., Indiana University, 1988), 172.

100. John Picton, ed., *The Art of African Textiles: Technology, Tradition, and Lurex* (London: Barbican Art Gallery, 1995).

3

Muslim Garments and the Morality of Dress

Over the past millennium, as Islam began to take root south of the Sahara, men in West Africa who practiced the Muslim faith set themselves apart from other West African men by, among other things, their dress. It usually included garments that were sewn and tailored, such as a robe or gown and trousers, accompanied oftentimes by a cap or turban. The focus of this chapter is a very wide pair of handwoven, handsewn, cotton drawstring trousers covered almost completely with vibrantly colored embroidered imagery (fig. 3.1). Against a field of dark and light indigo pinstripes, clusters of free-floating motifs jostle alongside densely patterned interlacing bands. Forms seem to tilt, float, and bob, their corners and edges sprouting loops, spirals, and other flourishes here and there. Added to this complex visual interplay of texture, shape, and line is color. In an intense arrangement of polychrome embroidery, outlines are drawn and spaces filled in with gemlike hues of red, green, orange, magenta, and salmon, heightened by contrasting touches of black and white. The overall effect is lively, pulsating, and lush.

In contrast to the cloth wrapper discussed in the previous chapter, the colorful imagery adorning these trousers was applied after the weaving and tailoring processes had already been completed. Embroidery, as a separate postloom process, allows for much more freedom in the way shapes are created and arranged, since they are not bound within the strict horizontal and vertical structure of the woven web. In general, embroidered textiles can be seen as fiber "drawings," in that the woven cloth serves as the ground for a composition rendered rather freely in thread. Like marks on the surface of paper, the sewn pattern or picture appears on only one side of the fabric. In this case, the motifs are made primarily with two very different kinds of

Figure 3.1. Men's Cotton Trousers, Embroidered in Cotton and Wool, 39 Inches Long by 64 Inches Wide. Collected in Northern Nigeria, ca. 1930, by A. W. Banfield, Accession no. 950.126.3. Copyright R.O.M., Reproduced with Permission of the Royal Ontario Museum, Canada.

embroidery stitches: a chain stitch, which is used as the main technique for sewing lines and outlines; and *couching* (more specifically, *self-couching*), a type of stitch that is most effective for filling in spaces with solid areas of color. Two other types of stitches—feather and herringbone—are found much less often and only in particular sections of the garment. Herringbone stitching, for example, is used along with a chain stitch to make a pattern of magenta-and-black vertical stripes on the plain white cotton anklebands of the trousers.

Almost all of the visual features of this garment were made by hand processes, from the spinning to the weaving, and from the tailoring to the embroidery. The trouser cloth consists of strips of cotton woven on a treadle loom, at an average width of about two inches, which were then handsewn together edge-to-edge to form a large cloth rectangle. When folded in half, this rectangle serves as the main body of the garment. One of the most distinctive features of this style of trousers, a *crotch gusset*, was formed by cutting a square out of the center of the cloth, turning the square 90 degrees so that the strips ran crosswise, and then handsewing it back in with "French," or encased, seams.[1] The tailor added strips to each side, which extended the finished width of the trousers to about sixty-four inches. Finally, narrow anklebands, just over fifteen inches in circumference, were attached at the legs and a strip of cotton 3½ inches wide was added as a waistband casing for the drawstring. All of the warp and weft threads of the strip cloth are single elements made by handspinning in the z-direction. Specialization in spinning is indicated by the differentiation between warp and weft thread dimensions: warp yarns were spun tighter and finer, their diameters measuring about half those of the weft threads. The embroidery was carried out with a variety of factory-spun and synthetically dyed imported yarns. Most of them are worsted wool, spun in the z-direction and plied together in pairs in the S-direction. The colors of the wool yarns include five shades of red, two shades of green, magenta, orange, and black. The cotton threads range from 2-ply all the way to 6-ply with, again, single z-spun elements plied in the S-direction. Some of the threads are the natural undyed white of the cotton fiber, while others were dyed salmon and red, the latter in two different shades.

Many of the embroidered motifs, along with the garment style and the strip loom used to make the cloth, are strongly associated with the history of Islam in Hausaland (northern Nigeria) and its surrounding regions. This chapter seeks to portray some of the major contours of that history, in order to show that garments such as this one reflect certain Muslim cultural values, social conventions, and trading networks as they took shape in the lower Niger basin. It is a story that illustrates both the powerful universalizing principles of Islam and the multiplicities of peoples it came to embrace. Tracing the material, technical, and iconographic features of these trousers takes us into the many-layered history of Islam in West Africa where, over time, all sorts of cultural accommodations were reached between Muslims and the beliefs and practices of their various trading partners, slaves, and recent converts. Along the way, skilled embroiderers coming from different backgrounds, living at different times, created distinct variants of the type of garment illustrated here. Finally, in the first quarter of the twentieth century, a series of workers would spin and dye the threads, weave the cloth, and fashion this pair of trousers so that a Muslim man, perhaps in the northern Yoruba town of Ilorin, could adorn them with imagery drawn from the rich cultural heritage of that particular place.

MATERIALS: FIBER AND THREAD

These remarkable trousers are a product of the narrow horizontal treadle loom, sometimes called the Sudanese treadle loom (fig. 3.2). This loom has been noted in many parts of west and northeast Africa, with weavers using it to produce cloth strips in widths ranging from very narrow ones of about half an inch to much wider ones measuring up to thirty inches. On the basis of the way it operates—warp threads being controlled by harnesses suspended from a pulley and attached to foot-operated pedals—it can be classified as a counterbalanced treadle loom.[2] One of its most distinctive

Figure 3.2.   Man Weaving on a Treadle Loom, Nupe Country, Nigeria, 1903. Photograph by A. W. Banfield. Copyright the Estate of Frank Banfield, Canada.

features places it firmly in the cotton-producing areas of West Africa: in contrast to the vertical loom, which requires a long wooden sword or batten for beating in the crosswise weft threads, weavers using the treadle loom beat in the weft with a comb or reed. This feature makes it very difficult to weave with anything other than continuous lengths of smoothly spun threads since knotted or thickly twisted fibers would get caught in the teeth of the reed, possibly breaking them and slowing down the process. Hence it is highly unlikely that this type of loom has ever been used for weaving raphia, rough cordage, or cabled yarns of bast, the indigenous fibers of the forest regions. So far, I have not found any examples of these kinds of fibers being used to make cloth with the narrow treadle loom. Instead, the treadle loom is commonly associated with yarns spun out of cotton and, in some areas, wool or silk.

The antiquity of the treadle loom in the savanna and Sahel regions north of the confluence of the Niger and Benue Rivers has not yet been firmly established. The earliest, though indirect, evidence for styles of clothing in general comes from the environs of the Jos plateau, an area sandwiched between the Niger-Benue and the northern savannas. There, around two hundred fragments of terra-cotta sculptures have been unearthed since the first discoveries of them in the 1940s. Most are of the human figure, modeled in many different sizes. These are the famous Nok sculptures, which have been dated to the period 500 BC to AD 200. Among the visual concerns conveyed by the makers of these clay objects was a special attentiveness to particularities of dress and body adornment, such as precisely rendered details of hairdos, beaded jewelry, and, in some cases, clothing. Male and female figures alike wore waistbands, and there were also some examples of individuals wearing short rectangular pubic aprons.[3] One fragment of a lower torso shows what appears to be a length of cloth wrapped around the body and cinched at the waist. It has been dated to the first century AD[4] and leads some scholars to hypothesize a historical link between the Nok sculptures and art forms that arose in the Yoruba kingdoms. The argument centers on the particular way the maker of this figure represented the lower edge of the cloth, using a kind of ribbed line to suggest a band or hem, a visual convention resembling one used in Ife and Owo sculpture more than a millennium later.[5] Such a hypothesis is highly speculative. Moreover, this artistic convention tells us next to nothing about the actual fabric being depicted. It is not possible to discern any of the material, textural, or structural qualities of the cloths represented in any of these sculptures, and so it is unclear whether they were locally produced or not. There has been no evidence of the practice of weaving (such as spindle whorls) yet uncovered in any of the Nok sites. For these reasons, the question of where the cloths depicted in the Nok sculptures were produced, who made them, and, if they were woven, on what type of loom, must remain open.

What can be said with some confidence is that the most likely ancestor of the treadle loom is the Indian pit loom and others like it that originated in eastern and southern Asia. How, when, and by what routes it came into use in West Africa are issues that are far from being resolved. Two main theories have been proffered so far. Boser-Sarivaxévanis has advanced a theory that centers on wool production, Fulbe herders, and the inland Niger delta. She suggested that around the first several centuries AD, wool-bearing sheep, which had become important domesticated animals in Egypt during Hellenistic times, were transported across the Sahara, along with a treadle loom for weaving woolen cloth, and both the sheep and the loom were then established among Fulbe-speakers in tropical West Africa. Fulbe pastoralists subsequently became the disseminators of wool and wool-weaving technology, taking it from the upper Senegal valley and transferring it to the upper Niger. Boser-Sarivaxévanis proposed that by the eleventh century, the Fulbe pastoralists had adapted their loom for weaving cotton as well, which she believes came to sub-Saharan Africa later than wool. Cotton weaving was taken up by Mande artisans in the upper Niger region, and transfers of cotton-weaving technology into other parts of West Africa were then, in her view, henceforth carried out via migrations of various Mande-speaking peoples.[6]

Johnson took issue with Boser-Sarivaxévanis's theory, and she especially called into question the proposition that wool weaving preceded cotton weaving in West Africa. She noted problems with the evidence cited for wool and wool sheep in general, and challenged such a narrow emphasis on Fulbe pastoralists as specialists in raising and working with wool. Her own ideas took another approach, with a focus on cotton. Johnson argued that treadle looms have historically been associated primarily with cotton weaving, and her loom distribution map showed that pit looms were used in areas overlapping with the narrow treadle loom, suggesting a historical link between the two. Interpreting her map more broadly, she proposed that treadle-loom technology entered West Africa from the east, following the trade routes running along the Sahel, perhaps before the Muslim era.[7]

Neither of these two theories is entirely convincing on its own, and each strains what is still a very weak evidentiary base. What evidence there is at present for the raising of wool sheep in West Africa, for example, suggests a rather more complex picture than the one Boser-Sarivaxévanis presents. Ethnographic and linguistic data indicate that the thin-tailed hair sheep, not the wool sheep, is the variety most widespread in Africa and the one most closely associated with pastoralism. Wool-bearing sheep in tropical areas have been rare. They are more likely to be tied to urbanization and long-distance trade, and were firmly established in only two regions of the Sahara: in the far west around Mauretania; and to the east, in Chad. Smaller numbers of them were raised in the upper Niger delta and also the Lake Chad region.[8] Dating the introduction of sheep into sub-Saharan Africa is a major problem, and archaeological evidence does not help us very much here, since the reports from many sites do not distinguish between sheep and goat remains. Therefore, only a very general time frame can be suggested. Based on excavations very far away at the southern tip of the continent, in Western Cape, it has been estimated that sheep were being herded in parts of tropical West Africa before 200 BC, but it is not clear whether they were wool-bearing or not.[9]

Woolen textiles dating to the first millennium AD have been recovered from two separate archaeological sites, one in Burkina Faso and the other in Niger, but the processes and places of their manufacture are not yet known. At Kissi, in the northeast corner of Burkina Faso, fragments of wool have survived in contact with iron implements; samples from wood that was associated with these materials date between the fifth and seventh centuries. The cloth fragments are weft-face fabrics, with woolen warp threads spun in the s-direction and wefts spun in the z-direction. What the textiles were used for—whether as clothing or burial shrouds or as coverings for metalwork—is unclear. An embroidered woolen tunic and shawl, buried with the remains of a fifty-year-old Muslim woman, were unearthed in the Sahara at Iwelen. They appear to be of North African manufacture, and are dated to the second half of the eighth century.[10]

Cotton, too, is poorly documented. It is almost certain that the earliest domesticated forms came originally from India, the putative cradle of Old World cotton development, but the precise timing of transfers out of the subcontinent is not yet known. The botanical evidence is difficult to sort out, largely because the sources, whether they are historical accounts or archaeological reports, often fail to identify the particular species of cotton in question. Based mainly on inferences from present-day distribution patterns, it appears that the two major early forms of Old World cultivated cotton, *Gossypium arboreum* and *Gossypium herbaceum*, spread from India into well-watered areas of Malaya, south China, and northeast Africa in pre-Islamic times, that is, before the seventh century AD. However, it was not until annual varieties of each species had been developed that cotton could be cultivated during the shorter growing seasons of more northerly, temperate locales. This latter achievement apparently then touched off a second wave in the spread of cotton production, which carried the fiber and its technology throughout much of the Muslim world between the tenth and thirteenth centuries.[11]

There has been some disagreement on the role of Africa in the story of the rise and development of cotton cultivation. Some scholars have proposed that *G. arboreum* might be native to both Africa and India, while those arguing against this view favor an introduction of Indian cotton into northeast Africa via the Red Sea trade.[12] Again, neither of these theories can be confirmed, and what archaeological evidence exists so far is inconclusive. Cotton was certainly known and used in the Nile valley very early on, however.

Cotton fiber predominates among the textiles excavated from Nubian sites, especially those sites dating to the Meroitic period of cultural florescence from AD 200 to 330, and the presence of spindle whorls and loom weights at these sites indicates that cotton fabrics might well have been locally woven. Continuity of spin direction among flax, wool, and cotton fibers in ancient Nubian textiles supports this line of reasoning.[13] An alternative, though less likely, reading of the evidence suggests that either the textiles themselves or the raw cotton was imported into Nubia from India, via the Nile trading system. Again, we have insufficient evidence for resolving definitively these opposing views. What is most striking, however, is a change in clothing that occurred in mid-fourth-century Nubia, after which time wool, primarily from camels, not sheep, became the predominant fiber woven and worn there. What the change in textile fiber preference tells us about the era that followed is frustratingly unclear. It might possibly represent a demographic trend—the influx of an entirely new group of people—or it could indicate a shift in political relations within the Nubian populace that set off dramatic cultural and economic repercussions.[14] Whatever the case, it is not yet possible to discern what effect these events might have had in West Africa. The myth of Meroë, which claimed Nubia as the original source for major technological and cultural developments in the rest of tropical Africa, has never been effectively demonstrated.[15] Whether the older varieties of *Gossypium arboreum* and *Gossypium herbaceum* were established in other parts of Africa during this time is therefore another open question.

A similarly intriguing but ultimately frustrating set of fragmentary hints and glimpses comes from accounts written in Arabic about cloth and clothing in sub-Saharan Africa. The earliest accounts, from the ninth and tenth centuries, were compilations based entirely on scattered reports of observations made by merchants and others who made the long journey by caravan across the desert. Aside from some references to woven clothing worn by Berber groups, they described African peoples as either naked or clothed in leather or pelts. Presumably, those people considered naked included individuals such as the non-Muslim Tellem women who, from the eleventh century onward, wore twined G-strings or grass skirts made of bast and bark fiber.[16] An account completed by al-Bakri in 1068, and based on more reliable sources, stated that the people of Ghana wore cotton, silk, and brocade, and that the inhabitants of Tadmakka, a Saharan trade entrepôt further to the east, wore cotton clothing. He also provided the first written documentation of cotton textile production in West Africa. In his description of Takrur, an early Muslim kingdom that straddled the lower Senegal River, he gave details about the forms of currency that circulated there, which included cloths of finely woven cotton called *shakkiyyat*. There is some ambiguity about who the weavers of these textiles were. Al-Bakri seems to suggest that they were non-Muslims, but his account does not directly state the social identity of the weavers or the religious affiliation of the people in the town where they worked. He did go on to comment on the supply of cotton fiber, saying that although it was not very abundant, it was, in fact, rather widely grown on a small scale, with most houses having their own "cotton tree."[17] This description suggests that women might have been growing cotton in their household garden plots or among their food crops. It is also tempting to interpret the wording as a reference to trees bearing cotton fiber, which could mean they were growing the *G. arboreum* variety.

Later Arabic accounts begin to provide more detail, and they also reveal how and in what ways matters of dress and textile fibers were a critical concern to Muslim observers. Writing in 1154, al-Idrisi mentioned that silk was the type of cloth worn by the king of Ghana. In Gao, the dress of commoners was supposedly fashioned out of leather, while those higher up the social ladder wore woven cloth: merchants wore chemises and mantles, and nobles wore waist wrappers. The fiber of these textiles is not specified, but it may well have been cotton since in other parts of al-Idrisi's account he pointed out specifically where people wore cloth made of wool—in Kawar, north of Lake Chad, for example, and in the far western Sahara.[18] By the time Ibn Battuta made his journey to sub-Saharan Africa in 1352 and 1353, the fine white clothing that was deemed to be the most appropriate attire for devout Muslims was the dress frequently worn on special occasions in Mali, including Friday prayers, while the sultan and his officials were also observed wearing fancy imported woolens and silk brocades. Berber garments, namely, a wrap or robe, trousers, and turban, predominated in Timbuktu and Takedda.[19] Above all, what this brief survey of Arabic sources demonstrates is that there was a growing market for cotton, wool, and other woven textiles in these West African kingdoms and sultanates, especially among Muslims, which laid a foundation for the establishment of local cloth production workshops by at least the eleventh century.

Direct archaeological evidence for textile manufacture, in the form of spindle whorls, does not yet show a clear historical pattern either. It does suggest that there may well have been more than one center of development south of the Sahara and at least two main temporal phases in the spread of cotton production. Some of the earliest examples of spindle whorls, in the form of recycled pottery sherds, were found to have been used during the Daima III period (around AD 700 to 1200) in the environs of Lake Chad,[20] though it is not clear which fibers—cotton, wool, or perhaps bast—were being spun at this time. This particular type of spindle whorl has persisted over the intervening centuries, as attested in Kanuri vocabulary where the term *ngeiya* or *ngaiya* means both "sherd" and "weight affixed to spindles in spinning." In Hausa-speaking areas to the west of Lake Chad, large spindles with sherds were used for selling cotton thread.[21] Other examples come from sites located far to the west, such as Ogo in the Senegal River valley. There, grains of cotton pollen, along with spindle whorls and disc-shaped whorls for making twine, were found at levels dating to the eleventh century.[22] At Dia, in the upper Niger delta area, the earliest ceramic spindle whorls appear to predate the end of the first millennium.[23]

Another wave of technology transfers must have taken place by the fourteenth century, when there is evidence of cotton spinners and weavers working in many locales throughout West Africa. Small spindle whorls for spinning cotton—made of molded and baked clay and usually measuring just over an inch in cross section—were well represented at archaeological sites in Mauretania, Senegal, Guinea, and the delta and lakes areas of the upper Niger basin, at levels dating between the fourteenth and seventeenth centuries. Similarly, large numbers of them found at Begho, two hundred miles inland from the Gold Coast, dated from the fourteenth to eighteenth centuries, while at Bono Manso, approximately forty miles east of Begho, spindle whorls indicate cotton textile production was being carried out there from the late fifteenth to seventeenth centuries.[24] These isolated patches of evidence are certainly valuable but very difficult to interpret, especially since their paucity may only reflect the unfortunate fact that archaeological projects in West Africa have not been sufficiently concerned with recovering evidence of textile production.

An exceptional find among human burial remains in Mali does lend strong support to the antiquity of cotton weaving in the West African savannas. Close to five hundred textile fragments, mainly of cotton, were collected from a necropolis near the town of Sanga, in a region known as the Bandiagara escarpment. They are the oldest extensive set of sub-Saharan textiles yet uncovered, and analyses of them provide important baseline data for the history of cotton textile production on the West African treadle loom. These precious fragments were preserved mainly because of the low humidity and well-protected stone surfaces inside the caves. However, since they were not found in a stratigraphic context, and the contents of the caves were seemingly in a jumble, there was some initial skepticism about the possibility of dating them with any reliability. This problem was mitigated by several factors: first, the caves themselves were very remote, some almost entirely inaccessible, making it improbable that the contents had been contaminated with later materials; second, the Dogon populations living nearby revered these burial caves as the cemeteries of their predecessors in the region, the Tellem, and were therefore unlikely to have disturbed them; and third, relative chronologies proposed for the artifacts were later confirmed by absolute dates from carbon-14 analyses. The contents of the caves yielding textile fragments span seven hundred years, from the eleventh to the eighteenth centuries (see table 3.1 below).[25]

The woven textiles found within these caves, having been carefully and thoroughly examined since their discovery in the 1970s, are considered to be products of weavers in the upper Niger region, probably the non-Muslim

Table 3.1.　**Tellem Textiles, Bandiagara Escarpment, Mali, West Africa**
Average Woven Widths

		No. of Fragments			Cotton			Wool
					Tunics	Large Cloths		
Cave	Period	Per Fiber Category: Cotton / Wool / Both			Plain Weave*	Plain Weave*	Weft Face*	Weft Face*
A	11–12th c.	74	53			13"	7½"	11", >15", >25"
C	11–12th c.	175	15	2	9"	10"	9½"	>10½", >14"
Z	12–13th c.	59	1		9"	8¾"	8½"	
M	14th c.	16	1	1	8½"	8"	8¾"	>25"
Q	14–15th c.	13			8¾"	7¾"	7¾"	
Y	15th c.	17		2	7½"	8"	8"	
[F]	15–16th c.	33			7¾"		8¾"	
[H]	17–18th c.	17				5¾"		
		404	70	5				

Notes: *Plain-weave structures here should be taken to mean a balanced structure where both warp and weft are visible; weft face means that there are more wefts per inch than warps, and that the warps are not visible. Weft-face fabrics are thus heavier, and this tends to be the preferred structure for blankets, rugs, and other sturdy textiles.
[ ]Bracketed caves F and H are not consistent with the rest of the sample: in F, the bones were identified as Tellem, but cultural artifacts show Dogon features; in H, the bones were identified as not Tellem.
Source: Bolland 1991.

Tellem peoples themselves. Technical analyses reveal features of the loom used to make the cloths—harnesses and a reed—which indicates that they were made on the narrow horizontal treadle loom. The only exceptions to this type of manufacture were the woolen cloths, which were woven wider than twenty-five inches and hence were apparently made on vertical Berber looms and transported across the Sahara to the upper Niger region. As for fiber content, a majority of the textiles (over 80 percent) were cotton, and almost all the rest were wool except for some few cloths that combined both fibers. All the yarns were z-spun. Much of the cotton yarn was indigo-dyed, some was dyed brown, and other yarns, left in their natural color, had turned brown with age. The woolen yarns found at different sites were all similar in color range: green, yellow, red, and blue. The most frequently found items of dress were tunics, caps, and large cloths or blankets, all made of strips with similar widths averaging around eight or nine inches (see table 3.1).[26] Many of the cotton textiles had balanced plain-weave structures, with equal numbers of warps and wefts per inch, while others (some of the cotton and all the woolen ones) had weft-face structures, that is, fabrics with so many more wefts per inch that the warp threads were not visible. Viewed as a whole, this rare trove of textiles demonstrates that weaving cotton on the narrow treadle loom was already well established and highly developed by the eleventh century in the upper Niger region.

It is unlikely that this was the only center for the development of this technology in West Africa. However, the Tellem textiles do not directly address the question of the antiquity of cotton production and weaving on the treadle loom in other locales. They do, however, lend strong support to Johnson's contention that this loom was used primarily for weaving cotton. And if we consider them alongside several of the broad technological and economic trends already laid out above, a general time frame can be suggested for early cotton production in and around the Hausa-speaking areas of the lower Niger basin. Distribution patterns for wool-bearing sheep and the locations where early spindle whorls have been found indicate that there were at least two axes of technology transfer into West Africa: one across the western Sahara to the environs of the upper Senegal and upper Niger basins; the other across the central Sahara to Lake Chad. These two routes were also conduits for early trans-Saharan trade and the introduction of Islam to *Bilad al-Sudan*, the Lands of the Blacks; hence, it is reasonable to surmise that cotton technology may have followed the same routes. That would make it possible that cotton cultivation and processing skills were brought into areas around Lake Chad, for example, sometime during the second wave of technology transfers, between the tenth and thirteenth centuries, when cotton knowledge and expertise were being promoted throughout much of the Muslim world.

At present, however, there is very little direct evidence for early cotton textile manufacture in Hausaland, primarily because so little archaeological work has been done there. One excavation of settlements that formed the nucleus of the western Hausa kingdom of Kebbi turned up clay spindle whorls throughout the archaeological sequence, which was estimated to have begun around 1500.[27] This finding is not at all surprising. Oral traditions indicate that the Hausa peoples themselves consider cotton production to be an ancient practice in their homelands. Legends recounted about the earliest Hausa kingdoms, the "original seven," characterize Rano and Kano as important centers of indigo dyeing. Other anecdotes of past historical figures and their connection to locally made cloth add weight to the general supposition that indigo dyeing of cotton in Hausaland goes back at least five hundred years.[28] Indeed, Leo Africanus noted in his 1526 account that an abundance of cotton was produced around Kano and Zamfara.[29] But so far, the antiquity of cotton in Hausaland cannot be established with precision. Of the early Hausa kingdoms we know relatively little until the fifteenth century, except for what was recorded in the Kano Chronicle, a kinglist outlining the dynastic history of Kano and some of the major events associated with its rulers. Concerned above all with political developments and territorial expansion of the kingdom, this kinglist provides only a very general picture of the economy during this time. It does suggest, however, that by the fourteenth century, Kano was an important production and trading center with connections to long-distance commercial networks.[30] And certainly by the second half of the fifteenth century, the rulers of Kano, Katsina, and Zazzau (Zaria) were known to be practicing Muslims. For these reasons, an estimate that cotton cultivation was already well established in some parts of Hausaland by the fourteenth century does seem reasonable. The fact that textile fragments, which date to the thirteenth century and might include cotton, were excavated near the West African coast, in Benin City, strengthens the argument.

Evidence from historical linguistics lends support to the proposition that cotton could well have been introduced into Hausaland between the tenth and thirteenth centuries. However, this evidence is much clearer for the introduction of Islam than it is for indigo dyeing or cotton. It also adds another dimension to the view presented in the Kano Chronicle, which claims that the first Muslims to come to Hausaland came from Mali, sometime around the fourteenth century. What the linguistic evidence suggests is that there were even earlier ties with Muslims from Kanem, east of Hausaland. Hausa lexical terms for *writing, reading, market, town wall, gun, saddle*, and a number of political titles all derive from Kanuri or from Arabic through Kanuri, the predominant language spoken in Kanem.[31] It is believed that at least some of these particular Kanuri influences on Hausa-speakers occurred before the arrival from the west of Mande immigrants in Hausaland, since Islam was established relatively early in Kanem. The Sefawa dynasty that founded the kingdom of Kanem in the ninth or tenth century probably encouraged small communities of Muslim traders to settle in their midst, with the result that Kanem became known to Arab geographers from this time onward. Its rulers had converted to Islam by the eleventh century, making it one of the earliest Muslim polities in West Africa.[32] Shea has argued that the Hausa terms for "dyeing," "dyer," and "dyeing center," *rini, marini, marina*, and "prepared indigo," *shuni*, all come from Kanuri and that an alternative term for "dyeing center," *karofi*, is apparently derived from Mande (*kara fye* = dye place), leading him to conclude that there were aspects of indigo technology and expertise coming into Hausaland from both the east and the west.[33]

The lexical terminology for *cotton* appears inconclusive, with many specific Hausa words for Old World varieties of cotton suggesting a long and complex development but showing no clear pattern of relation with other languages (see chap. 2, table 2.3). One might expect the Kanuri term for "cotton," *kender*, to be related to a Hausa term, but that does not appear to be the case. The Mande terms (*kori, kwori, kônti, kotoundi, kotodin, fande*) appear to be unrelated to all of the Hausa terms as well. A linguistic relationship that does emerge is the one linking the Tuareg word for cotton and the general Hausa term: the Tamachek *ebduga* appears to be derived from the Hausa *abduga* or *auduga*.[34] Several different types of cotton plants have been identified in the Air massif, all of them Old World varieties that may have been established there very long ago.[35] Transfer of cotton expertise would be consistent with the longstanding historical connections between Hausa-speakers and the Tuareg and the Tuareg convention of hiring cultivators on contract, but it is difficult to place any such transfer in time or to establish for certain the direction of the transfer. Given what is known about the history of early Hausa communities, many of which were originally located in the desert-side areas around Air,[36] at least two possibilities can be suggested. One would be that cotton was first established in Air by early Hausa-speakers, with later immigrants borrowing their knowledge and terminology. It is reasonable to suppose that the Tuareg, being major traders and consumers of cotton but not producers of it, would promote cotton technology among Hausa-speakers in Air sometime after their arrival around the tenth century.[37] Another scenario would suggest that cotton technology was first established by Hausa-speakers south of Air, such as in the fertile agricultural lands around Kano, and was then transferred northward. It would not be at all surprising, in fact, to find that a variety of Old World cotton was one of the early crops grown around the walled towns of Hausaland even before those towns became kingdoms, but such precise details about this time period are so far unavailable. What can be said for certain is that the story of the introduction of cotton technology into Hausaland is more complex than a single wave of Mande migration, as Boser-Sarivaxévanis proposed in her theory.

NARROW COTTON STRIP CLOTHS, PLAIN AND PATTERNED

The introduction and dissemination of the treadle loom in West Africa was undoubtedly also a complex process. Its distribution tended to follow the networks of Muslim trade, but it was by no means confined to areas where Islam was practiced by a majority of the population. There are many variations of it all across the savannas and in many forest communities, suggesting multiple instances of technology transfer and subsequent adaptations made by weavers using the technology in different locales. Attempts therefore to classify the treadle loom's many forms have raised as many questions as they have tried to answer.[38] Nevertheless, there are some very broad historical trends that can be outlined here, based on certain basic features of the cloths these looms produced.

In terms of their width, textiles woven on the treadle loom were relatively stable and consistent. Such was the case for cloths discovered in the Tellem grottos (the dates of these cloths spanned over seven centuries), and a similar continuity can be observed in textiles produced and traded in the nineteenth and twentieth centuries. Strip cloth widths tended to fall within certain fixed ranges and varied only slightly, depending on the particular regions and subregions in West Africa where they had been woven. Also, and this is consistent with the Tellem textiles as well, they usually exhibited one of only two main fabric structures: either a balanced or a warp-face plain weave that was used for clothing; and a heavier weft-face weave that was suitable for blankets, rugs, and other furnishings. In other words, weavers were quite conservative when it came to making changes in the widths and structures of strip cloth they wove. It is very likely that an underlying reason for this apparent technological conservatism had to do with the role of narrow strip cloth as a form of currency in Muslim trading networks throughout West Africa. In use oftentimes alongside and in relation to other commodity currencies, strip cloths of one form or another were carried by caravans into the Saharan oases, along the desert fringes, over much of the savanna region, and into many parts of the forest zone. Even though they came to be produced and marketed in so many places, their monetary importance has not been very well recognized by scholars, especially when compared to the more conventional, durable, and better-documented metal and shell currency forms.[39]

The textiles themselves also suggest the existence of separate though over-lapping currency zones. If we survey a wide range of strip cloths produced in West Africa, taking note of the woven width and fabric structure, an interesting distribution pattern emerges. It appears that at least two major networks of strip cloth production and trade were at one time in operation south of the Sahara. My compilation of data on strip-cloth widths, taken from published and unpublished descriptions of cloths produced in West Africa during the late nineteenth and twentieth centuries, shows that west of Hausaland, they were rarely woven any narrower than about three inches, while to the east, in Kanem/Borno, strip cloths were woven as narrow as one inch (see table 3.2 below). And Hausaland, in the middle, was apparently

Table 3.2.   West African Treadle-Loom Strip Cloths: Widths and Structures

Peoples, Present Locations	Balanced / Warp Face	Weft Face
Mende, Sierra Leone	ca. 4" wide	*ca. 8" wide
Bambara and Mandingo, Mali	ca. 3" wide	*ca. 6" wide
MaabuBe Fulbe, Mali	—	*ca. 8" wide
Dyula, N. Ghana	7"–9" wide	—
Baule, Ivory Coast	*4"–8" wide	—
Ashanti, Ghana	*3"–4" wide	—
Ewe, Ghana/Togo	*ca. 4" wide	ca. 4" wide
Zarma (Songhay), S.W. Niger	*ca. 4" wide	—
Yoruba, S.W. Nigeria	*4"–7" wide	—
Hausa, N. Nigeria	1/2", 1"–2", 3"–5" wide also 6"–7", ca. 18" wide	*8"–12" wide
Kanuri, N.E. Nigeria	ca. 1"–2" wide	—

*= sometimes with supplementary weft patterning (continuous weft, selvage to selvage).
Sources: Picton and Mack 1979; Boser-Sarivaxévanis 1972; Menzel 1972–1974; Nachtigal 1971–1984.

Table 3.3. Standard Cloths Woven in Hausaland on the Treadle Loom

Cloth	Width	Structure	Consumers
turku'di, kore	1/2"–1"	balanced plain weave	Tuareg/Fulbe/Kanuri
sak'i/swaki	1 1/2"–2 1/2"	balanced plain weave	general
sawaye	3"–5"	balanced plain weave	general
mutukare	6"–7", ca. 18"	balanced plain weave	Bororo Fulbe, women
luru/nuru	8"–11 1/2"	weft-face plain weave	general (esp. north)

Sources: Bargery and Westermann 1934; Menzel 1972–1974; Lamb and Holmes 1980.

connected to both networks, since strip cloths of both dimensions were woven there. It appears too that the strips functioning as currencies were the ones with either balanced or warp-face plain-weave structures, since they exhibited these standard features most clearly and fully. In short, it was the strip cloths that were intended to be used for making items of clothing that served as money in Muslim trade (see table 3.3 above).

The narrowest strip cloths were associated with the *litham*, a turbanlike veil worn by men, which may well have been the first cloth currency form to be circulated in sub-Saharan Africa. The earliest reference to cloth currency comes from al-Bakri's eleventh-century account, where he described the production and circulation of *shakkiyyat*, a cotton cloth serving as one of the currencies in Takrur. The lexical term *shakkiyyat* raises some questions about just what kind of cloth this was. Levtzion and Hopkins noted that cloths called "shegga" have been variously described by other authors—as fine Moorish cotton cloth, in one case, or in another as indigo-blue cotton cloth imported by desert pastoralists from production centers in the tropical Sahel. They concluded that the word might be from Arabic, namely, the word *shiqqa*, as Briggs also concluded, adding that it was the cloth most preferred by Tuareg men for their turban-veil known as the *tagulmust*.[40] This terminology is not particularly informative, however, since *shiqqa* (pl. *shiqaq*) is an Arabic word used generally to refer to garment-sized pieces of cloth.[41] Nevertheless, it is reasonable to suggest that this early cloth currency was, in fact, an undyed cloth that could have been made into a *litham*. Men's veils would presumably have had a very high and stable value, given the close trading relations between Takrur and the Sanhaja Berbers at this time, for we know that the *litham* was no ordinary item of dress. It was so much a part of Sanhaja Berber identity that they were called the *Mulaththamun*, people of the veil. Others wore the *litham* as well, such as the Muslim Berbers who inhabited the desert-side entrepôt of Tadmakka, northeast of Gao. It is still worn by the so-called Blue Men of the western Sahara, and also by the Tuareg in the central Sudan region.[42]

This same type of veil was also produced in Hausaland, where it was known as *turku'di*, and only the narrowest cotton strips were used to make it. *Turku'di* cloths had very precise, standard measurements and operated as a currency in Tuareg trading networks. The specifications in the early twentieth century for these cloths were that they had to be made of twelve narrow strips, each eight cubits long, and after being dyed and beaten they were to be folded up and wrapped in paper.[43] It was in this packaged form that they circulated as currency.

Another cloth currency arose early in the Lake Chad region, and it too may have been related at one time to the *litham* or to some other specific garment form. The desert nomads who established the Sefawa dynasty of Kanem would probably have been familiar with veils, since groups of pastoral Tuareg may have lived in the Kanem area even before the dynasty was founded in the ninth or tenth century. By the fourteenth century, it was reported by Arab geographers that Kanem's military wore the *litham*, and that one of the country's currencies was a strip of cotton cloth woven there. This cloth served as a currency of account as well as a circulating currency, and it was measured in units of length, from a quarter of a cubit to ten cubits. The narrow strip cloth, known then as *dandi*,[44] has more recently gone by the name *gabaga*. Johnson has described it in some detail, including the wound rolls or "wheel" forms in which these strip cloths were transported and circulated. She also charted the fluctuating values of *gabaga* cloth units in relation to metal and cowrie currencies over the nineteenth century, concluding that the strip cloth may have been more stable than the other currencies.[45] What is most interesting, though, is an example of it brought back by Nachtigal to Europe, where it is now a part of the collections in the Museum für Völkerkunde in Berlin. Still in wheel form, wound into a roll as it came off the loom, the accompanying descriptive data notes that Hausa slaves wove it in Borno. Published catalogue information describes the cloth as plain white (undyed) cotton, measuring about $1\frac{1}{2}$ inches wide, and very densely woven with finely spun yarns.[46] This strip is slightly wider than the type commonly used for making nineteenth-century veils, which suggests that this particular unit of cloth might have been made according to specifications for some other textile product, such as a shirt or robe.

Strip cloths continued to be used as money in Borno into the twentieth century, but that was not the case in Hausaland. Johnson concluded that strip-cloth currency in the Hausa kingdoms was probably replaced by cowries during the eighteenth century, although traces of it do remain in Hausa vocabulary. For example, certain forms of plain, narrow strip cloth were still being transported and sold in wheel form in the twentieth century, a form referred to in Hausa and Nupe as *zugu*. And plain white *sawaye* cloth, often traded in wheels, takes its name from the plural of *sau*, a twenty-cubit length of measurement.[47]

This special role of strip cloth is, in my view, the key to understanding the relative continuity of its widths and structures in the manufacturing sector of the economy. Measured out or reckoned in terms of length, strip-cloth units had to be recognizably uniform over time and locale if they were to be also acceptable as money and stores of wealth. And to prevent fraud and trade disputes, which are so contrary to Muslim ideals, they had to be produced in accordance with well-established specifications. The net result would be to put a damper on individual weavers' innovations and production-maximizing strategies, such as increasing loom widths or altering major technical features of the cloth. What seems to be technological conservatism—stability in treadle-loom equipment and strip-weaving technology—could very well have come about because of the strips' dual role as garment fabric and money. The primary visual features of cotton strip cloth appear to have been conditioned by specific currency requirements and the importance of consistent manufacturing and market standards in *shari'a* law.

Over time, the production and circulation of strip-cloth currency in West Africa made a lasting imprint on many people's cultural values. The continuity of strip width and fabric structure dovetailed well with Muslim ideals of restraint and simplicity in dress, with the result that many people's fashion preferences leaned heavily toward garments made of narrow cotton strips woven in plain weave. But that is not to say that there was absolutely no scope for weavers to produce a variety of attractive cloth types. On the contrary, what was woven within these rather strict limits was an astounding array of subtle striped and checkered patterns, with fabric densities ranging from rather coarse to very fine. Such gradations of quality were clearly visible to the discerning consumer and were reflected in the prices of wrappers and garments that were sold in the market.

The Sokoto Caliphate, which incorporated much of Hausaland, Nupe, and northern Yorubaland in the nineteenth century, provides us with an illustration of how these well-established consumer tastes could affect textile production in particular and society in general. Looking at specific products from caliphate looms, it becomes quite evident that many variations in quality and price were possible, though not always achieved, in West African textile manufacturing. My documentation of major cloth types produced in the caliphate catalogs the major distinguishing features of a number of standard piece-dyed and patterned cloths made primarily of cotton. They were defined generally according to fiber content, color (or colors), and whether the cloth was loom-patterned or piece-dyed. *Gwanda*, or *gonda*, for example, was cotton strip cloth woven with blue and white stripes, while *ridi* had stripes of black and blue, sometimes with the addition of colored silk. *Kore* was the name given to tailored robes of strip cloth, the entire garment being piece-dyed deep indigo blue and then glazed to make it shine. *Turku'di* cloths, or veils, were also piece-dyed and glazed.[48] All of them could then range in price according to other factors such as fabric density and depth of color.

For our purposes here, however, only one type of strip cloth, called *sak'i* or *swaki* in Hausa, will be the focus of discussion. The trousers described at the beginning of this chapter are made of a variant of *sak'i*. This type of textile is sometimes referred to in the literature as "pepper and salt" or "guinea fowl," because of its small-scale pattern of dark and light checks. Early prototypes can be seen among the many plaid and checkered cottons that were found in the Tellem grottos, although most of those patterns are larger in scale, show irregularities in their repeat units, and appear to have been made according to a different counting system. Garments made of *sak'i* were favored by men all over West Africa in the nineteenth century, and the cloth was woven in many locales and traded widely. It took on different names in different languages—*katsi* in Kanuri, *etù* in Yoruba, and *zabo* in Nupe—all words meaning "guinea fowl."[49] Barth remarked that Tuareg men everywhere—as far west as Timbuktu, east to Lake Chad, and northward into the Ahaggar region of the Sahara—were particularly avid consumers of robes and trousers called *taylalt*, their own word for the speckled guinea fowl.[50]

Sak'i was one of the most important and prominent types of cloth produced in the Sokoto Caliphate. Robes made out of it were available in the markets of Kano, where Barth himself purchased one for traveling, presumably so that he might appear to be respectable and a man of means. There the robe was called *rigan sak'i*, or "guinea fowl shirt," and he noted that a "good one" cost between eighteen and twenty thousand cowries, a price well beyond the reach of most of the population. Imam Imoru, a Muslim merchant who described the textiles produced and traded in the Sokoto Caliphate, noted that many gowns of *sak'i* were made in Yoruba workshops specifically for caliphate markets.[51] Men's trousers as well, whether plain or embroidered, were often made of *sak'i*.

Over time, *sak'i* cloth became associated with caliphate officials and title-holders, lending it a very special aura of power, position, and prestige. On occasion, it served as a metonym, a sign of the ruling classes. One example of this phenomenon can be seen among the population of spirits included in Bori possession cults of the Maguzawa (non-Muslim or semi-Muslim) Hausa. The spirit of Dan Galadima, for example, was consistently associated with specific clothing—*sak'i* robe, *sak'i* trousers, and white turban—which identified him as a prince and heir apparent. The word *galadima* itself is derived from the Kanuri language, and the title was associated with high-level officials in the various subregional emirates. In his Bori spirit form, Dan Galadima represented a caricature of how the Maguzawa viewed some of their rulers: he was a bit of a dandy, a handsome young man who loved to gamble, and the son of a scholar and one of the scholar's concubines.

Devotees who became possessed by the Dan Galadima spirit first covered their head with a *sak'i* cloth; then, when the spirit arrived, a robe of *sak'i* cloth was brought to dress the devotee, along with a white turban, fan, kola nuts, and cowries for gambling. Other examples of the cloth's significance show up in the Hausa language. *Sak'i* became a vernacular term connoting intrigue and untrustworthiness: *Wurin nan da sak'i* means "There is a stranger present here," or "There is someone here we don't quite trust"; and *Ana sa hular sak'i a nan?* literally means "Is a cap of the material *sak'i* worn here?" that is, "Is there anyone here who is not quite one of us, who may tittle-tattle, give information against us?"[52] These instances of caricature by clothing, institutionalized in religious practice and in language, are richly suggestive, offering valuable glimpses of caliphate leaders as seen by some of their more critically minded subjects.[53]

To the founders and rulers of the Sokoto Caliphate, cotton cloth, including *sak'i*, surely signified much more than proper dress. A number of specific and deliberate government policies they put in place created a cotton boom that had a profound effect on the production, consumption, and trade of cotton textiles throughout West Africa. In doing so, they were following models that were enshrined in Islamic history.[54] As had been the case in the greater Muslim world during the golden age of the early caliphates, the scholarly elites who claimed caliphal authority in nineteenth-century Hausaland were connoisseurs of fine textiles who actively promoted their manufacture. Under their administration, the textile industry was given vital support through various institutions and incentives having to do with immigration, taxation, and labor organization. In the northcentral part of the caliphate, for example, plantations worked by slave labor intensified the volume of cotton and indigo production, while relatively low rates of taxation on craftwork encouraged merchants to establish workshops for spinning, weaving, and dyeing.[55] Tailoring and embroidery were often carried out by male scholars and their students in officially subsidized Quranic schools. Other encouragements came in the form of tribute requirements, which often stipulated that yearly payments to the administrative centers of Sokoto and Gwandu should be in the form of textile goods, slaves, and other commodities, often numbering in the thousands.[56] By the time of Barth's travels in northern areas of the caliphate in the mid-nineteenth century, he calculated that the caliphate's looms were supplying the clothing needs of much of the central and western regions of *Bilad al-Sudan*, and noted that its exports reached as far as the Atlantic coast of Senegambia.[57]

New textile traditions were made out of older ones, just as this cotton boom restructured and reoriented textile production in the entire region. Drawing on textile techniques and technologies that were already established in the lower Niger basin, caliphate merchants and officials engaged in importing and reexporting cloth as well as in organizing production to serve Muslim markets and trading networks all across West Africa.[58] *Sak'i* is only one of a number of textile products that demonstrates this nineteenth-century transformation. Looking at the terminology for major components of the treadle loom, we see that before the nineteenth century, this particular weaving technology seems to have developed along different lines in Hausa, Yoruba, and Nupe communities. Assuming that it was established first in Hausaland, it appears that the loom (or improvements to it) was then introduced into Nupe via Hausa intermediaries. In contrast, the Yoruba terminology suggests a different pattern of historical development (see table 3.4 below). With the founding of the Sokoto Caliphate, however, these separate technological histories converged into a single tradition as weavers from all three ethnic groups were recruited and their skills marshaled to manufacture the particular types of cloths that were most esteemed by the administration's elites. These cloths—whether plain, piece-dyed, or elegantly patterned, such as *sak'i*—were then consumed domestically in growing numbers or marketed widely as export products of the caliphate regime.

This intensive production of specific textile products led to demographic changes that are as yet only partially understood. There is indirect evidence that at least some administrators and merchants of the caliphate were intent on improving and monitoring quality by identifying skilled workers—free and enslaved—and relocating them in weaving and dyeing workshops.[59] For example, members of a British expedition in 1824 noted that male slaves of Nupe origin, who were considered the best weavers in the region, had been brought to the capital city of Sokoto and were producing *sak'i* cloth there.[60] This illustrates only one version—forced relocation—of a much more general process of labor mobilization. The most popular forms of trade cloth were often made in workshops that depended on slaves brought in from known textile-producing areas or on the special skills of free immigrants.

Table 3.4. Vocabulary for Treadle-Loom Technology

	Yoruba *(N-C, Kwa)*	Nupe *(N-C, Kwa)*	Hausa *(Chad)*	Kanuri *(Saharan)*
treadle loom	*ofi*	*masaka*	*masak'a* (weaving workshop)	
treadles/pedals	*itèse*		*mataki*	
comb/reed	*hasa*	*masefi, matsefi*	*masafi, matsafi*	
loom heddles		*nira*	*andira, allera, alera*	
shuttle	*oko aso*	*kosiya*	*k'oshiya*	*kabum*

*Kwa languages belong to the much larger family of Niger-Congo languages.
Sources: Bargery and Westermann 1934; Bowen 1858; Crowther and Sowande 1950; Fletcher 1912; Koelle 1970; Lamb and Holmes 1980.

Shea's study of dyed-indigo textile production in Hausaland demonstrated the complex and interlocking labor patterns, free and unfree, that characterized cotton cloth manufacture in the nineteenth and early twentieth centuries. He also showed in particular how volume production of certain types of textiles led to changes in the ethnic composition of workshops and communities. For example, the emirs of Kano periodically sent for certain groups of artisans to come and work for them, especially Nupe weavers and Tuareg smiths. In another case, many of the *turku'di* cloths produced in Hausaland for export to Tuareg and Kanuri peoples to the north and northeast were made by Hausa-assimilated members of those same ethnic groups. And a considerable number of textile workers in the town of Kura, famous for its *turku'di* production, were originally Tuareg, perhaps as the descendants of slaves owned by textile brokers.[61] These few well-documented examples probably reflect many others.

Textiles manufactured in the caliphate reveal that standard products were made to sell in a number of consumer markets and at different price levels. *Sak'i*, for example, had several variants. The name *sak'i* refers to a distinct type of strip cloth showing repeat patterns in the warp of thin white stripes on a deep indigo-blue ground. When this repeat pattern also occurred in the weft, a checkered pattern was created rather than a simple pattern of stripes. The *sak'i* described in dictionaries as "speckled" (and therefore named for the guinea fowl) was this checkered version. The striped version, which was used to make the embroidered trousers described at the beginning of this chapter, had its own special name. Known as *gansark'i* in Hausa, it was considered a poorer-quality *sak'i* and was described as having weft threads of a single color rather than alternating black and blue or black and white. In Nupe, the term was *zaboyeko*, which meant a *zabo* (guinea fowl) cloth characterized by a large design. Barth also mentioned another variation— the "tob-harir," which was a type of *sak'i* that included a stripe of red silk.[62] In the former example, *gansark'i* and *zaboyeko*, the visible difference was created by a laborsaving technique in which the weaver used a single-color weft and a single shuttle, which eliminated the need to switch shuttles in order to alternate between two colors. This technical change would make the weaving go much faster and lower the price of the final product. In the second example, the "tob-harir" cloth, it is presumed that value was added by including a more costly material, silk, in the weave. These variations suggest that a mercantile value system was in operation, one that placed an emphasis on incremental differences in quality that could be reflected in a broad range of prices.

Other specific features of *sak'i* cloth suggest that efforts were made to ensure some degree of quality control in textile production. But what is especially striking about nineteenth-century specimens is not only their standardization but also their variability. They exhibit a consistent pattern of indigo and white threads, while at the same time there are many clearly visible levels of quality, depending on the density of weave and fineness of thread (see table 3.5 below). Aside from one anomalous pair of *sak'i* trousers collected by the German traveler Flegel, the strips shown in the table were woven between 1½ and 2½ inches, or slightly wider than *turku'di* cloth. Their warp threads were arranged with three deep indigo-blue threads followed by two plain white ones, in repetition, creating a blue ground with thin white pinstripes. The wefts consisted of two threads of indigo followed by two plain white ones, which added the speckled "guinea fowl" effect. These thread counts, or pattern repeats, for both the warp and the weft were highly consistent within each strip and also across the entire sample of cloths, a uniformity that is impressive considering that the strips were products of different workshops spanning over a century in time. However, the warp-to-weft ratios varied considerably, with warp threads numbering

Table 3.5. *Sak'i* Strip-Cloth Patterns, Densities, and Widths

Type of Cloth, Collection Data	Width, Inches	epi, Warp	epi, Weft	sq. Inch	Warp Repeat	Weft Repeat
Robe, Stanger, 1841	2	81	40	121	3i,2w,3i [15 mag]	2i,2w,2i
Trousers, Stanger, 1841	2½	68	40	108	3i,2w,3i	2i,2w,2i
Trousers, Nig. Expd., 1841	2	76	43	119	3i,2w,3i	2i,2w,2i
Robe, Barth, 1850s	2	83	58	141	3i,2w,3i	2i,2w,2i
Robe, Dundas, bef. 1864	2	71	35	106	3i,2w,3i	2i,2w,2i
Trousers, Flegel, 1880	4¾	50	35	85	4i,2w,4i [32 viol]	all indigo
Robe (Salaga), bef. 1890	1½	60	33	93	3i,2w,3i	3i,2w,3i
Robe, diCardi, bef. 1896	2	38	20	58	3i,2w,3i	2i,2w,2i
Trousers, CMS, n.d.	2	66	25	91	3i,2w,3i	2i,2w,2i
Robe, CMS, n.d.	1¾	68	40	108	3i,2w,3i	2i,2w,2i
Robe, Beving, bef. 1934	1½	93	27	120	3i,2w,3i	2i,2w,2i
Robe, Banfield, 1928	1½	60	35	95	3i,2w,3i	all indigo
*Trousers, Banfield, 1928	2	43	25	68	2i,2w,2i	all indigo
Robe (Hausa), bef. 1964	1¾	55	30	85	3i,2w,3i	3i,2w,3i
Wrapper (Hausa), 1962	1½	45	20	65	2i,2w,2i	all indigo
Wrapper (Hausa), 1962	1¾	45	20	65	n.a.	all indigo
Wrapper (Hausa), 1962	2½	40	22	62	n.a.	all indigo
Range:		38–93	20–58	58–141		
Average:		61	32	93		

*The trousers described at the beginning of this chapter.
  epi = ends (threads) per inch
  Warp and weft repeats: numerals indicate number of threads; i = indigo; w = white; mag = magenta (silk?); viol = violet (silk?)
Sources: Menzel 1972–1974; and unpublished data from my analyses of collections in the Museum of Mankind, Royal Museum of Scotland, Museum for Textiles in Toronto, Royal Ontario Museum, and Wisbech and Fenland Museum, England.

from 38 to 93 threads per inch and weft threads numbering 20 to 58 threads per inch, the average being 61 and 32 respectively. Density per square inch is calculated as the number of warps and wefts added together. The average density of these fabrics came to 93. Textiles woven in the nineteenth century show much higher densities than those made around the mid-twentieth century.

These particular handwoven cotton fabrics compare very well to the famous trade textiles exported from India before the advent of industrialized cotton manufacture in Europe and North America. According to Pfister's classification of many such cloths that were unearthed by archaeologists at Fostat (old Cairo), there were three main categories of cloth density: Coarse, Medium, and Fine.[63] Using his thread counts, I have translated these categorical terms into quantitative measures for making comparisons, using the total number of threads per square inch. The categories are as follows:

Indian trade cloth, pre–17th century

Coarse	Medium	Fine
60–73	76–90	100–116

Most of the examples of *sak'i* from the nineteenth-century Sokoto Caliphate show densities over 90 threads per square inch, or within the Fine category. Several exceeded even that, however, with densities over 116.

Such a high quality of cotton cloth was possible only because of the high quality of the handspun cotton threads used to make that cloth. These cotton threads were spun by women and girls throughout the Sokoto Caliphate on a small handheld spindle called by the same name, *mazari* or *manzari*, in the Hausa and Nupe languages (fig. 3.3).[64] The level of yarn quality depended upon a number of factors, such as the variety of cotton used, how well the fibers were cleaned and processed, and, most importantly, the skill of the spinner. Women spinners interviewed in Sudan just after the First World War, some of whom were originally from the area of the Sokoto Caliphate, stated that whenever possible they preferred to spin directly from the boll, which could be done only with certain varieties of long-staple cotton.[65] Otherwise, the bolls had to be ginned, or cleaned of seeds, which was usually done by rolling a metal rod over the fibers. The next step was separating and fluffing the fibers, using a stringed bow made just for that purpose. The Hausa term for the cotton bow, *bakan shi'ba* (*baka* = bow; *shi'ba* = teasing cotton with small bow), corresponds with a Nupe word defined generically as a "ginning tool," *kpako*, suggesting a technology transfer of cotton processing between Hausaland and Nupe. As was the case with the terminology for the treadle loom, the Yoruba vocabulary for aspects of spinning indicates

Figure 3.3. Women Spinning and Grinding, Lokoja, 1903. Photograph by A. W. Banfield. Copyright the Estate of Frank Banfield, Canada.

that textile technology there underwent a separate historical development (*kekke* = spindle; *igbonwu* = bow for carding cotton).[66]

Spinning the fiber was demanding and exacting work. It was only the most highly skilled spinners who could produce the very fine, tightly spun threads that were used as the warp in the most densely woven cloth. Such threads were known as *arafiya, raskwai,* and *anyanyana* in Hausa, though it is evident from nineteenth-century textile products that women throughout the region, even outside Hausa-speaking areas, were able to attain the level of skill needed to produce very fine cotton yarns. Other threads were spun slightly thicker and looser, qualities that were suitable for the weft, and they took less skill to make. They too were known by specific names in Hausa, such as *abawa, bartake, aburduga,* and *burudu.* The fact that there were several lexical terms meaning "spinning for payment" in Hausa confirms what is suggested by the cotton textiles themselves: many women engaged in spinning as an income-generating occupation. And many pursued strategies that maximized their earnings, such as engaging child labor for cleaning and preparing the fiber and then, while spinning, using chalk on their fingers to speed up the process. Nevertheless, this very important and highly skilled work was not as remunerative as other occupations in textile manufacture.[67] It is also noteworthy that although the treadle loom

was introduced into Africa from India, the wheel for spinning cotton thread
was not.[68]

Textile manufacture in the Sokoto Caliphate was impressive not only because of the quantity of cloth produced but especially because of its recognizably superior quality. From the specialized yarns and densely woven
fabric structures to the elegant patterning and piece-dyeing, it can be said
for certain that the renown of caliphate products was indeed well earned.
They were certainly higher in quality than the Tellem cloths, and equal to
or finer than the best of the Indian cottons that were traded before industrialized cotton manufacture in Europe and North America. It also appears
that the finest cloth was selected to make garments and wrappers strictly for
Muslim consumers, both male and female.[69] For these consumers, dress was
an indicator of character, taste, acumen, and worldly achievement. Prominent Muslim men wore tailored clothing—as long as it was made of acceptable fabrics and in an appropriate style—as an outward sign of their
inner qualities and public position. And in the Sokoto Caliphate, *sak'i* cloth
in particular was reserved for the tailored robes and trousers that were
most esteemed—the ones destined to be embellished with embroidered
imagery.

NEEDLEWORK: TAILORING AND EMBROIDERY

English missionaries, evangelizing in West Africa in the late nineteenth century, took to disparaging their African male colleagues by calling them
"trousered Africans." By doing so, they were displaying their ignorance of
the fact that, for centuries, West African men had been accustomed to wearing trousers and other tailored garments. In other words, this was not a
specifically European or Christian form of dress. Al-Bakri, writing in the
eleventh century, noted that the people of Tadmakka wore veils and robes
and other garments of cotton, and that their king was handsomely dressed
in a red turban, yellow shirt, and blue trousers. Twelfth-century reports described the king of Ghana as a skilled horseman who dressed in trousers
and a mantle, while far to the east the king of Kanem wore trousers of wool
along with wraps of wool and brocade. In the fourteenth century, Al-Umari
provided more detail, writing that the clothing worn in Mali was white cotton that was locally woven and of very good quality. Trousers were worn,
though they were apparently reserved for men of the highest political ranks.
It was also said that soldiers who had performed heroic feats in battle were
awarded large drawstring trousers, and the greater the number of exploits,
the wider the trousers were. These trousers were described as having an
ample seat and very narrow leg openings. The largest trousers, made up of
twenty pieces of cloth, were apparently reserved exclusively for the king.

Ibn Battuta described the Sultan of Takedda wearing a wrap, trousers, and a turban, all dyed blue; and when in Timbuktu, he witnessed the investiture of an emir who, to mark the occasion, was presented with a dyed garment, turban, and trousers.[70]

In these instances, trousers were part of a clothing ensemble that marked royalty and military leadership primarily, but not exclusively, in Muslim society. Indeed, wide and roomy trousers were considered an important component of elite dress, sometimes for women as well as men, throughout much of the greater Muslim world from its early beginnings.[71] In West Africa, they appear to have been worn primarily by men, and came to be closely associated with cavalry warfare and ceremonial displays of horsemanship (fig. 3.4). The use of billowing riding pants may have preceded the formal organization of cavalry troops, however, and could well have been introduced into the Sahara and Sahel via camel-riding nomadic Berber groups. In other words, trousers were probably known and worn in pre-Islamic times, though the production and use of them undoubtedly became much more common in West Africa when Islam was firmly established and as the influence of Muslim elites grew.

The earliest extant example of a pair of West African trousers comes from the grottos of the Bandiagara escarpment. Among the textiles found in the Tellem burial caves there were numerous examples of tailored garments, namely, tunics and caps, dating between the eleventh and fifteenth centuries. In contrast, there was only one pair of trousers, and they were found in cave Q, which was dated to the fourteenth and fifteenth centuries. In its general style and design, the garment is very similar to the trousers that are the focus of this chapter. The main body is made up of ten vertical strips of cotton cloth, with a large crotch gusset cut out, turned, and sewn back in with the strips running horizontally. Along the edge of the very wide waist is a hem for a drawstring, and the leg openings are narrow. The weaving structure is a plain weave of brown cotton yarns that are spun in the z-direction.[72] Given how well made and sturdy the garment is, and the lack of any embellishment, it was probably intended for everyday use.

The time during which these trousers would have actually been worn, the fourteenth or fifteenth century, was a time of political transformation in much of West Africa. It was an era that saw the rise of great Muslim empires, which also carried a number of cultural changes in their wake. One of these changes was in the domain of dress, whereby consumer demand for tailored garments, including trousers, increased substantially. Several factors combined to generate this demand. One major contributor was military expansion, especially the creation of cavalry forces and the development of equestrian skills. By the fourteenth century, the leaders of Kanem and Mali had cavalry units that required regular supplies of equipment and suitable apparel. Law suggests that it may have been Mansa Musa's pilgrimage to

Figure 3.4. King of Pategi (Nupe), on Horseback, 1903. Photograph by A. W. Banfield. Copyright the Estate of Frank Banfield, Canada.

Mecca in 1324, or more specifically his observations of military practice in Mamluk Egypt, that prompted the development of cavalry operations and equipage in the Mali Empire. While in Cairo, Mansa Musa was awarded gifts of horses, saddles, and bridles by the sultan, which he brought home along with newly purchased Turkish slave soldiers. Horses were used militarily around this time in the lower Niger region as well, first in Nupe perhaps as early as the 1400s, and then in Hausaland and the northern Yoruba kingdom of Oyo by at least the sixteenth century.[73] Important as they were, royal and military elites were not the only ones lending prestige to the wearing of tailored garments. This period was a time that also saw significant growth in West Africa's international trading centers where worldly and well dressed Muslim merchants rose to positions in the upper strata of society. Even more prominent were the professors, scholars, and judges who traveled the intellectual circuits that connected many of the centers of learning in the Muslim world, including those that had been established in West Africa. All of these men, as model members of society, contributed in their own ways to the rise of cosmopolitan and urbane cultural values that were signified by, among other things, admirable demeanor and impressively tailored dress.

This growing appreciation of and demand for robes, trousers, and other sewn garments meant that tailors had a steady supply of work. The most striking early example to be documented of this appreciation and demand can be found in the city of Timbuktu in sixteenth-century Songhay, under the Askia dynasty. Viewed through the eyes of Muslim clerics, this was a golden age—after the death of Sonni Ali in 1492 and before the Moroccan invasion of 1591—when classical Islamic law and custom were being actively promoted. As remembered by Leo Africanus, who traveled in West Africa during the early years of the Askiyas, Timbuktu was a thriving city with imposing architecture, a wealthy merchant community, and a powerful sultan, backed by military strength and gold currency. Cloth consumption reflected this prosperity. There were textiles made by local weavers, of cotton and bast as well as all sorts of imported textiles brought across the Sahara. Many of the women were attired with veils. Timbuktu was also a center of learning, with a significant population of scholars and legal experts supported by the sultan himself.[74] The large number of tailors' workshops at that time attests to a high demand for tailored clothing. It was said that in the city of Timbuktu itself there were twenty-six such establishments, each one having fifty, and sometimes up to one hundred apprentices who worked under the close supervision of a skilled master. In at least some instances, those master tailors were also themselves well known and respected scholars.[75]

After the fall of Songhay, another two hundred years would pass before the next era of great Muslim empires in West Africa. Certainly tailored garments continued to be made and worn during the interim, even in the face of

increasing textile imports from India and Europe, though there is insufficient
evidence for determining volume or centers of manufacture. A Muslim king
from the West African interior, visiting the Sierra Leone estuary in the 1640s,
was described as barefoot and dressed in a "typical" long gown, presumably
of local make.[76] Two examples of seventeenth-century robes, housed in the
collection of the Ulmer Museum in Germany, consist of narrow cotton strips
sewn together into a straight, tunic-like shape. One robe is made entirely of
strips in balanced plain weave, about six inches wide, and then piece-dyed
in indigo. The other robe is made of similar strips dyed deep indigo-blue
alternating with strips of weft-face plain weave that are almost eight inches
wide. These garments were acquired in the coastal port of Allada, but their
place of manufacture has not been identified.[77] Other sources indicate that
tailored garments remained a common form of dress, especially for Muslim
men. Salih Bilali, a Fulbe captive who was sold into slavery and shipped
to the Caribbean, described the clothing worn by Muslims in his homeland
of the upper Niger basin, the kingdom of Massina, in the late eighteenth
century. Men's dress consisted of a large pair of cotton trousers, a shirt, and
a conical straw hat. Women spun the yarn, men wove it into cloth, and some
of it was dyed blue.[78] Similarly, Mungo Park, traveling in West Africa in the
1790s, noted that men all across the savannas from Senegambia to Jenné
wore loose shirts or robes with trousers that reached halfway down the leg,
both garments being made of locally manufactured cotton cloth. Again, the
women spun, the men wove the cloth into strips about four inches wide,
and some cloth was dyed blue. The fabric was then cut and sewn into garments using locally made needles. Park also passed along an interesting
and amusing comment, somewhat at his own expense, about trouser styles.
While staying in a Muslim encampment in the vicinity of Kaarta, between the
upper Senegal and upper Niger rivers, he described how he was subjected
to mild criticism by his hosts who voiced their opinion about the kind of
trousers he wore. The pants were too tight-fitting, in their view, and therefore made him appear "inelegant" and "indecent."[79] Later explorers in the
West African savanna such as Barth, Mischlich, and C. H. Robinson, to name
just a few, abandoned their European clothing for the loose, layered Muslim styles, considering them much more respectable garments and better
adapted to the tropical climate.

Dress could thus be a contentious issue, especially in Muslim circles, and
it was a matter of some concern to the creators and administrators of the
Sokoto Caliphate in the early nineteenth century. Among their major goals,
they were intent on reviving what they considered to be the past greatness of
Islamic governance, learning, and culture. Restoring the appropriate mode
of Muslim dress—robe, trousers, and turban made of the proper, religiously
permitted fabric—surely was central to that vision. It had already played
a role in setting off the jihads in 1804, when the small community of Sufi

scholars in Gobir, who had long-harbored grievances against their king, were finally provoked into waging war after being persecuted and attacked for, among other things, wearing turbans and veils.[80] And in their writings, where they attempted to explain and legitimize their jihad, they leveled a series of harsh criticisms against the Gobir court that included the court's practice of "wearing whatever clothes they wish, whether religiously permitted or forbidden."[81]

But attitudes about dress within the Muslim community at large were never monolithic. The spiritual and intellectual leader and founder of the Sokoto Caliphate, Shehu Uthman dan Fodio, drew from his deep knowledge of scholarly and religious texts to write a summary opinion on what was permissible Muslim dress. He declared that the wearing of silk was a sin for men, adding that the preferable dress for scholars and students was white clothing, though other colors were permitted.[82] There were plenty of other Muslims, however, who were either unaware of or unconcerned by the Shehu's pronouncement and opted to take the risk of wearing their silk here and now, rather than later on in paradise. Table 3.6 below illustrates one example, a high-ranking official in Kano whose wardrobe included an impressive number of garments made from a wide variety of cloth types. And as can be seen in many garments now in museum collections, clothing created and worn by elite men in the caliphate was often woven or embroidered with locally produced and imported silk. That there would be such a range in attitudes toward the proper mode of dress should not be at all surprising. For despite the recommendations reputedly made by the Prophet Muhammad, that clothing be simple and modest, and despite periodic attempts to single out certain types of luxury fabrics as strictly forbidden, tastes for sumptuous textiles, especially among the wealthy elites, had always been avidly cultivated in the Muslim world.[83]

The making and embellishing of garments, from simple ones for Sufi ascetics to elegant robes for powerful emirs, was generally considered to be a very respectable occupation. Tailoring and embroidery were both done primarily by men, many of whom were also highly educated Quranic scholars and teachers.[84] The close historical connection between tailoring and Islam left its imprint in language, with words for "scissors" throughout the caliphate and neighboring regions all clearly related to the Arabic term *al mik'ass* (in Yoruba, *àlúmágàjí* and *àlúmógàjí*; in Nupe, *alumakasi*; in Hausa, *al-makashi*; and in Kanuri, *mágase*).[85] The terminology for "needles," however, shows differences between these same languages, suggesting that there was a longer, more locally based history of sewing in the region. Needles were made by local blacksmiths, but by the middle of the nineteenth century increasing numbers of industrially produced needles from Europe were also available in the markets, their smaller size and smoother surface making it possible for tailors and embroiderers to create ever more finely detailed,

**Table 3.6.   Garments Listed in the Estate of a Kano Emirate Official,
Late Nineteenth Century**

Garment	Estimated Value
Trousers, "katif" (broad)	40,000 cowries
Trousers, yellow satin	40,000 cowries
Trousers, "Duma"	20,000 cowries
Trousers, black *mulufi* (wool)	10,000 cowries
Trousers, black	10,000 cowries
Trousers, *samazadawa* cloth (imported white brocade)	10,000 cowries
Trousers, *samazadawa* cloth	10,000 cowries
Trousers, *sak'i* cloth	10,000 cowries
Trousers, white	10,000 cowries
Trousers, yellow	5,000 cowries
Trousers, *yaminu* (imported white cotton?) cloth	5,000 cowries
Trousers, red	5,000 cowries
Trousers, *samazadawa* cloth	2,000 cowries
Gown, velvet shot with red	80,000 cowries
Burnus, indigo and decorated w/copper wire	80,000 cowries
Burnus	50,000 cowries
Burnus, red	50,000 cowries
Gown (*gare*), *sak'i* cloth	40,000 cowries
Gown (*girke*), white (from Nupe)	40,000 cowries
Gown (*jibba*), yellow	40,000 cowries
Burnus (2), red	40,000 cowries each
Gown (*girke*), white (from Nupe)	30,000 cowries
Gowns (*gare*) (3), from Nupe	30,000 cowries each
Gown (*gare*), *algasa* cloth (from Nupe)	30,000 cowries
Burnus, yellow	30,000 cowries
Burnus, black	30,000 cowries
Gown (*gare*), *sak'i* cloth	20,000 cowries
Burnus, red	20,000 cowries
Burnus, black	20,000 cowries
Burnus, yellow	20,000 cowries
Gown (*gare*), *bullam* (white) strip cloth	15,000 cowries
Gown (*gare*), white	10,000 cowries
Gown (*jibba*), indigo	10,000 cowries
Burnus, indigo	10,000 cowries
Gown (*jauha*), red	5,000 cowries

Source: Hodgkin 1975, 378–84. Of the total value of the estate, about one-third was in the form of slaves, one-fourth in cloth and clothing, and just under one-fourth in livestock and equipment.

higher quality goods. Needlework of all kinds required careful thought and planning, sometimes requiring the coordination of skilled labor in several different workshops. In some instances, for example, weavers were commissioned to make narrow cloth strips that were specifically designed for an elaborate tailoring method, half of the strip being woven in a different color so that it could be folded to form a lining on the inside of the garment.

Clothing made in this unusual way was, of course, destined only for the wealthy few who could afford it. Most tailors, producing goods that would be within the reach of the majority of male consumers, used simpler and therefore quicker sewing methods.[86]

Among the products of tailors' workshops there were many styles and sizes of trousers, as is attested to by the numerous individual names for them in the Hausa and Yoruba languages. The embroidered examples I have surveyed in museum collections fall into two main groups, each having a distinct set of features. One of these groups, called *wando mai surfani* in Hausa (*wando* = trousers; *mai surfani* = with open chain stitch), consists of trousers made from a large rectangle of vertically arranged narrow strips. The garment structure required minimal tailoring, with the cloth simply folded in half and sewn together at the sides. At the top edge a hem was sewn for a drawstring and narrow leg openings were then cut out at each lower corner. Embroidery stitching on this style of trousers was in a single color, often green, and the patterns were sewn in with open chain stitches and eyelet stitches.[87] An example collected by Flegel before 1880 is extremely wide, being made up of thirty vertical strips, each almost five inches across.[88] Merchant-scholar Imam Imoru described two versions of *wando mai surfani*, one made of cloth with silk in it, the other made of cotton *sak'i* strips. He stated that at the time of his observations (1880–1910), many such trousers were being made in Yoruba and Nupe workshops to be traded northward and sold throughout the caliphate.[89] Fragments from both types, showing just the embroidered areas, were collected in Bida (Nupe) workshops by Frobenius in 1911, although museum accession information mistakenly describes them as examples of robe embroidery.[90]

The other group includes the trousers that are the focus of this chapter, which have a more complex garment form and a distinctly different type of embroidery. The tailor began with a large rectangle of strip cloth, but then two distinctive features were added: a square crotch gusset and narrow anklebands. As I noted above, the crotch gusset was formed by cutting out a diamond shape from the center of the rectangle, turning it 90 degrees, and then sewing it back in with the strips running horizontally. After that, the trousers were folded in half and the sides were sewn together, with the upper edge hemmed for a drawstring, just like the *wando mai surfani*. Finally, narrow anklebands were sewn in at the lower corners to fit tightly around the leg, and it was these that gave the trousers their name: *wando mai kamun k'afa*, or "trousers with anklebands." Examples from museum collections show that the ground cloth used for this type of pants was either plain white cotton (local or imported) or *sak'i*, the "guinea fowl" cloth. Embroidery on the anklebands consists of dense herringbone stitch, outlined with chain stitch, while a variety of motifs were sewn onto the body of the trousers with chain stitch and feather stitch and couching, using polychrome threads, usually of wool.[91] Imam Imoru commented on this type of pants as well, stating that the emir of Kano wore them and they were very much in demand among the Kano populace. Some of the nicer ones were apparently made in the emir's palace by his own sons. The most painstaking work of all was the embroidery on the anklebands, which could require over a week to complete. Differently priced versions of *wando mai kamun k'afa*, from the minimally decorated to the most elaborate, were available in caliphate markets.[92]

Members of the 1841 Niger Expedition bought two examples of them at the town of Eggan on the Niger River and brought them back to England. One, though unembroidered, was made of very high-quality *sak'i* cloth (about 119 threads per square inch). Sturdy in construction (the gusset sewn back into the fabric with encased seams), this garment was identified as "Hausa trousers worn by higher classes, made at Egga [*sic*]," and it cost four thousand cowries. The second example was part of an entire costume purchased from the wearer, presumably a Tuareg nobleman. His trousers were also made of high-quality *sak'i* strips (twenty of them, each just over two inches wide), though in this case the anklebands were elegantly embroidered in herringbone stitch with magenta silk (fig. 3.5). This Tuareg nobleman's associated gown was superb. It was tailored with gusset inserts so that the body of the gown flares out, and a band of colorful silk

Figure 3.5. Trousers Made with *Sak'i* (Guinea Fowl) Cloth, with Anklebands Embroidered in Magenta Silk, 36 Inches Long by 43 Inches Wide. Collected in 1841. Stanger Collection, Accession no. 1.xii.1856. Photograph by the Author. Copyright the Wisbech and Fenland Museum, UK.

lining glimmers along the inside hem. The *sak'i* strips have a narrow stripe of magenta silk in the center, and the delicate embroidered motifs on the body of the gown were sewn with open chain and eyelet stitches in white silk. The cost of the man's clothing and sword was not documented, but it must have been a considerable sum.[93] According to Imam Imoru, such trousers, with only the anklebands embroidered, were called *dungun k'afa*.[94]

In contrast to certain types of embroidered robes made in the caliphate, the arrangement of motifs embroidered on *kamun k'afa* trousers was not always consistent. The most stable portion of the imagery was regularly placed on a diagonal axis along the gusset seam, and it consisted of a series of several *interlace forms* topped off with a motif shaped like a cloverleaf (fig. 3.6). This motif, known in Hausa as *kan kiski* (head of the male rainbow lizard), suggests that interlace forms, frequently used to decorate pages of the Quran, could also be interpreted by the general populace as references to lizards.[95] It is quite possible that the interlace was considered to have talismanic properties, and was a sub-Saharan variant of the dragon/serpent motif incorporated into Islamic visual traditions during the Mamluk Empire (1250–1517). Originating in Hindu and Persian mythology, the dragon/serpent was

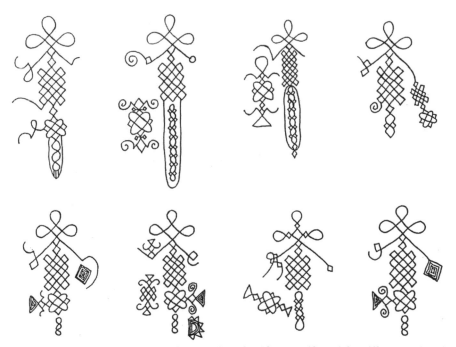

Figure 3.6.   Variations of *Kan Kiski* (Lizard) Embroidery Motif on Eight Different Pairs of Trousers in Museum Collections, Late 19th and 20th Centuries. Drawing by the Author.

thought to cause eclipses and other natural disasters, and it was depicted as a pair of intertwined serpents. This imagery was often placed on gates as a protection against the entry of evil spirits. Similarly, interlace and knot motifs could be seen on the facades of mosques, palaces, and houses in Hausa towns and cities, suggesting that this talismanic function, if not the precise historical meaning of the imagery, had been incorporated into the visual vocabulary of the region.[96]

Another motif, commonly referred to as the "northern knot," was also frequently included in the imagery on the most densely embroidered trousers. In some cases it would be attached to a more elaborate interlacing pattern, in others it was isolated. It has been called different names in Hausa: *dagi*, meaning "knot," *tafin musa*, meaning "cat's paw," and *dagin mussa*, which also is translated as "cat's paw."[97] Two trouser fragments, brought back to Europe by Frobenius, show examples of this motif sewn in polychrome on *sak'i* cloth, and the motif is described in the museum accession information as "Solomon's knot."[98] Variations of the knot form were important elements of Islamic iconography at least from Mamluk times, and in West Africa they were often sewn onto multicolored beaded vests and other paraphernalia of the Yoruba thunder god, Sango, as well as onto the regalia of Yoruba kings (fig. 3.7). Single-knot forms were also embroidered in monochrome on the fronts of round-necked, gusseted *agbada* gowns, as was, less frequently, a related pattern based on the *three-by-three square*. The latter consists of a square divided into nine smaller squares, with the corner and center portions filled in with embroidery stitches. It has been known by two different names in Hausa: *gidan zuma*, meaning "house of bees," and *gidan biyar*, meaning "house of five."[99] The motif, in the latter name and in its visual structure, refers to the number five, which, in Muslim numerological belief, signifies a charm against the "evil eye." It also belongs to a large and ancient family of magic squares that entered Islamic iconography from Asia, and was further developed and elaborated on by Sufi mystics and philosophers. Drawn, painted, etched, or embroidered, the magic square was adopted widely in Saharan and sub-Saharan Africa as an amulet, offering various protections to its bearer.[100]

One more motif, added to the imagery of the most densely and elaborately embroidered *kamun k'afa* trousers, was the six-pointed star. It too has a complex set of historical associations. Called *danko* in Hausa, it makes reference to the Bori spirits of Maguzawa religious practice. *Danko* was a spirit that was believed to assume the form of a snake and engage in conversation with Bori devotees. It could possibly be linked historically to *Donko*, a deity associated with thunder and lightning in the Zarma/Songhay pantheon. According to another source, *danko* was another name for the Bori spirit *Dan Musa* (Son of Moses), who was the "possessor of the spear" and the cause of stomach ailments.[101] Five- and six-pointed stars were known in

Figure 3.7. Chief of Shagamu (Yorubaland) in Beaded Regalia, 1925. Photograph by A. W. Banfield, Accession no. 950.257.26. Copyright R.O.M., Reproduced with Permission of the Royal Ontario Museum, Canada.

Islamic iconography by the name "Solomon's seal," and they were thought to endow their owners or wearers with power over terrestrial and supernatural beings. There was a generally held belief among many Muslims that Solomon had been able to acquire magical powers and special amulets from the jinn, and that this particular motif was inscribed on his ring as one such device. Versions of the motif thus show up in talismanic contexts, from battle flags carried by warriors to charm gowns worn by Muslims for supernatural protection.[102]

Most of these very same motifs were also embroidered onto caliphate robes. In all cases, the imagery provided various supernatural protections and assurances of good fortune to whoever wore the garment. I have argued elsewhere that robe embroidery was practiced well before the nineteenth century, but that officials of the Sokoto Caliphate created and promoted their own distinctive imagery to represent their administration. This was a well-known and longstanding practice in the greater Muslim world, as is evident in the institution known as the "robe of honor."[103] What is note-worthy for our purposes here is that although the robes shared motifs in common with *kamun k'afa* trousers, the motifs were not rendered in the same way. The composition itself was arranged quite differently and more consistently on the robes, and the embroidery stitching was entirely different. Looking strictly at the technical features of the embroidery of these robes, we see that they are very similar to *mai surfani* trousers. Both the robes and *mai surfani* trousers were embroidered in monochrome cotton or silk with chain stitches used as an outline and eyelet stitches as a filler. The overall effect is restrained, refined, and delicate—a sharp contrast to the bold poly-chrome wool and heavy couching stitches that characterize the embroidery on *kamun k'afa* trousers.

That there were such striking technical and material differences between these two trouser forms suggests that both forms—*mai surfani* and *kamun k'afa*—probably came about through different historical developments. Sur-veying embroidery stitches and their histories adds strength to this sugges-tion. Embroidery techniques were perfected and disseminated throughout the Muslim world thanks in large part to the importance of embroidered in-scriptions and imagery on the robe of honor, or *khil'a*. Embroidered robes of the Sokoto Caliphate show some similarities, in techniques and materials, to eastern variants of the *khil'a*, that is, those coming out of workshops in Turkestan, Persia, Iraq, and Yemen. These variants were woven in cotton, or cotton and silk, embroidered with chain stitches, and finished with a glaz-ing process. In contrast, the Egyptian robes were mostly made of linen, and were embellished with tapestry-woven bands until the Mamluk period. The history of the chain-stitch technique, known as *surfani* in Hausa, goes back at least two millennia to China, central Asia, and Syria. The eyelet stitch is not as fully documented, but it appears to have central and western Asian origins. Sometimes referred to in the literature as the "Algerian" or "Turkish" eyelet stitch, it appears in the embroidery traditions of Algeria, Morocco, Cyprus, the Ukraine, Romania, and Mamluk Egypt, and may well have been popularized during the Ottoman Empire.[104] The earliest extant examples of

Sokoto Caliphate robes, collected in 1841, were embroidered with chain and eyelet stitching, and were therefore clearly part of this pan-Islamic tradition.

Kamun k'afa trousers, however, display some idiosyncrasies among their embroidery features. More specifically, the use of wool threads for couching stitches appears to be a most unusual combination of material and technique in the history of textiles. Couching is used when threads are either too cumbersome to be stitched through the fabric or when they are so precious and dazzling that they ought to be kept fully visible on the outward-facing side of the cloth.[105] Indeed, my survey of published data on Middle Eastern and North African embroidery revealed that couching was principally done with silk, gold, or silver threads. Wool was rarely used in embroidery at all, and when it was, it was done in cross stitch or straight stitch on a sturdy ground fabric, in imitation of heavily woven wool tapestry.[106] There apparently are no historical precedents for the kind of wool embroidery that we see on these trousers.

A plausible explanation for this anomaly has to do with changes in international trade during the final years of the caliphate and the early colonial era. Of the two earliest known examples of this type of trousers, collected in 1841, only one of them was embroidered at all. Its anklebands were almost completely covered in magenta silk. Brightly colored waste silk, especially magenta, was imported from across the Sahara from at least the middle of the nineteenth century.[107] It was spun into various types of yarns—some to be used as warp threads in fancier kinds of strip cloth, others spun more thickly to be used as embroidery thread. Hence it may well be that the patterns and motifs first embroidered onto the main body of such trousers were also done with imported, locally spun silk, using a couching stitch to emphasize the silk's vivid, gemlike color. But with British colonial rule came changes in trading patterns and imported commodities. By 1906, more overseas goods were coming into Nigeria from the port of Lagos than from across the Sahara, and in 1912, with the opening of the Kano railway, Lagos became the major entrepôt for European, especially British, merchandise.[108] Multicolored woolen yarns were among the imported products carried northward to the former caliphate, and they were available at relatively low cost. Nigerian brokers might well have imported them with local weavers in mind, since there already had been such a long history of unraveling woolen blankets to use their threads for fancy brocaded textiles. Whatever the case, from this time if not before, trouser embroidery was carried out mainly with wool.[109] It seems reasonable to assume then that either waste silk was no longer available as before, or that the cheaper price of the wool made it a more attractive choice for most embroiderers. In any case, what was important was that the sheen and the color of this thread produced much the same strong visual effect as would waste silk.

PIETY AND PROPER ATTIRE

It is still very unclear when and where the first examples of elaborate *kamun k'afa* trouser embroideries were made. In contrast to embroidered robes, trousers have not very often been the subject of scholarly study. Examples in museum and private collections are relatively rare, and the documentation of them is usually minimal. Nevertheless, some historical interpretations will be offered here primarily to provoke debate and encourage further research. My suggestion that these heavily embellished, vividly colored trousers were embroidered in the Emirate of Ilorin rather than in the more obvious choice of Bida[110] is highly speculative, though it is based on several lines of visual evidence. The composition of the trouser imagery varies from rather simple examples showing interlace motifs along the gusset seam (fig. 3.8) to very elaborate examples like the garment described at the beginning of this chapter, which shows practically the entire body of the trousers covered in clusters of motifs (fig. 3.9). In the latter case, if we look carefully at the specific motifs and how they are arranged, they resemble the imagery on Yoruba beaded regalia much more than they do the patterns seen in Quranic illumination and robe embroidery. The iconography of objects associated with Sango, the thunder deity and legendary king of the northern Yoruba kingdom of Oyo, was especially rich in interlaces and knot forms, and would have been well known among Ilorin artisans, many of whom originated in Oyo.[111] Moreover, the use of glossy, brightly colored wool and a style employing the couching stitch can be considered consonant with Ilorin weaving traditions, where brocading on one side of the fabric was done from at least the late nineteenth century.[112] The couching stitches on such trousers, with the stitching worked in parallel lines perpendicular to the laid threads, produces the same kind of visual effect as that seen on Ilorin brocaded cloths, where supplementary wefts are held in place with "tie-down" warps. Also, the beadwork on items of Yoruba regalia bears some technical similarities to this type of couching. In my view, the most elaborately embellished trousers appear to be Yoruba-influenced versions of this Muslim garment tradition. If so, it is possible that some of these densely embroidered trousers were made in Ilorin workshops, during the caliphate period and after.

Much more certain are the ceremonial contexts in which men wore these kinds of elaborate trousers. As Law's research made clear, the display of horsemanship has a long history in West Africa and was not confined to predominantly Muslim societies. In the lower Niger region, kings and chiefs rode horses on formal public occasions, as was witnessed in the seventeenth century when the king of Benin made his yearly appearance on horseback.[113] The king of Idah was described in the mid-nineteenth century wearing his riding apparel, which included "Hausa trousers like a

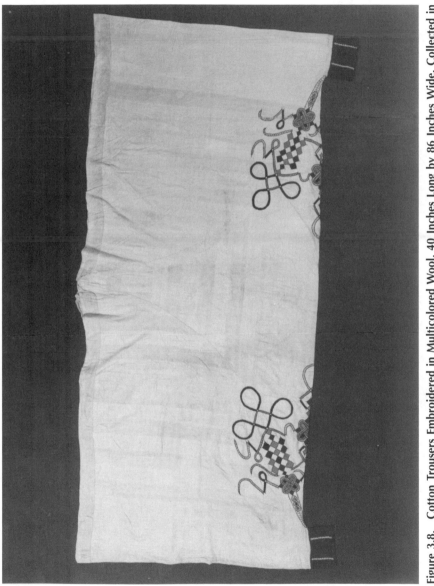

Figure 3.8. Cotton Trousers Embroidered in Multicolored Wool, 40 Inches Long by 86 Inches Wide. Collected in Kano by J. M. Freemantle before 1906, Accession no. 5.10.1906.3b. Copyright National Museums Liverpool, UK.

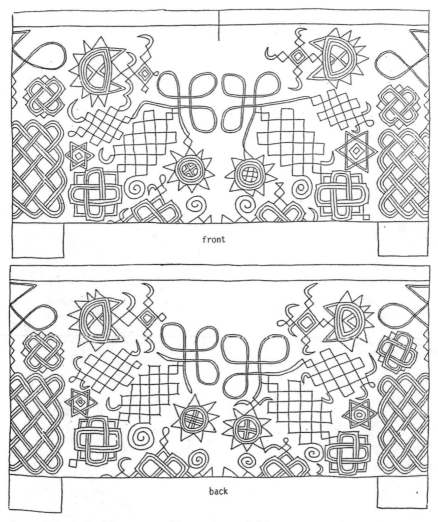

front

back

Figure 3.9.   Embroidery Composition on the Banfield Trousers, Royal Ontario Museum. Drawing by the Author.

petticoat, only tight at the ankles."[114] More commonly, however, the trousers were worn by men taking part in equestrian games and displays of riding prowess. Such games and displays usually took place at the time of initiation celebrations, religious rituals, or, in the case of non-Muslim areas such as the Jos plateau, at the appointment of priests or chiefs, and at analogous public events in Muslim communities in and around the Sokoto Caliphate and Borno. Some of these were organized competitions where high-precision skills and daring acts of horsemanship were rewarded with prizes.[115] It is at least conceivable that lavishly embroidered trousers might even have been, at one time, the prerogative of champion riders.

The most prominent and regularly occurring occasions for public equestrian displays in the Sokoto Caliphate were two major Muslim holidays, *'id al-fitr* and *'id al-kabir*. In the first case, the ending of the period of fasting during the month of Ramadan was celebrated with communal prayers, followed by ceremonial parades and dramatic performances of cavalry charges on horseback. In the second, there were similar displays presented at the closing of the annual time of pilgrimage.[116] Both of these holy occasions would have required that proper garments be worn, that is, the white clothing of the devout Muslim. Indeed, my survey of embroidered trousers revealed that they were regularly made from two types of cloth, white and *sak'i*. The former would certainly have been the most appropriate choice for religious ceremonies; the latter would likely have been reserved for secular ones.

A century has passed since the Sokoto Caliphate fell to the British. For reasons that have yet to be fully explained, elegantly tailored and embroidered garments of *sak'i* cloth, which signified the caliphate administration and its elites, are only rarely made now by special order.[117] Islam remains strong, however, and proper dress is still an issue. In the 1980s, celebrations of *'id al-fitr* and *'id al-kabir* in Kano demonstrated that white clothing was still deemed the dress to be worn by true believers, especially the emir and other aristocrats, on the day of prayers and in the procession leading from the mosque back to the palace.[118] Descriptions of palace wardrobes and photographs of equestrian parades affirm that careful attention was paid to dress—not only for elite men and their entourages but also for their horses. Correctly attired in their elegant white clothing, the brightly embroidered talismanic imagery on their trousers barely visible under the folds of their ample robes, Muslim leaders rode forward on their mounts, their bridles and saddles also laden with colorful triangular charms for protection against malevolent spirits.[119] The textile components of these ensembles were, as we have seen, the end result of a long history of trade, currency exchange, textile manufacture, and religious pluralism in West African history. And viewed all together, the message is clear. Such formal visual presentations make powerful public statements about the splendor and dangers of horsemanship, the dignified comportment of Muslim believers, their devotion to Allah, and also their awareness of the ever-present jinn.

NOTES

1. "French," or encased, seams are made by folding two fabric edges each inside the other so there is no seam allowance on either side of the garment.

2. Agnes Geiger, *A History of Textile Art* (London: Pasold Research Fund, 1979), 33–37.

3. Thurstan Shaw, "The Nok Sculptures of Nigeria," *Scientific American* 244 (1981).

4. Musée National des Arts d'Afrique et d'Océanie, *Vallées du Niger* (Paris: Réunion des Musées Nationaux, 1993), 571.

5. Ekpo Eyo and Frank Willett, *Treasures of Ancient Nigeria* (New York: Alfred A. Knopf, 1980), 36–37.

6. Renée Boser-Sarivaxévanis, *Les tissus de l'Afrique Occidentale* (Basel: Pharos-Verlag, 1972); Boser-Sarivaxévanis, "Recherche sur l'histoire des textiles traditionels tissées et teints de l'Afrique Occidentale," *Verhandlungen der naturforschenden Gesellschaft in Basel* 86, nos. 1 and 2 (1975); and Boser-Sarivaxévanis, "Research on the History of Traditional Woven and Dyed Textiles of West Africa," in *West African Textiles and Garments* (Minneapolis: University of Minnesota, 1980).

7. Marion Johnson, "Cloth Strips and History," *West African Journal of Archaeology* 7 (1977).

8. Roger Blench, "Ethnographic and Linguistic Evidence for the Prehistory of African Ruminant Livestock, Horses, and Ponies," in *The Archaeology of Africa: Food, Metals, and Towns*, ed. Thurstan Shaw et al. (London: Routledge, 1993), 78–80.

9. Juliet Clutton-Brock, "The Spread of Domestic Animals in Africa," in Shaw et al., *The Archaeology of Africa*, 69–70.

10. S. Magnavita et al., "Nobles, guerriers, paysans: Une nécropole de l'Age de Fer et son emplacement dans l'Oudalan pré- et protohistorique," *Beiträge zur Allgemeinen und Vergleichenden Archäologie* 22 (2002): 28, 36–37; Musée National des Arts d'Afrique et d'Océanie, *Vallées du Niger*, nos. 86 and 87, 547–48; François Paris, "Les sépultures monumentales d'Iwelen (Niger)" *Journal des Africanistes* 60, no. 1 (1990). I thank Graham Connah for passing on the information about the Kissi excavation.

11. Andrew Watson, "The Rise and Spread of Old World Cotton," in *Studies in Textile History: In Memory of Harold B. Burnham*, ed. Veronika Gervers (Toronto: Royal Ontario Museum, 1977); Watson, *Agricultural Innovation in the Early Islamic World: The Diffusion of Crops and Farming Techniques, 700–1100* (Cambridge: Cambridge University Press, 1983).

12. F. L. Griffith and G. M. Crowfoot, "On the Early Use of Cotton in the Nile Valley," *Journal of Egyptian Archaeology* 20 (1934); Thomas Bassett, *The Peasant Cotton Revolution in West Africa: Côte d'Ivoire, 1880–1995* (Cambridge: Cambridge University Press, 2001).

13. Ingrid Bergman, *Late Nubian Textiles* (Stockholm: Scandinavian University Press, 1975); and Christa C. M. Thurman and Bruce Williams, *Ancient Textiles from Nubia* (Chicago: Art Institute of Chicago, 1979).

14. Michael Gervers, "Cotton and Cotton Weaving in Meroitic Nubia and Medieval Ethiopia," *Textile History* 21, no. 1 (1990).

15. Bruce Trigger, "The Myth of Meroë and the African Iron Age," *African Historical Studies* 2, no. 1 (1969).

16. Rogier Bedaux and Rita Bolland, "Vêtements féminins médiévaux du Mali: Les cache-sexe de fibre des Tellem," in *Man Does Not Go Naked*, ed. Beate Engelbrecht and Bernhard Gardi (Basel: Museum für Völkerkunde, 1989).

17. Nehemia Levtzion and J. F. P Hopkins, eds., *Corpus of Early Arabic Sources for West African History* (Cambridge: Cambridge University Press, 1981), 77–85.

18. Levtzion and Hopkins, *Corpus of Early Arabic Sources*, 110–28.

19. Levtzion and Hopkins, *Corpus of Early Arabic Sources*, 290–303.

20. Graham Connah, *Three Thousand Years in Africa: Man and His Environment in the Lake Chad Region of Nigeria* (Cambridge: Cambridge University Press, 1981), 159, 165.

21. Sigismund Koelle, *African Native Literature: Or, Proverbs, Tales, Fables, and Historical Fragments in the Kanuri or Bornu Language* (1854; repr., Freeport, N.Y.: Books for Libraries Press, 1970), 376; Michael Bross and Ahmad Tela Baba, *Dictionary of Hausa Crafts: A Dialectal Documentation* (Cologne: Köppe, 1996). I am grateful to Phil Jaggar for informing me of the latter source.

22. Bruno Chavane, *Villages de l'ancien Tekrour: Recherches archéologiques dans la moyenne vallée du fleuve Sénégal* (Paris: Karthala, 1985), 110–12, 143–52, 170.

23. Shawn Murray, "Medieval Cotton and Wheat Finds in the Middle Niger Delta (Mali)," poster presented at the Fourth International Workshop of African Archaeobotany, Groningen, NL, 30 June–2 July 2003. Thank you to Shawn Murray for providing me with this paper, and to Kevin MacDonald for informing me about this evidence.

24. Rogier Bedaux, "Les plus anciens tissus retrouvés par les archéologues," in Musée National des Arts d'Afrique et d'Océanie, *Vallées du Niger*, 456–57, 560; Susan K. McIntosh and Roderick J. McIntosh, "Cities without Citadels: Understanding Urban Origins Along the Middle Niger," in Shaw et al., *The Archaeology of Africa*, 635; Susan McIntosh, ed. *Excavations at Jenné-Jeno, Hambarketolo, and Kaniana (Inland Niger Delta, Mali): The 1981 Season* (Berkeley: University of California Press, 1994), 216, 392, plates 33 and 34; James Anquandah, "Urbanization and State Formation in Ghana during the Iron Age," in Shaw et al., *The Archaeology of Africa*, 649; K. Effah-Gyamfi, *Bono Manso: An Archaeological Investigation into Early Akan Urbanism* (Calgary: University of Calgary Press, 1985), 197–98. For a study of male specialists making spindle whorls, see Leonard Crossland, "Traditional Textile Industry in North-West Brong Ahafo, Ghana—the Archaeological and Contemporary Evidence," *Sankofa* 1 (1975).

25. Rita Bolland, *Tellem Textiles: Archaeological Finds from Burial Caves in Mali's Bandiagara Cliff* (Leiden: Rijksmuseum voor Volkenkunde, 1991).

26. Bolland, *Tellem Textiles*.

27. Ade Obayemi, "Archaeology and the History of Western Hausaland: An Introductory Contribution," *Fourth Interim Report, Northern History Research Scheme* (Zaria, Nigeria: Ahmadu Bello University, 1977), 75–76.

28. Philip Shea, *The Development of an Export-Oriented Dyed Cloth Industry in Kano Emirate in the Nineteenth Century* (PhD diss., University of Wisconsin, Madison, 1975), 58.

29. Leo Africanus, *The History and Description of Africa and of the Notable Things therein Contained* (1896; repr., New York: B. Franklin, 1963), 3:829, 831.

30. Abdullahi Smith, "The Early States of the Central Sudan," in *History of West Africa*, ed. J. F. A. Ajayi and Michael Crowder (New York: Columbia University Press, 1976), 1:191–92.

31. Smith, "Early States of the Central Sudan"; and Joseph Greenberg, "Linguistic Evidence for the Influence of the Kanuri on the Hausa," *Journal of African History* 1, no. 2 (1960).

32. Smith, "Early States of the Central Sudan."

33. Shea, *Development of an Export-Oriented Dyed Cloth Industry*, 145–47. The proposed etymology for the Hausa *karofi* is doubtful, however, since the "r-sound" is realized as a "flap" instead of the "trill/roll" it should be if it was a loanword. Personal communication, Philip Jaggar, 17 November 2004.

34. My data are from Tuareg (Air) and Hausa (Nigeria and Niger). Barreteau discusses the relationship using the word *tabdok*, presumably from Tuareg (Ahaggar), and suggests that the Tuareg borrowed the term from the Hausa. D. Barreteau et al., "Les dénominations du coton dans le bassin du lac Tchad," in *L'homme et le milieu végétal dans le bassin du lac Tchad*, ed. D. Barreteau (Paris: ORSTOM, 1997), 241.

35. Here too, there are conflicting interpretations of the evidence. See Johannes Nicolaisen and Ida Nicolaisen, *The Pastoral Tuareg: Ecology, Culture, and Society* (London: Thames and Hudson, 1997), 1:271. The source cited for claiming Hausa introduction of cotton to Air does not, in fact, make that claim. See Ph. Bruneau de Miré and H. Gillet, "Contribution à l'étude de la flore du massif de l'Aïr," *Journal d'Agriculture Tropicale et de Botanique Appliquée* 3, nos. 5–12 (1956): 243–44. The varieties of cotton grown in Air are related to Old World cottons. J. M. Dalziel, *The Useful Plants of Western Tropical Africa* (London: Crown Agents, 1937), 124.

36. Smith, "Early States of the Central Sudan"; Djibo Hamani, "Proto-Hausa et Hausa," in Musée National des Arts d'Afrique et d'Océanie, *Vallées du Niger*, 194–95.

37. Nicolaisen and Nicolaisen, *The Pastoral Tuareg*.

38. Venice Lamb and Alastair Lamb, "The Classification and Distribution of Horizontal Treadle Looms in Sub-Saharan Africa," in *Textiles of Africa*, ed. Dale Idiens and K. G. Ponting (Bath, UK: Pasold Research Fund, 1980); Karl-Ferdinand Schaedler, *Weaving in Africa South of the Sahara* (Munich: Panterra Verlag, 1987).

39. Marion Johnson, "Cloth as Money: The Cloth Strip Currencies of Africa," *Textile History* 11 (1980).

40. Levtzion and Hopkins, *Corpus of Early Arabic Sources*, 78, 385; Lloyd Cabot Briggs, *Tribes of the Sahara* (Cambridge, Mass.: Harvard University Press, 1967), 275.

41. R. B. Serjeant, *Islamic Textiles* (Beirut: Librairie du Liban, 1972); Yedida Kalfon Stillman, *Arab Dress: A Short History, from the Dawn of Islam to Modern Times* (Leiden: Brill, 2000).

42. Levtzion and Hopkins, *Corpus of Early Arabic Sources*, 85; Michael Brett and Elizabeth Fentress, *The Berbers* (Oxford: Blackwell, 1997), 102; Murphy Collection, accession no. 5-1968, Phoebe A. Hearst Museum of Anthropology, Berkeley, California.

43. G. P. Bargery and D. Westermann, *A Hausa-English Dictionary and English-Hausa Vocabulary* (London: Oxford University Press, 1934), 1063.

44. Smith, "Early States of the Central Sudan"; Levtzion and Hopkins, *Corpus of Early Arabic Sources*, 260.

45. Johnson, "Cloth as Money."

46. Brigitte Menzel, *Textilien aus Westafrika* (Berlin: Museum für Völkerkunde, 1972–1974), vol. 1, no. 1444.

47. Bargery and Westermann, *A Hausa-English Dictionary*; Menzel, *Textilien aus Westafrika*; A. W. Banfield, *Dictionary of the Nupe Language* (1914; repr., Farnborough, UK: Gregg International, 1969).

48. Colleen Kriger, "Textile Production in the Lower Niger Basin: New Evidence from the 1841 Niger Expedition Collection," *Textile History* 21, no. 1 (1990); Kriger, "Textile Production and Gender in the Sokoto Caliphate," *Journal of African History* 34 (1993).

49. Koelle, *African Native Literature*, 318–19; T. J. Bowen, *Grammar and Dictionary of the Yoruba Language* (Washington, D.C.: Smithsonian Institution, 1858), 34; Samuel Crowther and E. J. Sowande, *A Dictionary of the Yoruba Language* (1937; repr., London: Oxford University Press, 1950), 80; Samuel Crowther, *A Grammar and Vocabulary of the Nupe Language* (London: Church Missionary House, 1864), 205.

50. Heinrich Barth, *Travels and Discoveries in North and Central Africa* (1857; repr., London: Cass, 1965), 1:345.

51. Barth, *Travels and Discoveries*, 1:512–13; Nicolaisen and Nicolaisen, *The Pastoral Tuareg*; Douglas Ferguson, *Nineteenth-century Hausaland: Being a Description by Imam Imoru of the Land, Economy, and Society of His People* (PhD diss., University of California, Los Angeles, 1973), 374–77.

52. Joseph Greenberg, *The Influence of Islam on a Sudanese Religion* (New York: Augustin, 1946); R. S. Fletcher, *Hausa Sayings and Folklore* (Oxford: Oxford University Press, 1912); Bargery and Westermann, *Hausa-English Dictionary*.

53. For a more recent exploration of these issues, see Adeline Masquelier, "Mediating Threads: Clothing and the Texture of Spirit/Medium Relations in Bori (Southern Niger)," in *Clothing and Difference: Embodied Identities in Colonial and Post-colonial Africa*, ed. Hildi Hendrickson (Durham, N.C.: Duke University Press, 1996).

54. Stillman, *Arab Dress*.

55. Paul Lovejoy, "Plantations in the Economy of the Sokoto Caliphate," *Journal of African History* 19, no. 3 (1978). For an excellent introduction to the topic of slavery in Africa in general, see Patrick Manning, *Slavery and African Life: Occidental, Oriental, and African Slave Trades* (Cambridge: Cambridge University Press, 1990).

56. Colleen Kriger, *Garments of the Sokoto Caliphate: A Case Study from the Banfield Collection, Royal Ontario Museum, Toronto* (MA thesis, York University, Canada, 1985); Kriger, "Textile Production and Gender."

57. Barth, *Travels and Discoveries*, 1:511–13.

58. Colleen Kriger, "Robes of the Sokoto Caliphate," *African Arts* 21 (1988); Kriger, "Textile Production and Gender."

59. This historical example contrasts with what Esther Goody observed in Daboya during the 1970s. She encountered no evidence of entrepreneurial control over textile manufacture. Goody, "Daboya Weavers: Relations of Production, Dependence, and Reciprocity," in *From Craft to Industry*, ed. Goody (Cambridge: Cambridge University Press, 1982).

60. Dixon Denham, Hugh Clapperton, and Walter Oudney, *Narrative of Travels and Discoveries in Northern and Central Africa in the Years 1822, 1823, and 1824* (1828; repr., London: Darf, 1985), 2:336.

61. Shea, *Development of an Export-Oriented Dyed Cloth Industry*, 78–82, 101.

62. Bargery and Westermann, *Hausa-English Dictionary*; Banfield, *Dictionary of the Nupe Language*; Barth, *Travels and Discoveries*, 1:513.

63. R. Pfister, *Les toiles imprimées de Fostat et l'Hindoustan* (Paris: Les Editions d'Art et d'Histoire, 1938).

64. Bargery and Westermann, *Hausa-English Dictionary*; Bross and Baba, *Dictionary of Hausa Crafts*; Crowther, *Grammar and Vocabulary*; and Banfield, *Dictionary of the Nupe Language*.

65. Grace Crowfoot, *Methods of Handspinning in Egypt and the Sudan* (Halifax, UK: King and Sons, 1931).

66. Samuel Crowther, *A Vocabulary of the Yoruba Language* (London: Seeleys, 1852).

67. Kriger, "Textile Production and Gender."

68. The reasons for this are not known, although gendered work patterns and preferred thread quality may well have been contributing factors.

69. Kriger, "Textile Production and Gender," 376.

70. Levtzion and Hopkins, *Corpus of Early Arabic Sources*, 85, 110, 171, 265, 299, 303.

71. R. P. A. Dozy, *Dictionnaire détaillée des noms des vêtements chez les Arabes* (Amsterdam: Jean Müller, 1845), 203–9; Stillman, *Arab Dress*.

72. Bolland, *Tellem Textiles*, 226, 232, 237.

73. Robin Law, *The Horse in West African History* (Oxford: Oxford University Press, 1980), 17–19, 120–22.

74. Africanus, *History and Description of Africa*, 3:824–25.

75. M. Kati et l'un de ses petit fils, *Tarikh el-fettach* (Paris: Maisonneuve, 1981), 282, 315.

76. Adam Jones, *German Sources for West African History*, 1599–1669 (Wiesbaden: Franz Steiner, 1983), 101.

77. Bernhard Gardi, *Boubou, c'est chic: Gewänder aus Mali und anderen Ländern westafrikas* (Basel: C. Merian, 2000).

78. Philip Curtin, ed., *Africa Remembered* (Madison: University of Wisconsin Press, 1967).

79. Mungo Park, *Travels in the Interior Districts of Africa* (Durham, N.C.: Duke University Press, 2000), 80, 154, 168, 252–53.

80. Murray Last, *The Sokoto Caliphate* (New York: Humanities Press, 1967), 12.

81. Thomas Hodgkin, ed., *Nigerian Perspectives*, 2nd ed. (Oxford: Oxford University Press, 1975), 250.

82. Hodgkin, *Nigerian Perspectives*, 255–56.

83. Stillman, *Arab Dress*.

84. David Heathcote, "A Hausa Embroiderer of Katsina," *The Nigerian Field* 37, no. 3 (1972); Heathcote, "Hausa Embroidered Dress," *African Arts* 5, no. 2 (1972); Heathcote, "Hausa Embroidery Stitches," *The Nigerian Field* 39, no. 4 (1974); Heathcote, "Aspects of Style in Hausa Embroidery," *Savanna* 3, no. 1 (1974).

85. Crowther and Sowande, *Dictionary of the Yoruba Language*; Banfield, *Dictionary of the Nupe Language*; Bargery and Westermann, *Hausa-English Dictionary*; Koelle, *African Native Literature*.

86. Kriger, "Robes of the Sokoto Caliphate"; Kriger, "Textile Production and Gender."

87. Kriger, *Garments of the Sokoto Caliphate*.

88. Menzel, *Textilien aus Westafrika*, vol. 1, no. 594; vol. 2, no. 512.

89. Ferguson, *Nineteenth-century Hausaland*, 312.

90. Leo Frobenius Collection, accession documentation and photographs, Staatliches Museum für Volkerkunde, Munich, 1915.

91. Kriger, *Garments of the Sokoto Caliphate*.

92. Ferguson, *Nineteenth-century Hausaland*, 312.

93. Kriger, "Textile Production in the Lower Niger Basin."

94. Ferguson, *Nineteenth-century Hausaland*, 312.

95. David Heathcote, "Some Hausa Lizard Designs," *Embroidery* 23, no. 4 (1972).

96. Kriger, "Robes of the Sokoto Caliphate"; Labelle Prussin, *Hatumere: Islamic Design in West Africa* (Berkeley: University of California Press, 1986).

97. David Heathcote, *Arts of the Hausa* (London: World of Islam Festival Ltd., 1976); Adam Michlich, *Uber die Kulturen im mittel-Sudan* (Berlin: Dietrich Reimer, 1942); Menzel, *Textilien aus Westafrika*.

98. Leo Frobenius Collection, Staatliches Museum für Völkerkunde.

99. Menzel, *Textilien aus Westafrika*.

100. Kriger, "Robes of the Sokoto Caliphate"; Prussin, *Hatumere*.

101. Menzel, *Textilien aus Westafrika*; Bargery and Westermann, *Hausa-English Dictionary*; Ade Obayemi, "History, Culture, Yoruba and Northern Factors," in *Studies in Yoruba History and Culture: Essays in Honour of Professor S. O. Biobaku*, ed. G. O. Olusanya (Ibadan: University Press, 1983); Greenberg, *Influence of Islam*. Zarma live today mostly in southwestern Niger; alternative spellings are Dyerma, Djerma, and Zerma.

102. Kriger, *Garments of the Sokoto Caliphate*. Jinn (djinn, or genie) is a type of spirit mentioned in the Quran and fully accepted in Muslim belief. In Hausaland, jinns were incorporated into the pantheon of spirits in the Bori cult. Nehemia Levtzion, "Islam in Africa to 1800," in *The Oxford History of Islam*, ed. John Esposito (Oxford: Oxford University Press, 1999). For an example of a charm gown, see John Picton and John Mack, *African Textiles* (London: British Museum, 1979), 164.

103. Kriger, "Robes of the Sokoto Caliphate."

104. Kriger, *Garments of the Sokoto Caliphate*.

105. Irene Emery, *The Primary Structures of Fabrics* (Washington, D.C.: The Textile Museum, 1980), 247.

106. Kriger, *Garments of the Sokoto Caliphate*.

107. Barth, *Travels and Discoveries*, 1:518.

108. Marion Johnson, "Calico Caravans: The Tripoli-Kano Trade after 1880," *Journal of African History* 17, no. 1 (1970).

109. Constance Larymore, *A Resident's Wife in Nigeria* (London: Routledge, 1911).

110. I say obvious because it is well known that this type of work was done in Bida, oftentimes by former slaves of Yoruba ancestry. See Judith Perani, *Nupe Crafts: The Dynamics of Change in Nineteenth and Twentieth Century Weaving and Brasscasting* (PhD diss., Indiana University, 1988), 82; Leo Frobenius Collection, Staatliches Museum für Völkerkunde.

111. Ann O'Hear, *The Economic History of Ilorin in the Nineteenth and Twentieth Centuries: The Rise and Decline of a Middleman Society* (PhD diss., University of Birmingham, 1983).

112. Ann O'Hear, "The Introduction of Weft Float Motifs to Strip Weaving in Ilorin," in *West African Economic and Social History: Studies in Memory of Marion Johnson,* ed. David Henige and T. C. McCaskie (Madison: University of Wisconsin, African Studies Program, 1990).

113. Law, *The Horse in West African History,* 164; Jones, *German Sources,* 38.

114. T. J. Hutchinson, *Narrative of the Niger, Tshadda, and Binue Exploration* (London: Longman, Brown, Green, and Longman, 1855), 50.

115. Law, *The Horse in West African History,* 165.

116. Law, *The Horse in West African History.*

117. Judith Perani, "Northern Nigerian Prestige Textiles: Production, Trade, Patronage, and Use," in Engelbrecht and Gardi, *Man Does Not Go Naked,* 72–73.

118. Judith Perani and Norma Wolff, "Embroidered Gown and Equestrian Ensembles of the Kano Aristocracy," *African Arts* 25, no. 3 (1992): 81.

119. Kojo Fosu, *Emblems of Royalty (Kayan Sarauta)* (Zaria, Nigeria: Fine Arts Gallery, Ahmadu Bello University, 1982); Musée Royal de l'Afrique Centrale, *Des fils de l'émir de Gombe* (Nigeria), published photograph, Tervuren, Belgium, 1972.

4

The Worlds of Indigo Blue

In the poetic world of art and literature, the word *indigo* evokes a host of potent images and symbolic meanings. The color, which signifies depth and richness, comes from plants originating in the tropics, and in the world of commerce they have long been the stuff of legend. Known widely as an effective drug and dye good, indigo was one of those highly profitable tropical cargoes that beckoned European maritime explorers into the Indian Ocean in the fifteenth and sixteenth centuries. At that time, centers of indigo production included parts of Africa as well as Asia and the Americas, and they were often closely connected to cotton growing and cotton textile manufacture. This chapter explores certain aspects of the history of indigo dyeing in West Africa by focusing on a women's cotton wrapper that was made during the 1970s in the Yoruba city of Ibadan (fig. 4.1). Viewing the cloth from a distance, one sees its delicate tonal gradations of blue merge into a single rectangular expanse of glimmering color. Up close, these varied tones of blue separate into areas of repeat patterning produced from only two shades—light blue on a dark blue ground. What appears to be differences in tone are, in fact, a range of differences in the types of pattern and how they were made. At one end of the range there are areas of floral motifs and checkerboards that create a clear and dramatic interplay of light and dark. At the other end are areas where light and dark alternate in small-scale all-over repeats that the eye effortlessly blends together into a field of texture and hue. Combined, they present the viewer with a subtle and gently rhythmical arrangement of seemingly endless indigo blues.

This wrapper was dyed "in the piece," that is, the woven cloth was dipped into the dye pot to color it all over with indigo. Its patterns were made by a process called *resist dyeing*, a method of preventing the dye from coming

117

**Figure 4.1. Indigo-Dyed Women's Wrapper, *Olokun*. Starch Re-
sist and Indigo on Factory-Woven Cotton, Ibadan, Nigeria, 1975,
79 Inches Long by 64 Inches Wide. UCLA Fowler Museum of
Cultural History, Colleen E. Kriger Collection of Nigerian Textiles,
X2005.24.42.**

into contact with selected areas of the cloth by either tying and binding
those areas (a process known as tie-dye or *plangi*) or painting them with a
dye-resistant substance (a process often called *batik*).[1] After dyeing, when
the bound areas are unbound or the dye-resistant substance is removed, the
undyed areas are revealed as motifs or patterns on a colored background.
Tie-dyeing produces patterns on both sides of the fabric, which is not always
the case with batik. In the case of this wrapper, white cotton cloth was
painted by hand with a starch paste—*eko*—probably made from cassava
flour. The working process thus gives the textile its generic name in the
Yoruba language: *adire eleko* (*adire* = resist dyeing; *eleko* = with paste).

The overall design composition painted on this cloth was carefully
planned and structured, and it shows on only one side. Patterned areas

were laid out in a central grid of twenty squares, all surrounded by a border of smaller squares and rectangles. The complete wrapper consists of two separate pieces of factory-woven cotton yardage sewn together by machine, each piece measuring about 32½ inches wide by about 86 inches long. Each piece was painted with starch paste in precisely the same way, then dipped repeatedly in an indigo dye bath to achieve a very deep shade of blue and, after drying, was scraped clean of starch and rinsed before they were sewn together. On each piece, ten squares of pattern—each about twelve-by-twelve inches—were outlined in an arrangement of two rows of five squares each. This grid, the focus of the design composition, was bordered on three sides—the two crosswise ends and one of the lengthwise edges—with smaller pattern areas forming six-by-six-inch squares, or six-by-twelve-inch rectangles. Once they had been dyed, scraped, and rinsed, the two patterned cloths were sewn together with one of them rotated 180 degrees so that the twenty large squares would make up the center, completely enclosed by a narrow border. The two pieces were joined by sewing an encased seam, and the cloth was then machine-hemmed along the cut edges. The final result was a wrapper with finished dimensions of sixty-four inches by seventy-nine inches.

Patterns within the individual squares, though varied, share some general features and structural principles. Each of the ten large squares on each half of the wrapper is singular, having a distinctly different design composition made up of linear and geometric motifs such as checkerboards, stripes, crosshatchings, squares, circles, and lozenges, and nonlinear, or biomorphic motifs, such as birds and plant forms, taken from the natural world. In almost all of the motifs, solid areas of light or dark blue were kept relatively small in scale and to a minimum, while areas and spaces were meticulously filled in with parallel lines, fine crosshatching, or tiny circles and dots. The cumulative effect of this feature is a softening of the light/dark color contrasts and a harmonizing of the varied motifs and patterns. Another layer of harmony is created through similarities in the squares' design structures. All of the individual elements within the large squares were themselves organized into a grid or arranged diagonally or, in some cases, a combination of both. In its entirety, the cloth is a masterpiece of order, invention, variation, and repetition.

This particular wrapper is called *Olokun*, having been named for the god or goddess of the sea in the Benin kingdom and parts of Yorubaland. It is one of the most elaborate of *adire eleko* cloth designs, and may well be one of the oldest. Its imagery was hand painted by a woman who specialized in the craft, using chicken feathers, palm ribs, and small metal knives as tools to create the various outlines, motifs, and textural effects. After each piece was painted with starch and dried in the sun, it was then taken to another woman specialist for dyeing. The making of indigo-dyed cloth has a long history in the lower Niger region, and the making of *adire eleko* is firmly rooted in that history. At the same time, the *adire eleko* tradition owes much to the Atlantic trade along the Guinea Coast, which brought new types of patterns, techniques, and materials that transformed the way dyed wrappers were made and how they looked. This chapter traces the major features of *Olokun* to chart these changes over time, and to show again how particular textile forms represent a melding of local values and technologies with new ideas brought from near and far. What finally came about in this case was a specifically West African variant of chintz: cotton cloths with patterns painted or printed onto them after weaving.

MATERIALS: INDIGO AND SALT

Indigo is native to tropical areas of south Asia, the Americas, and Africa. Various parts of the plant yield medicines and dyestuff that came to be known and highly valued in the ancient Mediterranean world and were imported by the Greeks and Romans by at least the last few centuries BC. The Greek and Roman source of supply for indigo, the Indian subcontinent, gave its name to this costly luxury product, and since then, India has been acknowledged and appreciated as the world's earliest major center for indigo growing and processing. That reputation is indeed well earned, especially since the most important variety of indigo in early trading systems, *Indigofera tinctoria*, was domesticated there.[2] Less well known, but also historically significant in their own ways, are the indigo species that were domesticated in Africa and the New World. Of the former, *Indigofera arrecta* was native to eastern and southern Africa, though it has been widely cultivated in West Africa as well, and it was vigorously promoted in Nigeria after 1905 as a richer source of dye than *I. tinctoria*. Another species, from a different genus, *Lonchocarpus cyanescens*, has been harvested in the wild and also cultivated by farmers in the rainforests and moister savanna areas of much of West Africa. Its presumed antiquity and ubiquity in Yorubaland have earned for it the alternative vernacular term "Yoruba wild indigo." And yet another *Indigofera* species, *I. suffruticosa*, was originally native to tropical America and the West Indies before being introduced into certain parts of Africa during the Atlantic trade. It too has been an important indigo dyestuff of international commerce.[3]

While it is clear that indigo has played an important role in local, regional, and international economic histories, those histories are far from easy to trace. Material evidence of indigo cultivation and processing in the form of plant remains or prepared dyestuff tends not to survive in the archaeological record. If pollen from the indigo plant is an exception, I have not found it mentioned in archaeological reports and surveys. Dye equipment is a more promising lead, as fired clay pots do survive very well, but it is not certain whether dye pots would be identifiable as such or if they were similar to pots used for other purposes.

Lexical terms for indigo are also difficult to sort out and interpret, since it is not always stated whether the term refers to the plant, the prepared dyestuff, or the dye bath itself. It appears that in the lower Niger region, people regularly distinguished between varieties of indigo within the two separate genera, *Indigofera* and *Lonchocarpus*, by using different words for them (see table 4.1 below). In Hausa, for example, *baba* referred to species

Table 4.1. Indigo Species and Lexical Terms

Family Papilionaceae (= Leguminosae)

Indigofera species (general terms for indigo dyeplant or dye)
Hausa: *baba; baba rini* (*rini* = the dye); *baba kore* (*kore* = the color)
Kanuri: *alin*
Bagirmi: *alini*
Shuwa Arab: *nile* (Arabic *nil*)
Yoruba: *shenshe;* èlú-aja; *ewere*
Igbo: *uri*

Indigofera species (particular species used as dye, medicine, or other)

x	*I. arrecta* Hochst.	Yoruba: èlú-aja
o	*I. astragalina* DC.	Hausa: *baban marai*
xo	*I. diphylla* Vent.	Hausa: *tantaroba*
x	*I. endecaphylla*	reportedly grown and used in Benin (19th c.)
o	*I. hirsuta* L.	Hausa: *k'aik'ayi*
o	*I. pulchra* Willd.	Hausa: *bak'in bunu*
	I. simplicifolia Lam.	Hausa: *sagagi*
	(= *I. simplifolia* Lam.)	
x	*I. suffruticosa*	widely cultivated, including Nigeria
x	*I. tinctoria* L.	widely cultivated in savanna areas

Lonchocarpus species

xo	*L. cyanescens* Benth.	Hausa: *talaki, talagi; baban talaki; talakin yarabawa* Fulbe: *talakiri* Tiv: *suru* Yoruba: èlú Edo: *ebelu* Igbo: *anunu*
xo	*L. Philenoptera* Benth.	Hausa: *shunin biri; farin sansami* Fulbe: *folahi* (Sokoto and Yola) Mossi: *nangalanga*

x = used for dye
o = used medicinally

Note: Updated botanical terminology is in parentheses.
Sources: Beauvois 1804–1807, 2: 44; Dalziel 1937, 243–50; Usher 1974, 318, 361.

of indigo, both wild and cultivated, from the *Indigofera* genus, while the word *talaki* or *talagi* referred to *Lonchocarpus cyanescens*, or Yoruba wild indigo. However, the terminology has not always been so clear and consistent. There have been some reports of the Hausa term *talaki* having been used in reference to the species *I. tinctoria*.[4] Similarly, there were several terms used for indigo in the Nupe language: *babari* referred to block, or prepared, indigo; *cancaria* was the type of indigo from which the prepared blocks of indigo were made (for storage and trading purposes); *taleki* and *ecin koro* each referred to a species of indigo (not identified); and *ecin* was the general term for the indigo plant and dye.[5] In Yoruba, *èlú* was used to refer specifically to *L. cyanescens*, while the word *aró* meant the prepared dyestuff.[6] Still other words were used, at least in the Hausa language, to designate species of *Indigofera* whose uses were primarily medicinal. Knowledge of the cleansing and healing properties of indigo had been discovered by peoples all across West Africa, probably very long ago, and certain varieties were gathered or grown for just those purposes. They were effective treatments when applied externally to cure yaws, scorpion bites, and skin diseases, for example, and when used internally to induce abortion.[7] Several species of indigo served as both a dye and a drug.

Vocabulary items in Hausa do provide some indication of the range of conditions in which indigo was grown: *baban fadama* for "marsh indigo"; *baban rafi* for "stream indigo"; and *baban daji*, meaning "indigo of the bush."[8] Imam Imoru, in his descriptions of the late nineteenth century, offered rare and valuable testimony about indigo cultivation in the Sokoto Caliphate. He began by distinguishing wild indigo—which he called *talaki*—from the cultivated variety, which he called *baban gida*. He went on to describe two main planting practices. The first was marsh planting, which was done after water levels had sufficiently receded, and the second, which he considered to be preferable, was generally carried out in fields that were not seasonally inundated. In the latter case, workers mounded soil into long ridges into which were sown the indigo seeds. There were also at least two methods of harvesting and processing the leaves of the mature indigo plant, one involving a decomposition stage, the other not. In the first case, when the plants reached maturity, they were cut and massed together in piles and left to rot. Then, after separating out the wood, workers would pound the rotten leaves together into little round cakes of indigo. Imam Imoru claimed that the process of decomposition enhanced the indigo, making a better product than the indigo made from fresh leaves.[9] To date, there have been no attempts made to test these two alternatives, but it may well be that the so-called rotten leaves were actually partially fermented, which would indeed have improved the dye quality.

A number of discoveries were made over time about the particular varieties of indigo that could be used as a dyestuff, and differences were noted among them. The efficacy of indigo as a coloring agent varies with the species, growing conditions, and timing of harvest, and the resulting differences can be easily recognized in textile products by an experienced and discerning customer. Dyers, of course, would be especially conscious of these differences in visual qualities and so could be expected to work hard to achieve the deeper shades. Such differences would then be reflected in price, as was demonstrated in the marketplaces of Hausaland where prepared indigo from *L. cyanescens* was accorded a higher value than the more widely cultivated *Indigofera* species. This value judgment was based not merely on factors of supply and availability, but had to do primarily with widely held assessments about comparative quality, an observation that has been supported by laboratory analyses and experiments. The following figures, showing percentages of the actual dyestuff *indigotin*, give a general idea of the potential differences in color quality between the two main genera of indigo produced and used in the lower Niger region, as compared to the best Indian indigo.

N. Nigerian *Indigofera* species (prepared dyestuff)	27.5 percent indigotin
Lonchocarpus cyanescens (fresh leaves)	43 percent indigotin
Lonchocarpus cyanescens (experimental dye vat)	56 percent indigotin
Top-quality Indian indigo	60 percent indigotin

However, this comparison is not entirely reliable or definitive, since the prepared dyestuff contained quite a bit of sand and soil, suggesting the work of unscrupulous dye processors who deliberately added impurities to the indigo they prepared for market. Such practices might explain why West African dyers often preferred to use the fresh leaves, which makes the above comparison—prepared dye vs. fresh indigo—rather misleading. Yet another species of indigo, *I. arrecta*, the one that was native to Africa according to the colonial physician and botanist Dalziel, was the richest source of indigotin, though he did not provide the percentage. Dyers were aware of *I. arrecta*'s qualities, however, and would sometimes add it to their vats with other varieties of indigo, such as *I. diphylla* and *L. cyanescens*, in order to achieve a deeper, richer color.[10]

To further complicate matters, the efficacy of indigo dye also varied according to the composition of the dye vat and the particular qualities of the other ingredients. Precise data on these factors are hard to come by, however, since African dyers, like natural dyers the world over, preferred to keep their recipes and techniques secret. And in the case of indigo, additional ingredients especially are the key to generating a deep blue color and making sure it adheres well to the fiber of the cloth. Unlike most natural dye processes, which involve preliminary treatments of the fiber with a mordant to fix the color, indigo dyeing is based on an entirely different set of chemical principles and procedures. There are, in the most

general terms, two separate stages. Indigo dye is insoluble in water, hence
it must first undergo reduction to dissolve it, a procedure that also changes
the dye bath into a clear liquid called "indigo white." Fabric dipped into
this bath and taken out again has a yellowish color that soon changes to
green and then to blue. This second stage—the oxidation of the dye—
thus completes the dye process.[11] Creating a strong indigo blue was not
a simple or easy task, especially when using natural ingredients with all
their attendant irregularities and impurities. It is quite remarkable then, that
long before the chemistry of indigo dyeing was explicitly and scientifically
understood, dyers the world over, through trial and error and careful observation, had discovered various ways of creating effective dye vat solutions for reducing indigo. African dyers, many of them women, were among
them.

West African dyers used particular kinds of salts for making an alkaline
vat. Some indication of the complexities of indigo dye technology and its
history in the lower Niger region can be gleaned from the terminology used
for the various ingredients that were added to water to make it alkaline (see
table 4.2 below). These substances ranged from vegetable salts, produced by
roasting certain types of wood and leaching the ash, to mineral salts, including potash and several types of natron (a form of niter). The last mentioned
became an important item of regional and interregional trade, especially in
the nineteenth century. Dyers who did not have access to mineral salts from
long-distance trade, however, could use locally made alternatives, such as
lye and impure forms of potash. Potash could be produced by leaching ashes
and then roasting the remains.[12] All of these salts differed in their chemical
properties, depending on the type and where each one came from, and
certain ones were preferred over others. Natron imported from the eastern
shores of Lake Chad was valued highly, as was the natron from Mangari in
Borno, which was especially favored by indigo dyers in Kano and northern
Zaria. Two varieties of natron were carried by caravan from the famous salt
deposits in the Sahara around Bilma, while another type came from Muniyo,
just north of the Caliphate near Zinder. Salts used for dyeing were also used
in livestock production, as well as for cooking, medicine, and mixing with
chewing tobacco.[13]

That there was such a range of salts used in indigo dyeing, as indicated
by the different words for them in the languages of the lower Niger region, also suggests a long history of experimentation in local dye centers
prior to the twentieth century. The precise details of this history may never
be fully known. Nevertheless, the boom in indigo production, processing,
and dyeing in the nineteenth-century Sokoto Caliphate, which was so well
documented and analyzed by Shea,[14] does provoke some interesting questions from a technological standpoint. What large-scale indigo dyeing centers

Table 4.2. Vocabulary for Indigo-Dyeing Technology

	Yoruba *(N-C, Kwa)*	Nupe *(N-C, Kwa)*	Hausa (Chad)	Kanuri (Saharan)
indigo (general)	èlú	ecin, baba	baba	alin
prepared indigo	aró	babarı	shuni, kantunan baba, butuku (Sok.), allaka, kuntukuru	shuni
dye vat (pits)		mana, marina	marina (Kats.), korofi (Kano)	
dye vat (pots)	ìkòkò aró	ecin dukun		
potash/ash strainer	lokiti	sasanto		
ash for dyeing	lábú, lárú, lábúlábú	swaka	ganuwa, tokar itace	
potash (baked ash)	ayunre (Ibadan), lamu lamu	zanta	zarta (Sokoto, Katsina)	
potash/natron	kánwún		kanwa (from Borno)	
natron/trona	kaun (from Sahara)			kelfu, kalfu, zarafu

*Kwa languages belong to the much larger family of Niger-Congo languages.
Source: Banfield 1969; Barbour and Simmonds 1971; Bargery and Westermann 1934; Bowen 1858; Crowther and Sowande 1950; Dalziel 1937; Ferguson 1973; Keyes 1993; Koelle 1970; Nadel 1951; Wenger and Beier 1957.

required, before the age of synthetic dyes, was a regular supply of relatively standardized ingredients in order to help stabilize the inconsistent conditions of a very tricky chemical process.

One wonders, then, about the degree to which quality controls were established and monitored by caliphate officials and merchants, and how successful these controls were. Certainly, having access to good sources of mineral salts must have helped dyers prepare effective indigo vats on an ongoing basis, much more so than if they had had to contend with the highly variable properties of vegetable salts. Major surpluses of indigo crops and the systematic processing of them into uniform blocks for regional trade probably led to a greater degree of standardization in the dyestuff itself, and hence greater predictability of results from the dye process, as long as there were safeguards against the adulteration of prepared indigo. In short, it is very likely that the indigo boom of the nineteenth century was made possible at least in part through some increase in control over the ingredients of the dye vat. What we do know for certain is that a recognizably high level of quality in production was indeed reached in the numerous dyeing centers of the caliphate, and this in itself was no small technological achievement.

Imam Imoru stated that the best indigo was produced in Kano, with other important centers being Zaria, Zamfara, and Katsina. Shea concurred, adding that based on his research, there were probably tens of thousands of dyers in Kano during the heyday of export production in the nineteenth century.[15] A very general description of the dye process was included in the imam's account, and it closely parallels a well-documented sequence of photographs showing an indigo dyer at work in Zamfara in the 1960s.[16] The initial task was the making of the dye pit, which was a large and very deep hole in the ground. It was lined with three layers of *laso*, a form of cement that sealed the walls of the pit. There could be as many as fifty of these pits (sometimes more) in one location, each one owned by an individual dyer or merchant. When the dyeing was to begin, the pit was filled with water, and two sorts of ash—one from wood, the other from maize stalks—were poured in. Next, the blocks of indigo were added, the number varying depending on the dyer's experience and judgment of the desired strength of the dye bath. After this, the pit was left for two days, presumably to allow the blocks of indigo to ferment. The next stage began with the addition of *zarta*, the potash that turned the liquid into an alkaline bath. Workers then stirred the dye with a long pole, and repeated the stirring for about ten days until the vat was deemed ready for the dyeing process. Both cotton threads and woven cloth were dipped into the dye bath, with repeated dippings imparting a darker, richer color (fig. 4.2). The imam claimed that indigo dye could last up to ten days, after which time the vat was exhausted.[17] This description, valuable though it is, omits the most crucial aspects of the dye process, that is, the initial proportions of indigo to potash, as well as the various indicators—noted by sight, smell, or taste—that dyers relied on to make judgments about how conditions were developing in the vat. It is reasonable to conclude that the imam was, like many other observers, either not aware of or not privy to that kind of specialist technical knowledge.

Quite apart from the indigo centers described above, where the work was done by dyers using large-scale dye pits, there were also women dyers' workshops in and around Yorubaland and the Benin kingdom. Boser-Sarivaxévanis has called attention to some technological features of Yoruba women's indigo dyeing that, in her view, distinguish it from other known centers and may indicate that it was the result of a separate historical development. Specifically, it was the particular way that Yoruba women made *ikat* threads—yarns that are tie-dyed to make them variegated in color—and

Figure 4.2. Men Dyeing Cotton in Indigo Dye Pits, Mafara (Northern Nigeria), 1930. Photograph by A. W. Banfield. Copyright the Estate of Frank Banfield, Canada.

especially the way they prepared their indigo vats—using potash baked in a special kiln—that appear so unusual and distinctive. She proposed that Yoruba women created one of the three major indigo dyeing traditions and production centers in West Africa, and that these special techniques were then transferred eastward to Edo and Ebira communities as well.[18]

The core evidence for this proposition—the potash kiln—has not yet received the systematic study it deserves. Making potash was in many instances the work of women specialists who then sold their product directly to dyers.[19] Several examples of the kiln can be seen in photographs taken in the twentieth century, which are accompanied by brief descriptions of the firing process. The kiln was constructed out of mud and usually measured several feet high and wide, though very large ones of up to five feet in height have been observed. The interior of the kiln was equipped with a perforated shelf for holding the ash. Underneath the shelf was space for a fire, and at the base of the kiln was an opening for replenishing the dry wood fuel. Old ash—that is, ash that had already been leached once—was collected and formed into balls using the liquid residue of a dye pot. Green wood was placed on the roasting shelf, and the ash balls, after being dried in the sun, were placed on top. Firing the kiln lasted about twelve hours. The balls of ash glowed red during the roasting, and in the end they were left to cool, perhaps up to two days. Finally, the balls were pulverized, sifted into powder, and mixed with dye residue to form cakes of potash.[20] There have been no laboratory tests done on these various sorts of ash and potash to precisely identify their chemical components, nor has there been a general survey of sites where such kilns have been in operation in the past. Three sources[21] do mention exact locales—Ede, Igara, Igbetti, Iseyin, and Ibadan—although most captions for illustrations of the kiln do not provide specific documentation.

From the few general descriptions we have (they date from the twentieth century), the procedures women dyers followed in producing an indigo dye vat were slightly different from those followed by men. Women used smaller pots that were freestanding, though oftentimes the pots were set into the ground to stabilize them; and instead of adding salt or potash to pure water, women strained water through baked ashes, using the resulting alkaline liquid for making the dye bath. Only one way of processing the indigo leaves has been described: the pounding of fresh leaves into a thick blue-black mass that the dyer then formed into balls. This dyestuff was allowed to dry in the sun for several days, and afterward it was stored or sold in the market. Like their male counterparts, women dyers were careful to keep their pots in good repair, and they strengthened them with a coating of cement. Unlike the men, they had particular types of pots for particular tasks and kept them all separate—some large ones were set aside solely for dyeing and others were specially made for straining the potash. The latter pots came in pairs, and were nested like the pots of a double boiler, one on top of the other. The top pot had a hole in its bottom, over which the dyer stacked grasses, sticks, and fiber to serve as a filter. Then she added layers of potash and ash, leaving them to settle for a few hours. She returned to pour water over the ash mixture, and as the liquid gradually dripped into the lower pot it was drained off through a hole in the pot's side. The dyer periodically tested the strength of the alkaline solution by assessing its color and by tasting it from time to time, and when it was finally dark and bitter enough it was considered ready. To produce the vat, a dyer would clean her dye pot and set it into the ground to keep it steady. Then she would begin by placing the requisite number of indigo balls into the pot, breaking them up into small bits. The alkaline water was poured in and the liquid stirred. The vat was then covered, left to stand, and stirred only occasionally. After about three days, dyeing began. Threads or whole cloths were dipped into the bath, allowed to air, and dipped again and again, depending on the desired depth of color. It is estimated that these dye vats, being smaller than the ones used by men, could last about five days before being exhausted (fig. 4.3).[22]

Figure 4.3.   Women's Dye Pots and Drying Racks, Abeokuta, Nigeria. Photograph by Edwin and Emily Dean, May 1966, Image no. EEPA 2002-120065. Eliot Elisofon Photographic Archives, National Museum of African Art, Smithsonian Institution, USA.

Boser-Sarivaxévanis's intriguing proposition, that the women dyers of Yorubaland created an indigo dyeing tradition that was historically distinct from men's dyeing practices in the savanna regions to the north, cannot be substantiated at this time. Even so, it is worthwhile making comparisons because of some of the useful questions they raise. To start with, how might some of the more striking differences be explained? It is entirely possible that major distinctions in dyeing processes and equipment were primarily the result of adjustments made in response to differences in the types of products made, the market demand for these products, and other economic factors. For example, the impressive dye pits that were so characteristic of the Sokoto Caliphate might well have been constructed initially to accommodate volume piece-dyeing of whole fabrics and voluminous garments—turbans, veils, wrappers, and especially robes—which were the main exports of the northern dyeing centers. In other words, the practice of dyeing whole garments at a time, where evenness of color would be crucial and mistakes would be so evident, could easily have prompted a transition to very wide dye pits. In contrast, workshops in the Yoruba kingdoms and Benin, where hanks of thread and single breadths of cloth were dyed, would have had no need for such wide vats, at least until *adire eleko* production in the twentieth century.[23] Until that time, an expansion in the volume and profitability of indigo dyeing by women would have been registered in another way, through technological improvements such as the development of the potash kiln. This issue prompts additional questions, such as whether the potash kiln was devoted entirely to making potash for indigo dyeing, or whether it was originally made for producing salt for human consumption or some other purpose. Also, there are indications that such kilns were owned by women,[24] which raises questions regarding marriage and residence patterns and how they affected women's ownership of this kind of fixed property. It is important to note, however, that these two major distinctive features have little to do with the basic chemistry of the dyeing process proper, the basic elements of which—indigo and salt—appear to have been relatively similar throughout the region, whether it was carried out by men or women.[25]

INDIGO DYEING IN THE LOWER NIGER REGION

While it can be assumed that indigo dyeing has a long history in the lower Niger basin, its precise antiquity is not known for certain. Surviving physical remains of dye workshops, especially the dramatic clusters of abandoned dye pits that can sometimes still be surveyed across the Nigerian landscape, are important evidence of volume production but say little about when or where the beginnings of the craft might have been. Shea's statement that it was well established in Hausaland by the sixteenth century[26] is probably somewhat on the conservative side, especially if we take a step back and look at the whole of West Africa. There is, for example, that fortuitous archaeological evidence from the grottos of the Bandiagara escarpment in the upper Niger region, already discussed in chapter 3, which shows that from at least the eleventh century onward, handspun cotton yarns were often dyed with indigo and then woven into striped and checkered textiles. Moreover, Shea presented linguistic evidence that appeared to link dye technology in Hausaland with workshops in Kanem and Borno to the east. If there was such a connection, then indigo could have been grown and processed in some parts of Hausaland much earlier than the sixteenth century. However, some of the linguistic analyses cited by Shea are open to question.[27]

Certainly by the time of European trade and exploration, foreign visitors noted that in many locales throughout West Africa, the craft of dyeing with indigo had already been very well mastered. In making such assessments, these observers were motivated not by a curiosity about African technologies but by strictly commercial interests that reflected recent changes in European textile manufacture. Demand for indigo in Europe was on the rise, especially in the seventeenth century, as wool dyers came to prefer it to their traditional dyestuff, woad, which was a relatively weaker source of blue. Not long after, cotton dyeing and cotton textile manufacturing were getting underway in Europe, especially in England, which added another demand for reliable supplies of indigo.[28] These factors combined to generate ongoing interest in locating new sources of the dye, with seafaring merchants and travelers on the lookout for good quality indigo blues until a synthetic replacement for it was developed at the end of the nineteenth century.

Merchants' written accounts support Boser-Sarivaxévanis's observation that there were two main geographical areas in West Africa that stood out early on for the remarkably high quality of their indigo-dyed products. One area stretched from Senegambia to the upper Niger, and the other was the lower Niger basin. The former provided the skilled slave-labor force and technical expertise that generated the famed cotton textile exports of the Cape Verde Islands from the sixteenth through eighteenth centuries. These distinctive cloths, which blended elaborate Moorish loom-produced patterns with the color preferences and textile technologies of the upper Guinea Coast, gave the enterprising *lançado*[29] merchants a much-needed edge in their trading operations during the pivotal early period in Atlantic commerce. Cotton and indigo plantations supplied the many small workshops of spinners, weavers, and dyers, all of whom labored under merchant supervision. The indigo plant itself was a local variety imported to the islands from the mainland, as were the invaluable slaves who knew how to bring it to harvest and successfully prepare it for the vat. Indigo dyeing was the work of women slaves, who picked the leaves, pounded them into a paste, and pressed the indigo into cakes that were then dried in the sun. Dye vats were made in pots, the dye cakes placed in the bottom, water and ash added, and the entire mixture then left to steep and ferment. From start to finish, the dyeing process reportedly took about two weeks. There were some efforts launched in the early eighteenth century to export indigo internationally, but they came to naught as local markets absorbed almost all of the dye that was produced.[30]

Meanwhile, the manufacture and trade of Cape Verde cloths apparently stimulated textile production in several other locations nearby. Here too, dyers played an increasingly important role. Weavers on the mainland manufactured cloth with loom-produced patterns, which required steady supplies of indigo-dyed threads, while certain garments were made up of piece-dyed strip cloths alternating with plain white ones. Indications of the pressures that must have been felt by artisan producers can be seen in altered trading patterns, as surpluses of local indigo began to be exported from Senegal and Nunez to meet a growing demand from markets and dye workshops in and around Cacheu.[31] Indigo dyeing technology on the mainland appears to have been very similar to what was practiced on the islands. In the early eighteenth century, Labat recorded some extended comments and assessments of the "wild indigo" of Senegal, calling it a high-quality dye source. He considered it superior to the indigos from India and Guatemala, and had great hopes that it could be grown for export. In describing how local dyers worked, he noted the role of indigo in loom-patterned cloth and piece-dyeing: the local dyers used indigo to dye their cotton (thread), their wrappers, and the cloth that they bought from the Europeans.[32] Mungo Park, about seventy years later, had equally positive things to say about local indigo when he was traveling up the Gambia River. Park also left us with a brief account of the dyeing process, which he noted was the work of women. He observed that they preferred to use the fresh leaves of the indigo plant, pounding them into a paste and then mixing them in a large pot with ash water. The cloth was then dipped until it reached the desired shade. He added that sometimes urine was included in the vat,[33] presumably to induce the fermentation process.

As for the other major indigo center of the time, the lower Niger region, our earliest evidence comes mainly from written descriptions of cloth. European merchants' accounts mentioned that skillfully woven and dyed cloths were available in the markets of several ports along the Bight of Benin. Dapper, for example, noted in the seventeenth century that cotton textiles made upcountry and sold in Lagos and Benin were either completely blue or blue-and-white striped.[34] In 1702, van Nyendael itemized a range of dyes used on cotton cloths produced in Benin, which he aptly characterized as "calico wrappers." The cloths were patterned with checkerboards, and he seemed particularly impressed by the mastery of the dyers, who were able to produce green, black, red, and yellow, apparently from the bark, leaves, and other parts of various tree species. Their blue, of course, was made from indigo, which, he added, grew there in abundance.[35] Fifteen years later, another Dutch merchant saw indigo leaves being soaked and processed in a workshop further west along the coast in Keta, and went so far as to purchase some of the prepared balls of dyestuff. At the same time, however, he expressed doubts about its profitability as a trade item.[36] That comment may have come from knowledge about unsuccessful Dutch attempts to establish cotton and indigo plantations on the Gold Coast between the 1650s and 1730s. The Royal African Company tried their hand at it too, on the Gold Coast between 1700 and 1740, and at Ouidah between 1700 and 1730, but these schemes were not economically viable because of labor difficulties, among other things.[37] I have not come across any eighteenth-century eyewitness descriptions of precisely how the dyeing process was carried out in the lower Niger basin, although Landolphe commented that he saw Benin dyers pounding indigo with their feet rather than with mortar and pestle, which might indicate volume production of dyestuff for the textile export trade.[38]

In the eighteenth century, certain travelers' accounts exhibit a keener, more precisely described attention to matters of color quality. Adams, for example, praised the industrious peoples of Allada, who manufactured cotton cloths with patterns, using dyed threads. He hastened to add that the indigo they used was indigenous to the region, that the dye it produced was very well fixed, and that the dyers followed a process he claimed was similar to what Mungo Park had observed in the Senegambia and upper Niger regions. Clearly he had at least some knowledge of dye technology and could discern differences in the quality of indigo-dyed products. He gave his general opinion that indigo dyeing was done exceptionally well in Allada, Oyo, and Ijebu.[39] A similar evaluation was recorded in 1819, and once again dyeing was assumed to be of special interest and importance, especially in regard to the shades of blue that could be thereby obtained. This time, Porto Novo was mentioned as a place where the dyeing was very well done, particularly the color blue; and Ijebu was also mentioned, where again, the fastness of the blue was singled out from among the other textile colors.[40] In 1826, Clapperton passed through the Yoruba town of Ijanna, some forty miles or so inland from the coast, staying on long enough to visit several weaving and dyeing workshops to observe how the various manufacturing processes were carried out. Boys wove cotton strips, about four inches wide, while women were the dyers. For each dye workshop he counted at least twenty vats, each one being a large clay pot and all of them in full operation. He considered the indigo dyestuff produced in these workshops to be highly durable and of excellent quality.[41]

Indigo dyeing and cotton textile manufacture continued to be practiced in the lower Niger region throughout the nineteenth century, though under the very difficult and unpredictable conditions of recurring warfare. A series of major wars, from the fall of Oyo and the expansion of the Sokoto Caliphate southward into Yorubaland, to the founding and territorial expansion of Ibadan and the subsequent struggles for independence by the Ekitiparapo, finally came to an end in the 1890s with the social and political landscape of West Africa drastically changed.[42] Undoubtedly, the technological map was changed as well. Craft production and trade had been often disrupted, sometimes halted completely, and along with the social upheaval and slave capture of prolonged armed conflict came also the transfer of textile techniques and specialized knowledge. As was the case in Bida and other Nupe towns,[43] where women's indigo dyeing was introduced by skilled captives who had been seized in wars of the mid-nineteenth century, new centers of indigo processing and dyeing were created during this time in communities in and around Yorubaland. Indeed, two of the four well-known urban centers for production of indigo-dyed *adire* cloth were founded during this period—Ibadan in the 1820s, and Abeokuta in the 1830s. Then with yet another series of dramatic events, the expansion of British colonial rule in the 1890s and early 1900s, the stage was finally set for what would be a major transformation in women's work with indigo—the beginning of a new textile tradition, *adire eleko*.

RESIST DYEING

One of the most useful early articles about *adire*—Yoruba resist-dyed cloth—addressed a number of important historical issues, some of which still have not been fully resolved. The authors of the article, Wenger and Beier, drew an important technical distinction between the two primary methods of making patterns on woven textiles in Yorubaland—tie-dyeing and starch resist—and by explaining the literal meaning of the word *adire* (to take, to tie and dye), they proposed a technologically based relative chronology for resist dyeing in general, namely, that tie-dyeing preceded the process of starch resist. They also stated that the earliest patterns, presumably created by tying with raphia fiber, were produced on locally made country cloths, but they added that by the time of their writing (1957), all *adire* cloths were being made with imported factory-woven cottons. Then they went on to declare, without identifying their sources or outlining their reasoning, that the tradition of *adire eleko*—cloths patterned with starch resist—was not older than 1910. It is very likely that this assertion was based on oral testimonies, but these testimonies were not documented in the article. Equally intriguing but also undocumented was the authors' claim that *adire eleko* cloths were first made in Lagos and Abeokuta and then later on in workshops further inland.[44]

Before examining these issues more closely, it would be useful to survey what is known about the larger historical context of resist dyeing (whether by tie-dying or the use of starch resist) in West Africa. Direct evidence for filling in this picture is, however, very sparse indeed. The earliest extant example of a resist-dyed textile comes, again, from the Bandiagara escarpment in the region of the upper Niger, where an indigo-blue, tie-dyed cotton cap was found in a cave whose contents were dated to the eleventh or twelfth century. The cap was sewn from cloth made on the treadle loom.[45] Not until much later, in the period of Atlantic trade, do we have another example of resist-dyed cloth, but it is an impressive one. It is one of two robes brought to Europe from the Guinea Coast before 1659, and which became part of the Weickmann Collection, now housed in the Ulmer Museum in Germany.

This resist-dyed robe was tailored like its partner from cotton cloth woven on the treadle loom. It consists of ten strips of plain-weave cotton cloth, each just over six inches wide, all sewn together edge-to-edge. Its resist patterning was done after the tailoring work was completed, with long parallel lines of tiny bindings crisscrossing the garment body and sleeves, front and back. One large tie was bound in the center front and another in the center back. The entire garment was immersed in indigo, probably several times, and the ties were then undone to reveal the patterns in white on a deep blue ground (fig. 4.4). It was then beaten, most likely with a wooden mallet, to produce a glazed surface. Before the twentieth century, this special finishing process was only applied to textile products made from strip cloth, such as the *litham* and certain types of tailored robes. Information accompanying the Weickmann robes describes both of them as garments worn and distributed by officials in Allada, a major kingdom along the Bight of Benin in the mid-seventeenth century. It does not state where or by whom the robes were made.[46]

Jones has suggested, quite plausibly, that these so-called Allada robes, along with other West African objects in the Weickmann Collection, were acquired in Allada by a German man named Haintzel who worked for the Swedish African Company in the 1650s.[47] How the robes came into his possession is not at all clear, although some speculations can be offered here based on the way many such prestigious textiles circulated at the time. The collection information about the robes refers to one of them as a garment commonly worn by the king, and the other as one customarily presented by the king to a nobleman or knight, but it is not certain which robe is which. One possibility would be to interpret the crisscross pattern on the tie-dyed robe as a reference to the prestige and equipage of cavalry, who have been depicted in West African sculpture with crossed straps on their torsos.[48] But more importantly, it is not possible to determine the accuracy of the collection information or who provided it. Moreover, the robes themselves suggest either additional or alternative uses. The most careful and complete examination of them to date, carried out by Menzel, revealed that they were both in excellent condition and had been worn only rarely if at all.[49]

Figure 4.4.   Tie-Dyed Gown, Indigo on Cotton, Made of Narrow Strip Cloth, Collected before 1659. Weickmann Collection. Copyright The Ulmer Museum, Germany.

If we accept that they were indeed associated with the king of Allada, it may well be that they were presented to Haintzel or to an intermediary by one of the kingdom's governors. As already discussed in chapter 2, gift exchange between European traders and local officials was an important key to commercial relations. One English agent remarked in the 1680s that the Allada king's representative had given him an African-made textile gift— a "very handsome" cloth made locally with threads from imported wool cloth.[50] Hence it is quite possible that these robes once belonged to the rich collections of textiles and other goods—foreign and locally made—that accumulated in and around the courts of African kings, coming in and going out as gifts via diplomatic and commercial channels.

That would explain why these two robes do not look like they were manufactured in the environs of Allada. For if that had been the case, the robes would show at least some technical or visual continuity with strip cloth and garments made there more recently, say, in the nineteenth century. However, weavers in and around the Yoruba kingdoms wove strips that were narrower than the strips used in the Weickmann robes, and their loom-produced patterns show distinctly different technical and design features. It is also very likely that each robe originated in a separate locale, given the striking differences between the two in the kind of strip cloths and tailoring methods that were used. For example, all of the strips in the resist-dyed robe were the same, while the other robe was made up of three kinds of strip cloth, two of them loom-patterned and one indigo-dyed. Even more noteworthy are the differences in garment structure. The body of the resist-dyed robe was made of six cloth strips, and two more made up each sleeve, for a total of ten, all of them running vertically. Such an arrangement for constructing sleeves is highly unusual and would be structurally weak. The other robe exhibits a much more conventional tailoring method, its sleeves made of strips running horizontally along the length of the arm, a feature that is consistent with the Tellem tunics as well as most West African robes made in the nineteenth century. What is anomalous about this latter garment, though, is the number of strips used and their widths. It was made of over sixty pieces of cloth sewn together, some of them being strip cloth that, oddly enough, was cut in half lengthwise.[51] The visual and technical features of these robes, and their anomalies in particular, make it very difficult to link them firmly to any specific well-known textile traditions.

Jones has addressed this issue, pointing out that a number of scholars have tried to identify the place of manufacture for these robes. He found no reason to accept any of the attributions offered so far, and added that there was as yet no reason to rule out the possibility that they were made in or around Allada.[52] The question of how to locate these robes—culturally and socially—is not a simple one. One thing that can be stated at the outset is that the tailors who made them were attempting to replicate at least some of the conventions of Muslim dress and hence were operating within the range of Muslim commercial networks and cultural influences. Therefore, although the robes could have been made along the Guinea Coast, they were most likely products of textile workers in the West African interior. Moreover, each garment had to be made in a series of workshops, being passed from one set of skilled hands to another. These hands were gendered and specialized—women did the spinning and other women the dyeing, men did the weaving and other men the tailoring—and they could easily have been located in different villages or towns or even language groups. In other words, it is entirely possible that the tailoring workshops where the robes were assembled were not only in different urban locales, but they may have relied on trade cloth, that is, strips that were woven elsewhere. Attaching a shorthand term to such textile products—especially elaborate garments such as these—based on one single language group, for example, or one geographical location—might serve well as a rhetorical convenience but it would deny the garments their technological, economic, and cultural complexities. And it would be seriously misleading in its implication of a continuity or sameness in the social complexity of those garments' makers.[53]

Other visual evidence from the seventeenth and eighteenth centuries provides glimpses of that complexity. Descriptions of strip cloth from the treadle loom—how wide it was, whether it was plain, patterned, or dyed—suggest that there were various interlocking networks of textile trade and currency circulation operating in West Africa. Merchants' reports on specific strip-cloth dimensions are few, but they do indicate that west of the lower Niger, strips produced on the treadle loom usually ranged between four and eight inches. Relatively wide strips were produced in the interior of what is now the Ivory Coast, and five or six of them sewn together into wrappers were marketed along the Gold Coast as "quaqua" cloth. As described in the mid-seventeenth century, the individual strip widths were about eight inches.[54] Along the upper Guinea Coast and in the Cape Verde Islands, cloth strips were usually woven slightly narrower, about five or six inches wide, from at least the seventeenth century onward. They varied from plain undyed cloths and *barafulas*, which were standard six-strip cloths with alternating blue and white strips, to more expensive ones such as deeply dyed *panos pretos* (black cloths), and the famed *panos d'obra*, which were luxury textiles with ornate brocaded patterns.[55] These textiles too were traded at least as far as the Gold Coast.[56] Park reported even narrower strips in the upper Niger region, noting that men all across the savannas from Senegambia to Jenné wore garments made of strip cloth, plain or dyed, about four inches wide.[57] In all, the variety of such textile products and the manifold extent of their manufacture and trade owed much to the skilled work that went on at the indigo vats, where cotton threads, plain white cotton strips, and whole wrappers and garments were dipped and dyed. The skilled work of the dyers contributed shades of blue to the systems of dress that made rank and social position visible in West Africa.

Questions remain, though, about how frequently, when, and in which locales resist patterns were being created on finished cloths and garments. Some scholars have attempted to trace the particular resist technique that was used on the Weickmann robe, the most recent attempt being Gardi's. Referring to Boser-Sarivaxévanis's published survey of West African indigo-dyed cloth, which includes examples from the late nineteenth and twentieth centuries, he concluded that the robe was probably not tied and dyed in Yorubaland. His argument was based on visual evidence, contrasting the circular tie-dye patterns that Yoruba women customarily created, and which generally featured a star-shaped center (fig. 4.5), to the patterns on the Weickmann robe, which were small squares with very dark centers. The technique that resulted in this latter pattern was apparently practiced only in certain areas of what are now Guinea-Conakry, the Ivory Coast, and Mali, as well as in parts of North Africa.[58] However, another source complicates

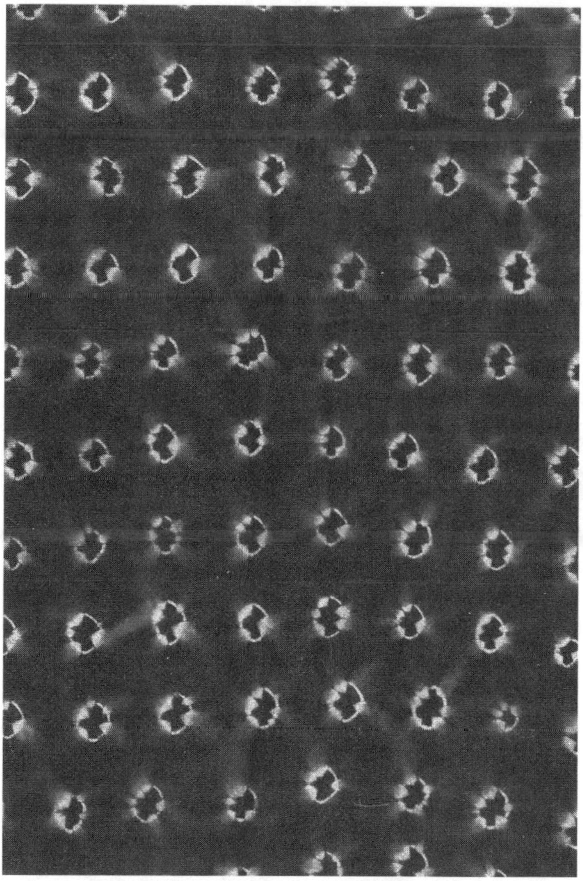

Figure 4.5. Detail, Women's Indigo-Dyed Wrapper. Tie-Dye Pattern "Little Fruits"; Circles Average ¹/₂ Inch in Diameter. Ibadan, Nigeria, 1975. UCLA Fowler Museum of Cultural History, Colleen E. Kriger Collection of Nigerian Textiles, X2005.24.33.

Gardi's claims about Yoruba women's tie-dyeing methods. An observer in the 1930s described several techniques used by Yoruba women and girls for making patterns of circles or dots, techniques such as tying raphia around small seeds or stones or gathering and tying little peaks in the cloth. She added that "by a cunning twist of the fingers" the tie-dye patterns could be made to look like a square or oblong.[59] So in certain respects Jones was right—even though the cloth might have been woven somewhere else, the possibility that the resist-patterned Weickmann robe was dyed somewhere in the vicinity of Allada cannot be ruled out.

FROM COUNTRY CLOTH TO "NATIVE CHINTZ"

Additional historical evidence of resist dyeing, especially to fill in the time
gap of several centuries between the Weickmann robe and the cloths surveyed by Boser-Sarivaxévanis, is very hard to come by. But once again,
there are some suggestive and intriguing, though intermittent, references to
consumer tastes that can be found buried in merchants' accounts of their
slave-trading operations on the Guinea Coast. What they show, among other
things, is that there was a growing demand in the Bight of Benin and its
hinterland by the late seventeenth century for particular kinds of painted
or printed fabrics from overseas. Later accounts mention African-made versions, perhaps tie-dyed, being traded or produced there by at least the 1730s.
In other words, the indications are that some forms of resist patterning could
have been done in the lower Niger region in the first half of the eighteenth
century, if not before. These would be early versions of *adire* cloth, and
they would signal a major transition in women's dyeing practice, from one
in which women specialized mainly in dyeing thread and piece-dyeing woven cloth solid blue to one that included making patterns on textiles by
using resist techniques. The story of this transition cannot yet be told in full,
but fleeting glimpses of it can be seen in descriptions of the textiles traded
in this part of West Africa.

Trade commodities, bundled into particular assortments that included
many textiles, made commerce between Africans and Europeans possible
on the Guinea Coast. Merchants' records are replete with complaints and
admonitions about striking changes in supply and demand for this or that
item. Requests made by European factors (for certain specified textile products known to sell well at a certain time) thus reflected trends and tastes
in consumer demand that differed from one port to another and among
distinct classes of people. Items that were requested to be used in gift exchange, for example, were not the same as those that were requested for
trade transactions, the former exhibiting the individual fashion preferences
of royal officials and elites, and their taste for luxurious and exotic fabrics.
Textiles that were necessary in assortment bargaining, however, represented
the preferences of an entirely different population. They were for the most
part commodities or currency items deemed most sellable among populations inland, whose commercial networks supplied the slaves and other
exports coming to the coast. That is, they were basic trade items, available in bulk, and not the one-of-a-kind novelties desired by kings and their
entourages.

Table 4.3 below, compiled from the published records of the Royal African
Company of England, presents a glimpse of consumer preferences in two
locales on the Guinea Coast in the late seventeenth century. It relies on
written requests for trade textiles sent to company suppliers by their factors

Table 4.3. Requests for Indian and European Trade Cloth, Bight of Benin and Gold Coast, Late Seventeenth Century

Cloth name	Fiber	Offra/Ouidah 1681–1698 (11 total requests)	Accra 1681–1683 (16 total requests)
*pintados/chints	C	13	1
long cloths	C	7	3
white bafts	C	7	0
linen/bedsheets	L	5	14
allejars	C	5	5
perpetuanas	W	5 (red)	5 (blue or green)
patterned silks	S	4	0
pautkes	C	4	1
scarlet cloth	W	3	0
salampores	C	3	0
sletias	L	3	10
satin	S	2	0
ginghams	C	2	1
chercolees	C	2	0
Holland	L	2	0
Muslins	C	2	0
tapsells	C/S	0	3
blanketts	W	0	3
brawles	C	0	2
carpetts	W?	0	2

*painted or printed cloth
Fiber: C = cotton, S = silk (from India); L = linen, W = wool (from Europe).
Source: Irwin and Schwartz 1966; Jones 1995, 313; Law 1992, 38, 40–41, 44, 52, 56, 57; Law 1997, 154, 156, 162, 168–69, 178, 179, 185, 187, 189, 191, 194, 196, 203, 204, 206, 210, 225, 228, 230, 237, 257.

on the Guinea Coast. Although much of this correspondence did not survive, those letters that did survive offer valuable evidence of African demand for particular types of cloth at major ports. It should be noted that since the company suppliers were based in Europe, any references to African-produced textiles were only occasional and in passing. Requests for overseas textiles, though, whether they were manufactured in Europe or India, were very clear and specified types of cloth by name. The table shows which ones were most preferred in Offra and Ouidah on the Bight of Benin versus the ones preferred in Accra on the Gold Coast. I should add here that there were more of these company records available for Accra in the years 1681 to 1683; therefore, in compiling the table, I chose to minimize this imbalance by adding requests from Offra/Ouidah in later years. As a result there is a problematic disparity in time periods for each locale (Accra, 1681–1683; and Offra/Ouidah, 1681–1698).

Admittedly, the table derives from a very fragmentary base of evidence. It does, however, give at least some indication of just what the local specifics of consumer markets on the Guinea Coast could be like at a particular point in time. West African consumers were not monolithic in their tastes. While there are areas of overlap in the two lists, the lists show distinct differences in the kinds of cloth that were most in demand in each locale. The types of textiles most requested in Accra were linens: linen cloth, secondhand linen sheets, and "sletias," that is, linen cloth originally made in Silesia and later copied by Dutch and English weavers.[60] In Offra and Ouidah, however, linens were much less in demand at this time, and one letter from 1686 noted that sletias were not selling there.[61] Instead, the textiles most in demand were painted or printed cloths, with ten requests for "pintados" and three for "chints." Plain white cottons—long cloths and white bafts—were also favored. We also see here the demand along the Bight of Benin for red wool that was discussed in chapter 2, with scarlet cloth and red perpetuanas together requested eight times. These repeated requests for certain items cannot be ignored or dismissed, though it is not clear how long they were sustained over time. Letters sent from Ouidah in 1727/1728, for example, show a marked change, with requests for linens (sletias) along with blue-and-white calicos.[62] Whether this change represented a shift in fashion or a revision of commercial relations inland remains an open question.

What exactly were these pintados and chints that were so coveted on the Bight of Benin? The several published editions of company correspondence that were used to create table 4.3 give only shorthand descriptions of trade cloth in their glossaries, and these descriptions sometimes disregard the histories of the cloths' manufacture and marketing networks. That is the case especially for painted and printed cloth. For example, in the most prominent of these publications so far, *pintados* was defined as "printed (batik) cloth from the East Indies," and *chintz* was defined as "Indian block-printed cotton cloth."[63] In fact, the two terms apparently meant the same thing, and referred to a general category of painted and printed cottons made in India. *Pintado* is the earlier term, having been used in the trade records of the sixteenth and seventeenth centuries, and it comes from the Portuguese *pinta* (spot, fleck). *Chintz* is the Anglicized version of the plural for *chint* or *chitta*, the Hindi and vernacular terms for "spotted cloth," and this word was current in the trade records of the seventeenth and eighteenth centuries.[64] Major centers of manufacture during the seventeenth century were in northwestern India, and many of these cloths were exported from the city of Surat, as well as from centers on the southeastern side of the subcontinent, in a stretch of territory known as the Coromandel Coast. The most costly *chint* or *chitta* was made by hand and underwent a number of different processes, including stencil work, hand painting, wax resist, and mordant dyeing. Cheaper versions were made in the same centers, using the quicker method of block printing, sometimes combined with hand painting.[65] None of these cloths can be called simply *batiks*, as that term refers to cloths patterned entirely by wax resist. It makes more sense, then, to group them all together under the more commonly used term, *chintz*, and it was during the last quarter of the seventeenth century that the chintz trade between India and Europe reached its peak.[66] Some of the items in this trade, of course, were destined to be re exported to places like Offra and Ouidah on the Guinea Coast of West Africa.

Summing up our evidence so far: we have a mid-seventeenth-century tie-dyed robe, said to be from Allada; the possibility that the robe could have been dyed and finished there; and reports of a demand for chintz in the environs of Allada in the 1680s and 1690s. Interestingly though, the seventeenth-century reports about locally produced textiles along the Bight of Benin make no mention of printed or resist-patterned cloth being made. So if indeed the Weickmann robe was tied and dyed in or around Allada, it was probably not a common practice. Instead, from what few descriptions we have, it appears that standard local textile products were quite different— they were either plain white cottons, cloths with loom-produced patterns of stripes or checks, piece-dyed cloths in solid blue, or mixed fabrics of cotton and raphia. Other references are inconclusive. A German merchant in the 1660s listed a wide range in prices for cloths from Allada and Benin, but did not provide details about what they looked like or why they were given such varying market values. The only adjective—*multicolored*—was applied to an Allada cloth.[67] In another account, Allada cloth was described as woolen,[68] undoubtedly in reference to special luxury textiles whose patterns were brocaded with wool unraveled from European yardage. One such cloth, a gift given to a Royal African Company factor in Apa (just east of Offra) in 1682, was described as handsomely made with "Welch plaine," that is, thread from a coarse woolen cloth from Britain. This account also noted the large numbers of Benin cloths that were traded by canoe along the rivers and lagoons of the area, but did not describe them.[69] Twenty years later, van Nyendael praised the textiles woven in Benin, singling out especially the ones worn by elite women. He described their locally made wrappers as "very fine" and "very beautifully chequered with several colours." Included in his comments on dress was a reference to "a great painted cloath woven here, which they wear like a cloak."[70] His enigmatic use of the descriptive term "painted" most likely came from a misreading of vividly colored brocaded imagery. As they stand, none of the seventeenth-century descriptions of locally made textiles fit with the specific visual qualities of fabrics patterned with resist techniques, and the cloths embellished for elite dress were apparently richly colorful, not elegantly understated like the glazed indigo-blue Weickmann robe. Hence there is, at present, no clear and convincing evidence of textile printing or resist dyeing being done in the Bight of Benin hinterland earlier than the eighteenth century.

By that time, though, all the necessary elements for production of resist patterns were well in place: a high market value placed on imported chintz textiles, workshops of skilled dyers, and surpluses of locally woven cotton cloth as well as plain-cotton yardage from India. Merchants' accounts regarding their transactions in Benin indicate that there, too, conditions were ripe for local dyers to develop their own versions of printed and resist-dyed cloths. The values assigned by Benin merchants to overseas textiles in eighteenth-century trade assortments were very similar to the preferences we saw in Offra and Ouidah in the late seventeenth century. Indian chintz was highly prized, and was second only to longer lengths of woolen yardage and finely patterned silk kerchiefs (see table 4.4 below). Plain white muslin, probably of very fine quality, was also much in demand, as was plain white baft. Most interesting are the passing references, in Dutch records from the 1730s, to stores of "native chintz" at their company post at Jakin (Allada).[71] Since the factor in charge included some of this cloth in gifts given to members of the bodyguard and interpreters of the Dahomey king, it is unlikely that they were low-cost or commonly available local products. It does seem certain, however, that since they were referred to specifically as "native," these were cottons printed or resist dyed in Africa, not in India.

Observations and records from the late eighteenth century show further developments on the Bight of Benin in consumer taste for patterned cottons. Even more importantly, one of the records contains the earliest eyewitness description of tie-dyeing in Allada. In his account of ten voyages to the Guinea Coast between 1786 and 1800, Adams wrote that in Allada, "kid-skins are tied all over in knobs very tight, then soaked for some days in a strong dye, which, when untied, exhibit a pattern resembling a star, or rays of blue and white radiating from round blue spots."[72] Adams also listed goods he recommended for successful trading in this particular locale, and here we see, in addition to chintz, two other types of patterned cloth that were made strictly with tie-dye techniques: "bandannoes" and "sastraundies."[73] The former, called *bandhani* or *bandhej* in India, was a tie-dyed silk fabric that was a major trade item in the eighteenth century, and when later imitated by English textile manufacturers went by the name "bandanna." This word originally came from the Sanskrit verb *bandhna* (to tie).[74] As for the latter cloth, also known as "sacerguntes," it was a cotton textile from south India woven with tie-dyed warp and weft threads. It too was shipped to England in the eighteenth century.[75] As reexports to Allada, these cloths may have provided the models for tie-dyeing cotton and silk yarns in neighboring Yorubaland. What these consumer trends do show quite clearly is a well-articulated and growing market on this part of the Guinea Coast for textiles patterned using various techniques, textiles that included Indian chintz, "native chintz," and tie-dyed cloths from India.

Until more primary data come to light, however, it cannot be determined exactly when and how resist dyeing began to be practiced in the Bight of Benin hinterland and lower Niger region in general. Some techniques could

Table 4.4. Values of Overseas Textiles Required in Trade Assortments, Benin Kingdom, Eighteenth Century

Cloth name (Indian cloth in **bold**)	Value, 1715 (in lbs. ivory)	Value, 1778 (in Benin cloth)	Value, 18th century (n.d.) (in Benin cloth)
broad says [wool]	70		
yellow perpetuanas (34 ell piece)	48		
Cholet kerchief		12 cloths	
Nîmes silk kerchief		12 cloths	
Indian chintz (14 ½ ell piece)	40		
(5 ell piece)		10 cloths	
(15 ell piece)			12 cloths
coarse muslin w/ stripes or spots (12 yd. piece)			12 cloths
Indian muslin (12 yd. piece)			12 cloths
good Coromandel, dyed blue			10 cloths
printed calico (7 ell piece)		7 cloths	
French linen	32		
white salempore	24		
lg. blue perpetuanas (14 ell piece)	18 2/7		
cambric [fine white linen]	16		
unbleached cloth	12		
platilhos [fine linen]	10		
dress Cholet (6 ell piece)		6 cloths	
Nîmes silk satin		6 cloths	
white bafts (6 ell piece)	10		
(5 ell piece)		6 cloths	
Rouen cotton cloth (6 ell piece)		6 cloths	
sm. red perpetuanas	9½		
sm. blue perpetuanas	9 1/7		
Surat coverlet			4 cloths
Breton linen (5 ell piece)		4 cloths	
Irish tablecloths	6		
king cloths	4		
red damask (18 ell piece)	4		
bedsheets	4		
lg. annebas [wool/linen]	3		
Irish sheets	2		
coarse linen w/ red edging			1 cloth
kerchief			1 cloth
rough Irish sheets	1		
sm. annebas	1½		

Source: Ryder 1969, 320, 208, 210–11; Reikat 1997, 237; Jones 1995, 312, 314, 322.

have been independently invented there, though more likely they were created in imitation of imports, the prototypes being either prestige cloths from elsewhere in West Africa or from India. It is certainly conceivable that all of the above took place. Nevertheless, there was no tie-dyeing whatsoever— of threads or of woven cloth—among the textiles brought back to England from the 1841 Niger Expedition, though several vertical loom cloths in the collection had been headed northward and were destined to be piece-dyed in indigo.[76] The fact that there were no resist-dyed cloths in the collection may have been because most of the cloth purchased by the expedition members was trade cloth, and resist dyeing at this time might well have been done only in dye workshops and then primarily for local clienteles. Whatever the case may be, the absence of evidence in this particular collection of textiles does not necessarily mean that resist dyeing was not being done anywhere in the region.

Oral histories and the visual evidence from individual textile products lend support to Wenger and Beier's claim that the earliest *adire* was made using locally woven cloth.[77] Unfortunately, however, only a few elderly dyers interviewed in the past several decades retained memories of resist dyeing on handwoven cloth. Their comments varied. In one case, a dyer said that *adire* was a practice used to improve the appearance of older textiles or garments that were wearing out. In another, the dyer was able to provide more detail about specific techniques, saying that tie-dyed patterns were made by sewing locally made cloth with a needle and raphia thread.[78] Boser-Sarivaxévanis's survey of West African indigo-dyed textiles, which focused mainly on regions west of the lower Niger, included some examples of resist dyeing on handwoven cloth, and they were all tie-dyed. At least four were from the late nineteenth century, and they reveal some interesting regional differences in dye practice. Two of them (identified as being from Liberia) illustrate the technique of tie-dyeing an entire textile. They were made up of narrow strips, all sewn together before being tied and dyed, and resemble two similar cloths collected in Liberia in 1879 and 1885 that are now in the Berlin Museum für Völkerkunde.[79] The same technique was used on a robe collected in 1840, which was made up of ten strips, each just over six inches wide, sewn together and then tie-dyed with an allover pattern. It was said to have been the garment of a Muslim cleric in Asante.[80] Another type of dyeing involved working with the individual strips rather than a larger textile or garment. Strips were folded in various ways, then tied, dyed, and sewn together afterward. This was a practice of dyers along the upper Guinea Coast.[81] Piece-dyeing of individual strips was probably also done at one time in Yorubaland, which would explain the peculiarities in making a cloth called *elelo*. Factory-woven yardage was in this case cut into narrow three-inch bands that were rolled lengthwise, tied with thread, and dyed. The patterned bands were then sewn back together (fig. 4.6). Finally, there was

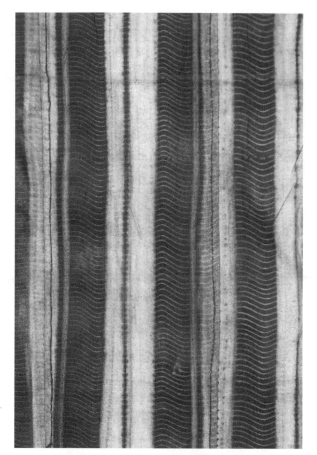

Figure 4.6. Detail, Women's Indigo-Dyed Wrapper. Tie-Dye Pattern *Elelo*, Seam-to-Seam Measurement Averages 3 Inches. Ibadan, Nigeria, 1975. UCLA Fowler Museum of Cultural History, Colleen E. Kriger Collection of Nigerian Textiles, X2005.24.32.

tie-dyeing done on cloth woven on the vertical loom as well, the example illustrated being a single-width cloth embroidered with raphia to produce linear patterns. The cloth is identified only very generally—as coming from the Benue area—and is very similar to twentieth-century women's title cloths in northern Edo communities.[82] In short, tie-dyeing was initially carried out on locally handwoven textiles, using several different techniques and with cloth from both treadle and vertical looms.

Then, in twentieth-century Nigeria, an explosion of resist dyeing took place. It was concentrated mainly in Yorubaland, but it also transformed

well-established northern dye centers such as Kano, where techniques originally introduced by Yoruba women immigrants were copied by Hausa artisans, male and female alike.[83] Much of this production relied on imported
factory-woven yardage, the most oft-repeated reasons for this being that
it was cheaper and easier to work with. While not untrue, both of these
reasons require some clarification. The first one, that imports were cheap,
does not take into account the changing values of textiles over time. The
prices of plain, locally made cloths were generally lower in relation to cotton
yardage woven overseas until the late nineteenth century, when European
factory-made cottons started to become more competitive.[84] This means
that if market production of resist-dyed textiles in Yorubaland depended
on cheap cotton cloth, then prior to the late nineteenth century that cloth
would have been made closer to home in West Africa, not overseas. And
that is indeed what the nineteenth-century evidence suggests. Second, there
is the question of fabric weight and pliability. It has already been shown in
chapter 3 that handspun, handwoven cotton textiles manufactured in and
around the Sokoto Caliphate in the nineteenth century showed fabric densities comparable to high-quality Indian trade cloth, much of which was
printed. Hence the notion that locally made cloth was inherently less suitable for resist dyeing is not entirely accurate. Locally made cloth did serve
very well for various tie-dye techniques, though it would not have worked
very well with starch resist, which explains why, as far as I know, there are
no examples of *adire eleko* on strip cloth or cloth woven on the vertical
loom. As was the case with handpainted and resist-dyed chintz made in India, starch resist—*adire eleko*—required very fine, thin fabric with an even,
smooth surface. Factory-woven imports fit the bill. And when they finally
became available at affordable prices in the early colonial period, there was
a boom in the production of *adire*.

Major centers of *adire eleko* manufacture developed in the southern Nigerian cities of Lagos, Abeokuta, Ibadan, and Oshogbo in the early twentieth
century as the import of plain, lightweight cotton yardage from Lancashire
rose steadily. This was cloth ideally suited to all sorts of resist-dye techniques, especially starch resist. Most importantly, as both production and
transportation costs declined, this cloth came within the reach of many more
people in West Africa—consumers and craftsworkers alike. The place and
date proposed by Wenger and Beier for the earliest *adire eleko* workshops—
Lagos, around 1910—seems reasonable then, since this was where and when
the right kind of cloth could be had for the right kind of price. Coastal ports
were the first places where prices of European factory cloth undercut those
of local cloth, a trend that set in during the 1880s and 1890s. Henceforth,
imports into Nigeria grew substantially, numbering 40 million square yards
yearly between 1896 and 1906, and increasing to 100 million square yards
per year by 1912.[85] A major contributor to this upswing was the construction

of a railway from Lagos northward, which made it possible for textile brokers inland to lower their prices for imported cottons as well in cities like Abeokuta, Ibadan, and Oshogbo. Women in these cities quickly took advantage of this promising new market opportunity and created another type of local "native chintz"—*adire eleko*—made with overseas cloth.

IMAGERY FROM NEAR AND FAR

Not everyone agrees about where in Yorubaland the first starch-resist cloths were manufactured, which is precisely what one would expect given the fierce competition between textile workshops and towns for product notoriety and market share. As already mentioned, Wenger and Beier proposed Lagos and Abeokuta as the earliest production centers, followed by workshops further inland.[86] Keyes proposed that *adire eleko* was invented in Ibadan, basing this judgment on interviews in Ibadan, Oshogbo, and Abeokuta, but without detailing the information those testimonies revealed.[87] Other competing claims were collected by Byfield in Abeokuta, with some dyers insisting that the first *adire* workshop was established in the compound of Madam Jojolola, a wealthy, prominent businesswoman-dyer, while others stated that the technique of starch resist was brought from Sierra Leone by Saro immigrants, who reputedly had learned it from Mende craftsworkers.[88] However and whenever the technique was first practiced, Wenger and Beier's proposed timeline for the establishment of major production centers does seem nevertheless to fit best with the general economic trends outlined above.

In making *adire eleko*, Yoruba women were developing their own textile tradition of starch resist, but they were not the only ones who practiced this special technique. Yet that is precisely what Wenger and Beier claimed in an endnote in their article on *adire*. They briefly compared the pattern dyeing of the Yoruba and that of the Sarakole[89] by pointing out that the Yoruba used imported cloth, but the Sarakole used locally made cottons; Yoruba women did both the tying and dyeing, while Sarakole men tied and the women dyed; and the method of starch-resist dying, though practiced by the Yoruba, was not practiced by the Sarakole.[90] Oddly, though, the source they cite does contain a description of starch-resist dyeing by Sarakole women, who used only imported cotton percale for this work. They painted the cloth surface with a paste made from cassava flour, and then ran a comb through the paste, making wavy and zigzag lines. De Zeltner described the same technique being used by Sarakole women in 1910, only with rice paste. Two examples of finished cloths made in this way, from workshops in Senegal and French Guinea, were illustrated in Boser-Sarivaxévanis's survey.[91] Moreover, the earliest extant example of starch resist known so far from the lower Niger area is a tailored cotton shirt, painted with "northern knot" motifs, purchased at Lokoja ca. 1909 or earlier.[92] Taken together, these examples show that even though resist dyeing with starch paste was nowhere near as widely known and practiced in West Africa as was tie-dyeing, it was clearly not the exclusive domain of Yoruba women. What Yoruba women did do was vigorously exploit the design potential of the technique, turning it into a vehicle for generating income and making their own distinctive visual statements on cotton cloth.

As was also the case with Indian chintz, there was a wide range in quality. Some versions of *adire eleko* featured intricate compositions that were superbly executed while others were quite obviously made more simply and quickly. Certain women and girls specialized in painting with starch by hand (fig. 4.7), taking their cloth to other women who were specialists in indigo dyeing. Very successful dyers often bought cloth in bulk and supervised teams of starch painters as well as cloth dyers in their own workshops. Men were the main specialists in faster production methods, which involved cutting stencils out of sheet metal for applying the starch in repeat patterns all over the cloth. Sometimes the stenciled designs were made to commemorate

Figure 4.7. Alhaja Fatilatu Adegbenla Painting Cassava Starch onto Cotton Shirting, Ibadan, Nigeria, 1976. Photograph by the Author.

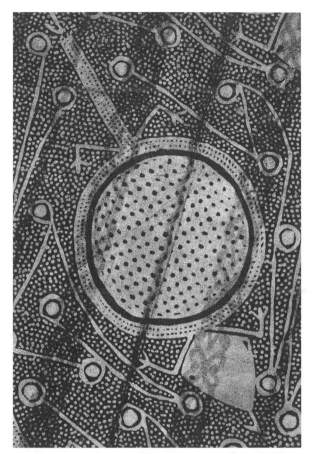

Figure 4.8. Detail, Handpainted "Tortoise" Motif on Textured-Cotton Shirting. *Adire Eleko* **Wrapper, Ibadan, Nigeria, 1975. UCLA Fowler Museum of Cultural History, Colleen E. Kriger Collection of Nigerian Textiles, X2005.24.39.**

a special occasion,[93] while others were made directly in imitation of hand-painted cloths (figs. 4.8 and 4.9). This more mechanized mode of manufacture also began in the early twentieth century, and was centered primarily in the town of Abeokuta.[94] Both types of *adire eleko* cloth—handpainted and stenciled—were unique to workshops in the lower Niger region.[95]

There is strong visual evidence that at least some painted versions of *adire eleko* were made originally in imitation of elaborate tie-dyed cloths. Each of the two main methods of tie-dyeing, either wrapping or binding with raphia or sewing stitches with needle and raphia, have their own names, *adire oniko* and *adire alabere*, respectively.[96] Certain *adire eleko* designs

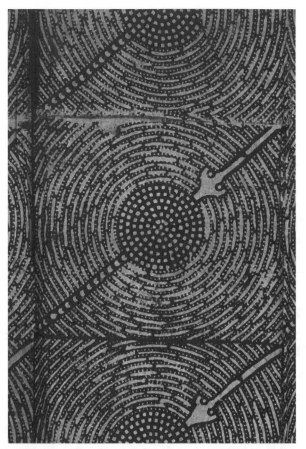

Figure 4.9.   Detail, Stenciled "Tortoise" Motif on Plain-Cotton Shirting. *Adire Eleko* **Wrapper, Ibadan, Nigeria, 1976. UCLA Fowler Museum of Cultural History, Colleen E. Kriger Collection of Nigerian Textiles, X2005.24.40.**

replicate both of these techniques, such as the cloth known as *sún bèbè*, which consists of delicate arrangements of circles and lines painted to look like the patterns that would result from tied and stitched cloths (figs. 4.10 and 4.11). No systematic studies have yet been done of *adire* costs and pricing, but it appears that labor inputs ranged much more widely than did the market price. Based on my own experience with *adire* techniques, painting the *sún bèbè* patterns, for example, would have been quicker than hand sewing them. In other words, just as applying starch with stencils was faster than handwork, painting the starch was faster than sewing and wrapping, an option that offered women savings in labor and thus greater potential profits. It has also been noted, though, that preparing the cloth by

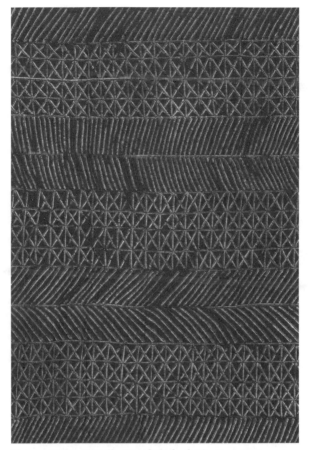

Figure 4.10. Detail, Handstitched Tie-Dye Patterns on Plain-Cotton Shirting. *Adire Alabere* Wrapper, Ibadan, Nigeria, 1975. UCLA Fowler Museum of Cultural History, Colleen E. Kriger Collection of Nigerian Textiles, X2005.24.29.

either method could take varying amounts of time and up to several days, depending on the complexity and quality of the work and the degree of mastery possessed by the artisan. Moreover, profits were sometimes divided if the work was organized by a dyer-entrepreneur.[97] All in all, it appears that the greatest laborsaving method by far was the one that was practiced by men, whose stenciled repeat patterning came the closest to a classic factory production model of industrial settings.

Olokun, the name for the particular *adire eleko* cloth that is the focus of this chapter, is one of the oldest of the women's handpainted versions. The earliest known photograph of an *adire eleko*—taken in Lagos,

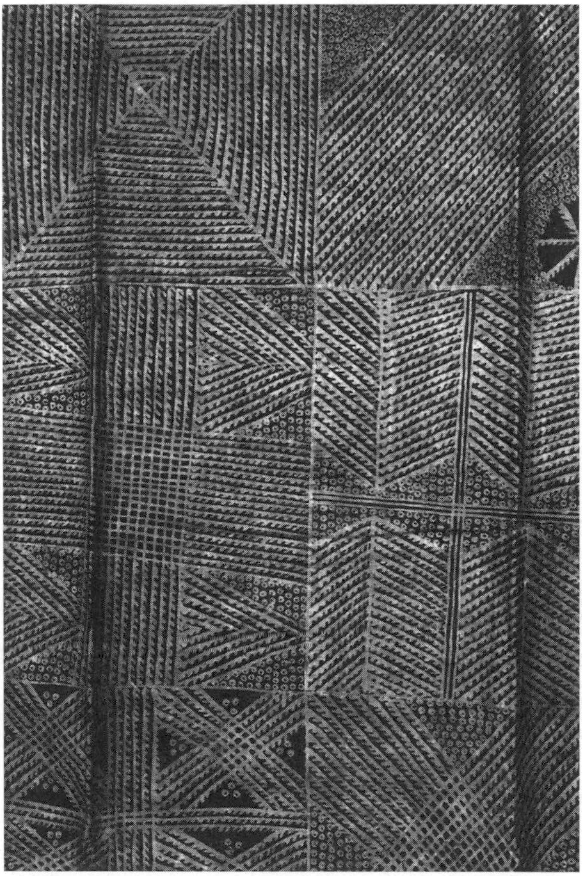

Figure 4.11. Detail, Handpainted Pattern, *Sún Bèbè,* on Plain-Cotton Shirting. *Adire Eleko* Wrapper, Ibadan, Nigeria, 1975. UCLA Fowler Museum of Cultural History, Colleen E. Kriger Collection of Nigerian Textiles, X2005.24.36.

ca. 1920—shows a woman wearing what appears to be an *Olokun* wrapper.[98] Given the history of Lagos as a seaport and its longstanding ties to the Benin court, Lagos would seem a fitting locale for the invention and first wearing of *Olokun* cloth. *Olokun* is the name for the god or goddess of the sea, as I've noted, a deity worshipped primarily in the Benin kingdom but also known in some parts of Yorubaland. This god was believed to provide wealth and many children, and hence had many female devotees.[99] An elite claiming legitimacy from and owing allegiance to the Benin king ruled the settlement of Lagos, which was said to have been founded in the sixteenth century as a Benin war camp. The camp grew into a city and prospered from maritime commerce, trading first in slaves and then in products like palm oil, ivory, and cotton. By the late nineteenth century the population of Lagos had become a cosmopolitan mix of peoples from the hinterlands—Yoruba, Hausa, Nupe, Kanuri, Fulbe—and immigrants from around the Atlantic basin—Sierra Leone, Brazil, and Cuba.[100] It makes sense, then, to view *Olokun* as a product of this multiethnic and multicultural city, and to argue that only later did the cloth come to be known as a traditional Yoruba women's wrapper.

The design elements of *Olokun* have been stable and are standardized enough to make it immediately recognizable to consumers. However, it differs markedly from other *adire eleko* cloths in the structure of its composition. It is divided into ten large squares with a border of smaller squares and rectangles, while other *adire eleko* compositions have much simpler grid arrangements with squares that are all the same size. *Olokun* also tends to have richer and more varied imagery, which consists of an intriguing mix of geometric and natural forms. The motifs and patterns painted within the ten squares of our *Olokun* cloth are shown in figure 4.12, and their names (collected in Ibadan in the 1960s, in Yoruba or English) are (1) *wáyà*, or "wire," (2) "mats," (3) name unavailable, (4) *bèlèké*, or "dividing into pieces," (5) *agboòrùn*, or "umbrella," (6) *onisóná*, or "matches," (7) "tops," (8) "stool," or *opón*, also named "wooden cover," (9) *olópà*, or "sticks," and (10) "leaves of a fig tree." When the two pieces of resist-dyed cloth are sewn together, motif number 3 appears twice in the center of the finished wrapper and it is usually (at least most recently) a variant of an eight-leafed plant or flower form. The motif that appears most consistently as number 8 is a large circular form with four radiating extensions. There has been some disagreement about what this motif represents, whether it be the cover for a pot or a stool or a visual pun on the word *bottom*.[101] A similar motif can be seen on the *adire eleko* cloth called *Ibadan dun*, where it is referred to as a Muslim writing board or divination tray.[102] Such inconsistencies are not surprising, as names were undoubtedly given to motifs and patterns after the fact and would be likely to vary from workshop to workshop and over time.

While certain design elements of *Olokun* imagery appear to have been quite stable over the decades between the 1940s and 1970s, it is not yet possible to say the same for the entire composition. It would therefore be useful to test just how consistent *Olokun* imagery has been by amassing and comparing a sample of cloths made over time in various production centers. My own preliminary survey (see table 4.5 below), based on eight examples, is skewed in time and place, being limited primarily to cloths made in Ibadan in the 1960s and 1970s. That limitation may well account for the strong consistency of motifs included and their stable positioning in the compositions. What the chart does show, however, are some important characteristics in the design of each individual *Olokun* cloth. Looking across the eight versions of *Olokun*, we find certain motifs and patterns that were always included, certain others that could be left out, and at least one that

Figure 4.12. Primary Motifs in *Olokun* Cloth. Drawing by the Author.

Table 4.5. Motifs in *Olokun* Cloths

Motif	Sieber (1972: 224) Coll. 1941	Barbour (1970: fig. 10; 1971: 78) Coll. 1960s	Barbour (1970: fig. 11) Coll.1960s	Barbour (1970: fig.12) Coll. 1960s	Menzel (Vol. 2, 257) Coll. 1965	Picton/Mack (1979: 158) Coll. 1970	Borgatti (1983: 53) Coll. 1974	Kriger Coll. 1975
(1) "wire"	X	X	X	X	X	X	X	X
(2) "mats"	X	X	O	O	O	O	O	X
(3) "pedals of a sewing machine" or		X						
(3) (8-leaf plant form)	O		O	O	O	O	O	O
(4) "dividing into pieces"	X	X	X	X	X	X	X	X
(5) "umbrella"	X	X	X	X	X	X	X	X
(6) "matches"	X	X	O	O	O	X	O	X
(7) "tops"	X	X	X	X	X	X	X	X
(8) "stool" or "pot cover"	O	X	X	X	X	X	X	X
(9) "sticks"	?	X	*(2) X, X	*(2) X, X	*(2) X, X	*(2) X, X	*(2) X, X	X
(10) "leaves of fig tree"	?	X	X	X	X	X	X	X

X = presence of motif.
O = absence of motif.
*"sticks" motif appears in position 2 and position 9.

was repeated in some instances. If we then examine more closely which ones were left out and which ones might be repeated, we begin to see that there could be a considerable variability in the time spent making *Olokun* imagery. The design compositions were all very similar, but the labor investment in painting the starch could differ widely.

Some women chose to paint more elaborate motifs and patterns and so worked with greater care overall, while others simplified and speeded up their work. My own replication experiment, in which I drew the imagery in figure 4.12, demonstrated that the most time-consuming designs to produce were numbers 2, 4, 5, and 6. Numbers 3 and 9 were the quickest. With this in mind, the data in table 4.5 can be interpreted to show several possible laborsaving strategies. One strategy would be to eliminate designs number 2 and 5 and include simpler ones in their place, such as "sticks," the design that replaced number 2 in five of the eight cloths. Another strategy would be to enlarge a repeat pattern so that fewer lines have to be drawn, which can be seen in designs number 4 and 6. In number 4, "dividing into pieces," the size and amount of squares could vary considerably from cloth to cloth, with some examples showing sixteen large squares and others showing ninety or over a hundred small squares. In design number 6, "matches," the range went from twelve large squares to one hundred small ones. Similarly, painting fewer plant forms in design 10 would have made the work go faster. It is not clear, however, what the reasons might have been for these differences in labor investment. Two possibilities come immediately to mind: one, that the versions that were quicker and easier to make were the work of girls who were still learning the craft; and two, that the same quicker and easier versions were used by women who were trying to turn a quick profit or increase their output. In any event, it is important to note that while the market prices of a variety of *adire eleko* cloths may not have varied much,[103] the profits for the individual craftswomen could vary a great deal according to how much time and skill they invested in their work and whether they owed any shares of the profits to anyone else. Moreover, the most elaborately and carefully made specimens were often only available in the workshops of certain *adire* masters, and as a result they could command higher prices.

Although the names for this cloth and its designs serve to localize and naturalize the imagery in Yoruba culture, visual evidence suggests the cloth belongs to a much larger family of West African textile traditions. An especially provocative illustration of this point is the resemblance of *Olokun* to *adinkra* cloth, another form of "native chintz," made by Akan craftsmen in the Gold Coast hinterland. Known primarily as a pigmented cloth patterned with stamped motifs, the earliest extant examples of *adinkra* are a combination of handpainted and stamped imagery. Many of them were made using factory-made cotton or linen yardage imported from Europe.

However, one *adinkra* cloth, collected in the Asante capital of Kumasi in 1817, was made of handwoven strip cloth—twenty-four strips about three inches wide, sewn edge-to-edge—that was said to have come from Dagomba in the north. The imagery was arranged in a grid of rectangles, each one about ten to twelve inches wide and fourteen to sixteen inches long, and each filled in with motifs or patterns that were either painted with a chicken feather or stamped. The two handpainted patterns resemble two of the most stable and consistent *Olokun* designs—number 1, "wire," and number 4, "dividing into pieces." A pattern related to number 4 was also painted on another *adinkra* cloth, made in the 1820s (fig. 4.13). There are other visual features shared by these two types of textiles: *Olokun* design number 2 is structured very much like the two-by-two grid pattern on both *adinkras*; and two other *adinkra* cloths, one of them photographed in the late nineteenth century, show a stamped pattern that is very similar to *Olokun* design number 10.[104] Altogether, there appears to be a cluster of similarities, visual and technical, between the two types of textiles, namely, division of the cloth into a grid; the use of the same scale for units of the grid; painting of the imagery with a chicken feather; and several shared or analogous designs, some of them also painted in the same way. It could well be then that there was some historical connection between *Olokun* and *adinkra* cloth, especially given the longstanding trade relations along the shore and caravan routes inland that linked the lower Niger to the Gold Coast.

It would be far too simplistic, though, to suggest that *Olokun* was invented as an imitation of *adinkra* cloth. While it is true that both textiles rely heavily on geometric repeat patterns, that is, designs with translation symmetry,[105] these are not the only visual principles at work in the *Olokun* imagery. Some of the motifs and patterns are very similar to magic squares and inscriptions drawn on Muslim charm gowns. One example is the squared lozenge of *Olokun* design number 5, a motif that can be seen on Muslim amulets and in a variety of other talismanic contexts.[106] *Olokun* designs also share some basic structural features with those designs made by tie-dyeing techniques. Numbers 1 through 6 all involve strong lines or axes running horizontally, vertically, and diagonally, each then further elaborated in a distinctly different way. Designs 7 and 10 have horizontal and vertical arrangements, while 8 and 9 involve diagonals. These same principles of linear organization can be seen in various tie-dyed patterns whose horizontal, vertical, and diagonal lines were made by folding and pleating the cloth before tying, or by stitching tucks along folded guidelines. An example of this close visual correspondence can be seen in *Olokun* motif number 3, an octagonal star or leaf form, which has been rendered also in tie-dye by using the stitching method.[107] All of this imagery was modified in the painting process through the addition of tonal shadings created by allover dots, crosshatchings, and

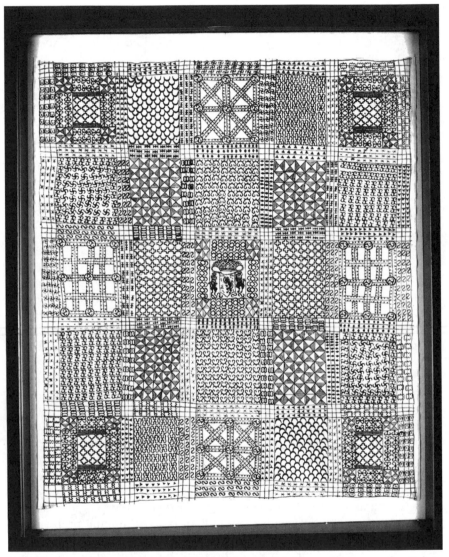

Figure 4.13. *Adinkra* **Cloth, Commissioned by a Dutch Representative on the Guinea Coast, and Sent to the King of the Netherlands before 1826, Accession no. 360-1700. Copyright the National Museum for Ethnology, Leiden, Holland.**

parallel lines. And in doing this, women *adire*-makers generated their own visual vocabulary based on several sets of familiar visual principles.

Geometry predominates in the *Olokun* imagery, with only a few of the main designs based on recognizable objects or natural forms. This feature is in striking contrast to another complex handpainted *adire eleko* cloth called *Ibadan dun*, or "Ibadan is sweet," which abounds in all sorts of stylized figural elements. One of the *Olokun* designs described above, number 3, appears to be a very simplified version of the leaf or flower form found in number 10, where it was called "leaves of a fig tree." The same design, when it was painted in an *Ibadan dun* composition, was referred to as "cassava leaves."[108] This prompts the question of whether there is any special significance attached to these plant forms. Turning our attention to the paraphernalia and imagery associated with the veneration of this god or goddess of the sea, Olokun, we find that the leaf motif could possibly allude to a particular type of river plant whose leaves were used in healing rituals by Olokun priestesses. Representations of it were frequently included as background on the elaborate brass plaques that once adorned the Benin king's palace, and also on other ceremonial objects, such as stools and containers, whose iconography linked Olokun to the court.[109] Other aquatic images commonly associated with the sea, such as pythons and crocodiles, can be seen in some of the border areas of the more elaborate *adire eleko* textiles bearing this name, but it is noteworthy that the mudfish, a major feature of Olokun iconography, is, as far as I know, totally absent. Searching these resist-dyed cloths for clear and direct visual correspondences to iconography related to Olokun worship is, in any event, bound to yield only mixed results. They are everyday wrappers, not ritual cloths. And as others have noted, Yoruba-speakers understood the name of the cloth as a figure of speech rather than as a literal reference to the deity, and translated it accordingly into the proverbial phrase "life is sweet."[110]

Historically, this deity of the sea was associated with fertility, prosperity, and riches, and was believed to have been responsible for the ebbs and flows of trade.[111] Hence the name *Olokun* for this particular variant of "native chintz" becomes entirely appropriate when understood in this context, as it is itself a complex amalgamation of local, regional, and international influences, many of them conveyed via trade and commercial relations. Its most essential material elements—indigo dyestuff that was locally grown and processed, boiled starch paste made from New World crops of corn or cassava, and lightweight cotton yardage woven in English factories—reflect the centuries-long period of Atlantic maritime shipping that has linked Africa with Europe and the Americas. Moreover, this richly designed wrapper bears visual evidence alluding to ongoing creative efforts that took place, over time and across language boundaries, among textile producers as they responded to changes and opportunities in the marketplace. One of the end results was something new to dip into the indigo dye pot, a distinctive version of West African chintz.

TRADITIONAL CLOTH AND MODERN TIMES

Adire cloth production in general—including all the various forms of tie-dye and starch resist—became a thriving artisanal industry in Nigeria at different times and locations during colonial rule and after. One major factor that helped to generate and sustain such high productivity was a change in the technology of dyeing with indigo. As I described earlier in this chapter, the making of these textiles had long relied upon women skilled in the tricky workings of the indigo vat, using locally processed indigo dye and salt. Without diminishing the historical significance of this indigenous technology, it must be pointed out that some features of it did set limits on the ability of dyers to expand their output. Workshops were relatively small in scale and the organization of manufacturing was based on artisanal skills and intensive labor inputs. If a higher volume of production was going to be achieved, there had to be an expansion of the labor force, but entry into the occupation of dyer was fraught with risk. Producing an effective dye vat was a challenge even for the master dyer, owing in large part to irregularities and inconsistencies in the dyestuff, the alkaline bath, and the reduction of the indigo itself. It was both a time-consuming and an unstable process, technically, and women complained that the contents of the vats could easily go bad.[112] New ingredients—caustic soda and synthetic indigo—transformed the technology of indigo dyeing, making it an easier and more stable process. And this, in turn, allowed less-skilled women to establish their own dye workshops.

The change did not come easily, all at once, or overnight. Byfield's important study of *adire* production in Abeokuta, one of the major centers of indigo dyeing, chronicles the struggles that ensued there between practitioners and admirers of the old process and promoters of the new one. Little did they know at the time that they were part of a much larger, worldwide revolution in the chemistry of textile manufacturing. Soda vats had been known and used in Europe from the late eighteenth century onward, but it was a breakthrough in 1900, the creation of a reliable and stable hydrosulphite vat, that greatly improved dye technology. Around that same time, recently invented synthetic indigo was becoming available at reasonable market prices, and by 1913 it had almost completely replaced natural indigo dye in Europe.[113] These two events ensured greater production efficiency and sealed the fate of natural dyestuffs. Indigo's long history as an important dye plant and lucrative tropical product was coming to an end, which meant that it would no longer be cultivated on a large scale.

All of these events converged in Abeokuta, sometimes in surprising ways. During the 1920s, Abeokuta's dye workshops were thriving, with *adire* being exported to consumers on the Gold Coast, and Senegalese buyers traveling to Nigeria to purchase dyed cloth in bulk for the markets back home. But due to this commercial success, dyers began to face difficulties in keeping up their supplies of potash and local indigo. Caustic soda was therefore taken up as an alternative to potash in 1924, and by 1928, at the height of the *adire* trade, dyers were using it extensively. Many of them also adopted synthetic indigo from 1932 onward, although local dyestuff continued to be available through the 1930s. These new techniques were soon one aspect of a debate between Abeokuta's indigo dyers and town officials over how best to support this important local textile industry. Dyers were experiencing economic problems brought on by the depression, and they sought advice and help from the king and the colonial resident of Abeokuta. But dyers and officials differed in how they defined the problem and in what they offered as solutions. Key to the dyers' argument were concerns over the shortage of credit for purchasing cloth, and the fact that the colonial government was cracking down on the use of nonfree (debt pawn) labor. Instead of addressing these concerns, local government officials brought up the question of dye quality and market standards, turning these factors into the focus of a public conflict over *adire*. Citing customer complaints that the level of quality of dyed textiles was declining, they issued a ban on the use of caustic soda in 1929, which was extended and applied to synthetic indigo in 1933. It remained in place until a Commission of Enquiry lifted it in 1937.[114]

Despite initial controversy over the new dye process, it quickly spread to other Nigerian dyeing centers such as Ibadan and Oshogbo. By the 1930s, *adire* production relied heavily on materials that were all imported: factory-made cloth as well as the caustic soda and synthetic indigo for the dye vat. Other innovations around this time included the design of commemorative cloths with human figures and written inscriptions, and the use of treadle sewing machines for stitching resist patterns. Another wave of innovation took place in the 1960s with the introduction of synthetic dyes other than synthetic indigo that were easier to work with and came in a wide range of colors. Some artisans also took up wax batik, which made it possible for them to exploit hot-dye bath methods.[115] Products made with these new methods and materials were counted, along with handwoven cloth, among the three million yards of indigenous textiles that were sold yearly through Ibadan's Oje market.[116] Meanwhile, questions about quality control in dyeing persisted. There remained some skeptical master dyers, mostly older women in rural areas, who steadfastly insisted that the old ways of dyeing resulted in higher-quality textiles. In their view, based on their own experience, using caustic soda shortened the dyeing time but did not fix the color as well, and the synthetic indigo faded easily and sometimes damaged the fabric.[117]

Nevertheless, *adire* textiles lived on, as dyers rode the ebbs and flows of economic trends and sought new markets at home and abroad. Although locally dyed cloth was said to be "despised" by wealthy, western-educated elites, it found enough buyers to survive and support thriving workshops in the major production centers of Abeokuta, Ibadan, and Oshogbo. There was some continuity in the industry as the older, labor-intensive patterns continued to be made in limited numbers, especially by Muslim women who were secluded and had little or no formal education. And there were some unexpected changes as well. In the 1960s, for example, certain groups of young Nigerian men broke the gender barrier and began to wear shirts made of machine-stitched *adire* cloth for the first time. Expatriates, too, added their own dimension to the growing consumer markets for certain types of *adire,* having tailored garments made from cloth purchased in the market.[118] During the 1980s, production expanded as a result of a Nigerian government ban on imported fabric and the devaluation of the local currency. As structural adjustment policies eroded the purchasing power of much of the population, many women opted to acquire additional income-generating skills such as dyeing.[119]

The current situation is no less complex. Those dyers—men and women—who work with a much wider range of materials and techniques are able to market their cloths internationally to the fashion industry and the art world. At the same time, there are other workshops where some of the standard resist-dyed patterns are still being produced in familiar, deep blue hues. However, it has been said very recently that traditional, handpainted *adire eleko* wrappers like *Olokun* are rarely being made, and that they are fetching high prices from discerning collectors.[120] One can hope, then, that they will eventually find homes in museums, where *adire* cloths of all kinds can serve as primary sources for histories of textile manufacture, much as their counterparts do in India and other parts of the world. What we already know for certain is that dyers of indigo, who helped to pattern the woven webs of country cloth and went on to play a central role in the creation of resist-patterned chintz, lent a special richness to the economic and cultural history of West Africa.

NOTES

1. *Plangi* and *batik* are the words most commonly used by English-speakers for these techniques, though the words originally come from Indonesian languages. See Mattiebelle Gittinger, *Master Dyers to the World: Technique and Trade in Early Indian Dyed Cotton Textiles* (Washington, D.C.: The Textile Museum, 1982).

2. W. A. Vetterli, "The History of Indigo," *CIBA Review* 15 (1951), 3066–68.

3. J. M. Dalziel, *The Useful Plants of Western Tropical Africa* (London: Crown Agents, 1937), 245–50.

4. Brigitte Menzel, *Textilien aus Westafrika* (Berlin: Museum für Völkerkunde, 1972–1974).

5. A. W. Banfield, *Dictionary of the Nupe Language* (1914; repr., Farnborough, UK: Gregg International, 1969).

6. Samuel Crowther and E. J. Sowande, *A Dictionary of the Yoruba Language* (1937; repr., London: Oxford University Press, 1950); Dalziel, *Useful Plants of Western Tropical Africa*, 244, 249.

7. Vetterli, "The History of Indigo"; Dalziel, *Useful Plants of Western Tropical Africa*, 246–49.

8. Dalziel, *Useful Plants of Western Tropical Africa*, 244.

9. Douglas Ferguson, *Nineteenth-century Hausaland: Being a Description by Imam Imoru of the Land, Economy, and Society of His People* (PhD diss., University of California, Los Angeles, 1973), 81–82.

10. Dalziel, *Useful Plants of Western Tropical Africa*, 244–50.

11. R. Haller, "Production of Indigo," *CIBA Review* 15 (1951).

12. C. A. Folorunso, "The Archaeology and Ethnoarchaeology of Soap- and Dye-Making at Ijaye, Yorubaland," *African Archaeological Review* 19, no. 3 (2002); John Picton and John Mack, *African Textiles* (London: the British Museum, 1979), 38.

13. Paul Lovejoy, *Salt of the Desert Sun: A History of Salt Production and Trade in the Central Sudan* (Cambridge: Cambridge University Press, 1986).

14. Philip Shea, *The Development of an Export-Oriented Dyed Cloth Industry in Kano Emirate in the Nineteenth Century* (PhD diss., University of Wisconsin, Madison, 1975).

15. Ferguson, *Nineteenth-century Hausaland*, 82; Shea, *Development of an Export-Oriented Dyed Cloth Industry*, 60.

16. Menzel, *Textilien aus Westafrika*, vol. 2, nos. 189–97, nos. 199–203.

17. Ferguson, *Nineteenth-century Hausaland*, 306–7.

18. Renée Boser-Sarivaxévanis, "Recherche sur l'histoire des textiles traditionels tissées et teints de l'Afrique Occidentale," *Verhandlungen der naturforschenden Gesellschaft in Basel* 86, nos. 1 and 2 (1975): 319–32.

19. Folorunso, "Archaeology and Ethnoarchaeology of Dye-Making," 138–42.

20. S. Wenger and H. Ulli Beier, "Adire-Yoruba Pattern Dyeing," *Nigeria Magazine* 54 (1957): 223–24; Nancy Stanfield, "Dyeing Methods in Western Nigeria," in *Adire Cloth in Nigeria*, ed. Jane Barbour and Doig Simmonds (Ibadan: Institute of African Studies, 1971), 18–23; Picton and Mack, *African Textiles*, 38–40; Boser-Sarivaxévanis, "Recherche sur l'histoire des textiles traditionels," 330–32, 339.

21. Folorunso, "Archaeology and Ethnoarchaeology of Dye-Making," 140–41; Stanfield, "Dyeing Methods in Western Nigeria," 20; Boser-Sarivaxévanis, "Recherche sur l'histoire des textiles traditionels," 339.

22. Folorunso, "Archaeology and Ethnoarchaeology of Dye-Making," 136–40; Wenger and Beier, "Adire-Yoruba Pattern Dyeing," 223–24; Stanfield, "Dyeing Methods in Western Nigeria," 18–23; Boser-Sarivaxévanis, "Recherche sur l'histoire des textiles traditionels," 330–32, 339.

23. *Adire eleko* (starch resist) was done on factory-made cloth, which was wider than the textiles woven locally by men and by women. Hence piece-dyeing of the narrower local cloth would not have necessitated a change to very wide pots.

24. Philip Shea, *Collection of Notes on Interviews Concerned with the History of Production of Indigo Dyed Cloth in Kano Emirate, Nigeria* (manuscript, 1970–1971), 175.

25. By this I mean that West African dyers used a different technology from what was practiced in India and Europe: in India, the indigo dye vat was made using trisulphite of arsenic; in Europe, the methods of dyeing with woad, by using lime, were adapted to indigo vats in the late sixteenth century. See Haller, "Production of Indigo," 3077; Vetterli, "The History of Indigo," 3068.

26. Shea, *Development of an Export-Oriented Dyed Cloth Industry,* 146.

27. Philip Jaggar, personal communication, 17 November 2004.

28. Vetterli, "The History of Indigo," 3068–70; Florence Pettit, *America's Indigo Blues: Resist-Printed and Dyed Textiles of the Eighteenth Century* (New York: Hastings House, 1974).

29. *Lançados* were Portuguese men who married West African women, and the term also was used in reference to their Luso-African descendants. George Brooks, *Eurafricans in Western Africa: Commerce, Social Status, Gender, and Religious Observance from the Sixteenth to the Eighteenth Century* (Athens: Ohio University Press, 2003), 27.

30. António Carreira, *Panaria Cabo-Verdiano-Guineense* (Lisboa: Museu de Etnologia Ultramar, 1968); T. Bentley Duncan, *Atlantic Islands: Madeira, the Azores, and the Cape Verdes in Seventeenth-century Commerce and Navigation* (Chicago: University of Chicago Press, 1972).

31. Carreira, *Panaria Cabo-Verdiano-Guineense;* Duncan, *Atlantic Islands;* Charles Monteil, *Le coton chez les noirs* (Paris: Librairie Emile Larose, 1927).

32. J. B. Labat, *Nouvelle relation de l'Afrique Occidentale* (Paris: G. Cavelier, 1728), 1:74–79.

33. Mungo Park, *Travels in the Interior Districts of Africa* (Durham, N.C.: Duke University Press, 2000), 72–73, 252–53.

34. Adam Jones, trans. and ed., *Olfert Dapper's Description of Benin* (Atlanta, Ga.: African Studies Association Press, 1998), 18. It is not clear if the blue cloths were made entirely of dyed threads or if they were dyed "in the piece" after weaving.

35. David van Nyendael, "A Description of Rio Formosa, or the River of Benin," in *A New and Accurate Description of the Coast of Guinea,* ed. William Bosman (1705; repr., New York: Barnes and Noble, 1967), 440, 459. See also Carolyn Keyes Adenaike, "Putting the Color Back in the History," in *Paths toward the Past: African Historical Essays in Honor of Jan Vansina,* ed. Robert Harms et al. (Atlanta, Ga.: African Studies Association Press, 1994).

36. Albert Van Danzig, *The Dutch and the Guinea Coast 1674–1742: A Collection of Documents from the General State Archive at The Hague* (Accra: Ghana Academy of Arts and Sciences, 1978), 206.

37. Robin Law, "King Agaja of Dahomey, the Slave Trade, and the Question of West African Plantations: The Embassy of Bulfinch Lambe and Adomo Tomo to England, 1726–32," *Journal of Imperial and Commonwealth History* 19 (1991), 154–58.

38. J. F. Landolphe, *Mémoires du Capitaine Landolphe contenant l'histoire de ses voyages pendant 36 ans, au côtes d'Afrique et aux deux Amériques* (Paris: J.S. Quesne, 1823), 2:49.

39. John Adams, *Sketches Taken during Ten Voyages to Africa between the Years 1786 and 1800* (1822; repr., New York: Johnson Reprint, 1970), 19, 61.

40. G. A. Robertson, *Notes on Africa, Particularly Those Parts Which Are Situated between Cape Verd and the River Congo* (London: Sherwood, Neely, and Jones, 1819), 264, 301–2.

41. Hugh Clapperton, *Journal of a Second Expedition into the Interior of Africa* (1829; repr., London: Cass, 1966), 15–16.

42. S. A. Akintoye, "The Economic Background of the Ekitiparapo, 1878–1893," *Odu* 4, no. 2 (1968); Bolanle Awe, "Militarism and Economic Development in Nineteenth Century Yoruba Country: The Ibadan Example," *Journal of African History* 14, no. 1 (1973); Toyin Falola, "Warfare and Trade Relations between Ibadan and the Ijebu in the Nineteenth Century," in *Warfare and Diplomacy in Precolonial Nigeria*, ed. Toyin Falola and Robin Law (Madison: University of Wisconsin, African Studies Program, 1992).

43. S. Nadel, *A Black Byzantium. The Kingdom of Nupe in Nigeria* (London: Oxford University Press, 1951).

44. Wenger and Beier, "Adire-Yoruba Pattern Dyeing," 213.

45. Rita Bolland, *Tellem Textiles: Archaeological Finds from Burial Caves in Mali's Bandiagara Cliff* (Leiden: Rijksmuseum voor Volkenkunde, 1991), 55, 164; Rogier Bedaux, "Les plus anciens tissus retrouvés par les archéologues," in Musée National des Arts d'Afrique et d'Océanie, *Vallées du Niger* (Paris: Réunion des Musées Nationaux, 1993), 461.

46. Adam Jones, "A Collection of African Art in Seventeenth-century Germany," *African Arts* 27, no. 2 (1994): 35–36; Bernhard Gardi, *Boubou, c'est chic: Gewänder aus Mali und anderen Ländern westafrikas* (Basel: C. Merian, 2000), 52–53.

47. Jones, "A Collection of African Art," 41–42.

48. See for example, the terra-cotta horsemen pictured and described in Musée National des Arts d'Afrique et d'Océanie, *Vallées du Niger*, 370–71 and nos. 89 and 107; they were excavated in Bura, southwestern Niger, and are dated between the third and eleventh centuries AD.

49. Gardi, *Boubou, c'est chic*, 50, 52, 186–87.

50. Robin Law, ed., *The English in West Africa, 1681–1683: The Local Correspondence of the Royal African Company of England, 1681–1699, Part I* (Oxford: Oxford University Press, 1997), 237.

51. Gardi, *Boubou, c'est chic*, 50–53.

52. Jones, "A Collection of African Art," 35–36.

53. For a valuable study of the complexity of twentieth-century textile production (in this case, by men) in which the technology and skills were embedded in social relationships as well as mediated by market conditions, see Esther Goody, "Daboya Weavers: Relations of Production, Dependence, and Reciprocity," in *From Craft to Industry*, ed. Goody (Cambridge: Cambridge University Press, 1982).

54. Adam Jones, trans. and ed., *German Sources for West African History, 1599–1669* (Wiesbaden: Franz Steiner, 1983), 64.

55. Duncan, *Atlantic Islands*, 212; Carreira, *Panaria Cabo-Verdiano-Guineense*, 84–95.

56. Law, *The English in West Africa*, 209.

57. Park, *Travels in the Interior Districts*, 252–53.

58. Gardi, *Boubou, c'est chic*, 49.

59. F. Daniel, "Yoruba Pattern Dyeing," *Nigeria Magazine* 14 (1938), 126.

60. Law, *The English in West Africa*, xix.

61. Robin Law, ed., *Further Correspondence of the Royal African Company of England Relating to the "Slave Coast," 1681–1699* (Madison: University of Wisconsin, African Studies Program, 1992), 43.

62. Robin Law, ed. *Correspondence of the Royal African Company's Chief Merchants at Cabo Corso Castle with William's Fort, Whydah, and the Little Popo Factory, 1727–1728* (Madison: University of Wisconsin, African Studies Program, 1991), 9, 15, 17, 27.

63. Law, *The English in West Africa*, xviii–xix.

64. John Irwin and P. R. Schwartz, *Studies in Indo-European Textile History* (Ahmedabad: Calico Museum of Textiles, 1966), 15; John Irwin and Margaret Hall, *Indian Painted and Printed Fabrics* (Ahmedabad: Calico Museum for Textiles, 1971), 176, 180.

65. Irwin and Hall, *Indian Painted and Printed Fabrics*.

66. Irwin and Schwartz, *Studies in Indo-European Textile History*, 17.

67. Ray Kea, *Settlement, Trade, and Polities in the Seventeenth Century Gold Coast* (Baltimore: Johns Hopkins Press, 1982), 319.

68. Jones, *German Sources for West African History*, 302.

69. Law, *The English in West Africa*, xix, 234, 237.

70. van Nyendael, "A Description of Rio Formosa," 439–40.

71. Van Danzig, *The Dutch and the Guinea Coast*, 265, 297, 305.

72. Adams, *Sketches Taken during Ten Voyages to Africa*, 20.

73. Adams, *Sketches Taken during Ten Voyages to Africa*, 106.

74. Veronica Murphy and Rosemary Crill, *Tie-Dyed Textiles of India: Tradition and Trade* (New York: Rizzoli, 1991), 9, 127.

75. Irwin and Schwartz, *Studies in Indo-European Textile History*, 70.

76. Colleen Kriger, "Textile Production in the Lower Niger Basin: New Evidence from the 1841 Niger Expedition Collection," *Textile History* 21, no. 1 (1990).

77. Wenger and Beier, "Adire-Yoruba Pattern Dyeing," 212.

78. 'Bisi Akpata, "Comments on Adire in Western Nigeria," in Barbour and Simmonds, *Adire Cloth in Nigeria*, 97; Judith Byfield, *The Bluest Hands: A Social and Economic History of Women Dyers in Abeokuta (Nigeria), 1890–1940* (Portsmouth, N.H.: Heinemann, 2002), 89.

79. Renée Boser-Sarivaxévanis, "Aperçus sur la teinture à l'indigo en Afrique Occidentale," *Verhandlungen der naturforschenden Gesellschaft in Basel* 80, no. 1 (1969), 218, figs. 19, 20; Menzel, *Textilien aus Westafrika*, vol. 2 nos. 244, 245.

80. Gardi, *Boubou, c'est chic*, 130–31.

81. Boser-Sarivaxévanis, "Aperçus sur la teinture à l'indigo," 211, fig. 5; Carreira, *Panaria Cabo-Verdiano-Guineense*, fig. 89.

82. Title associations offered high status and leadership positions in society, and special cloths were awarded to titleholders as signs of their positions. Boser-Sarivaxévanis, "Aperçus sur la teinture à l'indigo," 228, fig. 38; Jean Borgatti, *Cloth as Metaphor: Nigerian Textiles from the Museum of Cultural History* (Los Angeles: UCLA Museum of Cultural History, 1983), 22–25.

83. Shea, *Development of an Export-Oriented Dyed Cloth Industry*, 91–93.

84. Marion Johnson, "Technology, Competition and African Crafts," in *The Imperial Impact: Studies in the Economic History of Africa and India*, ed. C. Dewey and A. G. Hopkins (London: Athlone Press, 1978), 265, Martin Lynn, *Commerce and Economic Change in West Africa. The Palm Oil Trade in the Nineteenth Century* (Cambridge: Cambridge University Press, 1997), 68, 84–85.

85. Johnson, "Technology, Competition and African Crafts," 265; Johnson, "Cotton Imperialism in West Africa," *African Affairs* 73 (1974): 185–86.

86. Wenger and Beier, "Adire-Yoruba Pattern Dyeing," 213.

87. Carolyn Keyes, *Adire: Cloth, Gender, and Social Change in Southwestern Nigeria, 1841–1991* (PhD diss., University of Wisconsin, Madison, 1993), 91.

88. Byfield, *The Bluest Hands*, 89.

89. *Sarakole* is the Wolof term for the Soninko people (sing. Soninke) who today live mostly in the upper Senegal and upper Niger river basins.

90. Wenger and Beier, "Adire-Yoruba Pattern Dyeing," 225.

91. Monique de Lestrange, "Les Sarankole de Badyar," *Etudes Guinéennes* (Conakry) 6 (1950): 25–26; Fr. de Zeltner, "Tissus Africains à dessins réservés ou décolorés," *Bulletins et Mémoires de la Société d'anthropologie de Paris*, sér. 6, no. 1 (1910): 226; Boser-Sarivaxévanis, "Aperçus sur la teinture à l'indigo," 216, figs. 15, 16.

92. Keyes, *Adire: Cloth, Gender, and Social Change*, 500, plate 74. It is possible that the starch resist painted on this shirt was the work of a Yoruba woman.

93. George Jackson, "The Devolution of the Jubilee Design," in Barbour and Simmonds, *Adire Cloth in Nigeria*.

94. Stanfield, "Dyeing Methods in Western Nigeria," 10; Byfield, *The Bluest Hands*, 90, 102–3.

95. Boser-Sarivaxévanis, "Aperçus sur la teinture à l'indigo," 204.

96. Stanfield, "Dyeing Methods in Western Nigeria," 10; Jane Barbour, "The Origin of Some Adire Designs," in Barbour and Simmonds, *Adire Cloth in Nigeria*, 52.

97. Stanfield, "Dyeing Methods in Western Nigeria," 11; Byfield, *The Bluest Hands*, 90, 101.

98. Betty Wass, "Yoruba Dress in Five Generations of a Lagos Family," in *The Fabrics of Culture*, ed. Justine Cordwell and Ronald Schwarz (The Hague: Mouton, 1979), 336.

99. Hans Melzian, *A Concise Dictionary of the Bini Language of Southern Nigeria* (London: Kegan Paul, 1937), 144; Crowther and Sowande, *Dictionary of the Yoruba Language*, 172.

100. Titilola Euba, "Dress and Status in 19th Century Lagos," in *History of the Peoples of Lagos State*, ed. Ade Adefuye et al. (Lagos: Lantern Books, 1987), 142–43; A. F. C. Ryder, *Benin and the Europeans, 1485–1897* (New York: Humanities Press, 1969), 14.

101. Jane Barbour, "Nigerian 'adire' Cloths," *Baessler-Archiv*, N.F. 18 (1970), 369, 371; Barbour and Simmonds, *Adire Cloths in Nigeria*, 100–104.

102. Wenger and Beier, "Adire-Yoruba Pattern Dyeing," 220–21; Barbour, "Nigerian 'adire' Cloths," 372–73.

103. Stanfield, "Dyeing Methods in Western Nigeria," 11.

104. J. G. Christaller, *A Dictionary of the Asante and Fante Language called Tshi (Twi)* (Basel: Basel Evangelical Missionary Society, 1881), 84; T. Edward Bowdich, *Mission from Cape Coast Castle to Ashantee* (1819; repr., London: Cass, 1966), 310; Daniel Mato, *Clothed in Symbol: The Art of Adinkra among the Akan of Ghana* (PhD diss., Indiana University, 1986), 78, 98, 171; Museum voor Land- en Volkenkunde, Rotterdam, *Een Adinkra doek van de Goudkust in het Museum voor Land en Volkenkunde te Rotterdam* (Rotterdam: Gemeente-Drukkerij, 1954).

105. Designs with translation symmetry are repeated patterns that extend to infinity. Examples are *Olokun* number 2 (p4m), number 4 (p4g), number 6 (p1), number 7 (p4m), and number 10 (p4m). See Dorothy Washburn and Donald Crowe, *Symmetries of Culture: Theory and Practice of Plane Pattern Analysis* (Seattle: University of Washington Press, 1988); Washburn and Crowe, eds., *Symmetry Comes of Age. The Role of Pattern in Culture* (Seattle: University of Washington Press, 2004).

106. Claudia Zaslavsky, *Africa Counts: Number and Pattern in African Culture* (1973; repr., Westport, Conn.: Lawrence Hill, 1979), 137–51; Labelle Prussin, *Hatumere: Islamic Design in West Africa* (Berkeley: University of California Press, 1986), 238–43.

107. Stanfield, "Dyeing Methods in Western Nigeria," 62–63.

108. Barbour, "Nigerian 'adire' Cloths," 371–72.

109. Paula Ben-Amos, *The Art of Benin* (London: Thames and Hudson, 1980), 28–31; Kate Ezra, *Royal Art of Benin: The Perls Collection in the Metropolitan Museum of Art* (New York: Metropolitan Museum of Art, 1992), 239.

110. Barbour, "The Origin of Some Adire Designs," 54.

111. Ryder, *Benin and the Europeans*, 205–6.

112. Byfield, *The Bluest Hands*, 97.

113. Haller, "Production of Indigo," 3077–78; Vetterli, "The History of Indigo," 3071.

114. Byfield, *The Bluest Hands*, 110–14, 141–48, 158, 182.

115. Keyes, *Adire: Cloth, Gender, and Social Change*, 92–99, 231.

116. B. W. Hodder, "The Markets of Ibadan," in *The City of Ibadan*, ed. P. C. Lloyd et al. (Cambridge: Cambridge University Press, 1967), 176.

117. Wenger and Beier, "Adire-Yoruba Pattern Dyeing," 223; Stanfield, "Dyeing Methods in Western Nigeria," 23.

118. Barbour, "Nigerian 'adire' Cloths," 364–65. For an overview of the artistic explosion during the early postcolonial period in Nigeria, see Ulli Beier, "A Moment of Hope: Cultural Developments in Nigeria before the First Military Coup," in *The Short Century: Independence and Liberation Movements in Africa 1945–1994*, ed. Okwui Enwezor (Munich: Prestel, 2001).

119. Byfield, *The Bluest Hands*, 227–28.

120. See for example, www.adire.clara.net (last accessed 31 August 2005).

5

Textiles, Culture, and Historical Change

A groundbreaking exhibition of African textiles went on view in London in 1995, bringing together two types of woven cloth that are usually viewed and studied quite separately: the so-called traditional, handcrafted textiles manufactured by artisans all over the continent and modern industrial products, in this case the factory-made yardage designed specifically for African consumers. One of the exhibition's stated aims was to call into question the utility of categorical terms such as *tradition* and *authentic*, words that have often been used to assess, divide, and classify textiles and other art forms created in Africa. What the exhibition organizers were getting at was the fact that such broad-stroke terminology presumes some sharply drawn opposition between a "genuinely African" culture and a totally alien, western modernity.

Offering an alternative view, the show's organizers took deliberate care to situate examples of both types of African textiles in their particular historical moments and contexts, highlighting at the same time how the textiles had undergone change by the incorporation of new ideas, techniques, and imagery over time. The end result was a demolition of well-worn colonial myths such as the claim that European imports did irreparable harm to African craft production, or that, by some miracle, certain traditions had been able to survive in their seemingly pure (and supposedly static) forms. As stated in the exhibition catalogue, a major goal of the exhibit was to articulate the agency of African artists and craftsworkers as historical actors by demonstrating "the particular range of African responses to and demands upon textiles as a medium of art, especially in the present century."[1]

The contributions of a variety of specialists reiterated these themes in detail and with copious illustrations. Over and over again the exhibition catalogue presented instances of innovation and change in African textiles, revealing both the resilience of people's aesthetic preferences and technological practices as well as people's decidedly keen interest in novelty. Perhaps the most salient example of this was the adoption of a certain type of synthetic imported thread—a shiny, metallic-like plastic material called Lurex—by handweavers in Nigeria, which led to the creation of a whole new genre of locally made cloth called *shain-shain* (shine-shine). The new cloth was such a major hit with African consumers that by the 1990s it held a dominant position in the African textile market.[2] In other cases, careful documentation of work by individual producers uncovered how their technical choices were linked to marketing strategies. Interviews with well-known artist Nike Olaniyi-Davies revealed her shrewd decision to switch from doing embroidery work to the making of handpainted and stenciled starch-resist cloth, a change that allowed her to increase her volume of production.[3] Even in the industrialized domain of European factory-made cloth could be found evidence of African input. Cotton prints manufactured in Europe from the mid-nineteenth century onward targeted particular African markets by embracing the specific design and color preferences of different groups of African consumers.[4] All in all, the message of the exhibition came across emphatically that thinking of African tradition and western modernity as mutually exclusive is to miss the point entirely. And the myth that European imports had at some point destroyed local production was exposed as false. African textile producers welcomed selected materials, techniques, and ideas from overseas, while the visual acuity of the African consumer was acknowledged and taken well into account by European merchants and manufacturers.

The present book has shown that these kinds of exchanges, and the politics of dress, predate the past one hundred years.[5] Over centuries of history, West African textile workshops have served as an important locus of both continuity and innovation, where workers maintained many of their society's most ingrained visual preferences while also choosing to embrace selected novelties. Production and trade are, of course, a two-way street. By weaving, dyeing, sewing, and embellishing such a rich variety of cloth and clothing, African artisans helped to facilitate the workings of local, regional, and international commerce over time. And along the way, they were able to gain access to new fibers, techniques, and imagery, which opened up possibilities for the invention of new products and the alteration of standard ones. In other words, the phrase "local craft production" is something of an oxymoron, for textile manufacturers were neither insulated from external change nor impervious to it. One factor that contributed much to this dynamism was an especially high cultural value placed on cloth. Peoples in West Africa, and in many other parts of the continent, shared an avid appreciation of the powerful sensual qualities of woven fabric and the serious matters of proper and stylish dress and public display. Even those recently made textiles exhibited as art in London arose from values and processes that were rooted in a much deeper past. Whether hung on a wall or worn, West African textiles owe their existence to a long history of body adornment and the making of visual social statements through clothes.

According to the archaeological record, this history goes back very far indeed. Ancient terra-cottas unearthed at the Nok sites give us our earliest indications of the cultural importance of dress in the lower Niger region. Many of the individual sculptures convey an air of privilege, wealth, and elevated social position, and the figures they depict are represented as being elegantly adorned with items of clothing, beaded jewelry, and elaborate headdresses and hairstyles. Although we will probably never know the origins and precise material features of these various elements of dress, their significance is undeniable. Further evidence, coming later and from other locales in the region, follows along similar lines. The revered personage buried at Igbo Ukwu in the ninth century, whoever he was, must also have been richly attired, given the thousands of imported trade beads, metal jewelry, and other impressive treasures placed with him in his grave. But we know nothing about his clothing. Several centuries later, artisans in Ife were sculpting figures in terra-cotta and cast copper alloy, some of them depicted with simple dress and others gracefully draped and belted in cloth, covered with layers of beaded ornament, and bearing royal insignia. Our earliest direct evidence of textiles used as clothing comes from an event around this same time, when a number of women were ceremonially sacrificed at the court of the Benin king. Surviving fragments of their garb reveal a variety of fabrics, from simple to complex, suggesting a well-articulated consumer market for cloth. Using different types of yarns, made with fibers that might have included cotton, weavers produced textiles having different densities and thread counts, some woven into plain-weave structures while others included areas of openwork or brocade. This technological sophistication could not have developed without an equally sophisticated population of consumers who could appreciate a variety of cloth types and their many social meanings. Finally, a rich trove of cast metalwork made in the kingdom of Benin during the era of European trade provides us with an even more extensive set of visual evidence that amplifies and conveys in greater detail the important role of dress in this region's cultural history. Articles of clothing served to distinguish rank in the social and political hierarchy, to divide people along age and gender lines, and to mark the collective identities of local and foreign social groups. Taking all of these sources together, it is clear that certain specific items of dress signified status and social position in societies of the lower Niger region from very early on.

Acknowledging the cultural significance of dress and visual presentation may seem so obvious as to be unnecessary. It is given special mention here to provide a reference point for understanding in general what drove historical change in West African workshops and textile markets. Placing this history in relation to broad cultural values is necessary because the specific actors, along with their names and their individual desires and motivations, elude us. They did not leave written records behind, and we cannot travel back in time and interview consumers and producers of cloth to inquire as to what was driving their behavior. This book is therefore based on inferences about their collective values and achievements, inferences that are drawn from the visible results of their choices, conventions, and actions, the things we can see that they did in their lives as wearers and makers of cloth. And what they did was a lot—much too much to fit into one single grand history of textile consumption and production. By focusing here on three particular products from one important textile-producing region in West Africa, it has been possible to present three interrelated narratives of just how cloth fit into the flow of general historical trends and events. The wearing of clothing was not simply a practical matter guided by environmental and climatic factors—human factors such as trade, travel, religious beliefs, and social differentiation played their part as well. And for cloth to hold such a high cultural value meant that purchases and gifts of textiles, whether of local products or imports, were subjected to careful scrutiny and selection. What cloth looked like and how it was made was considered to be of major significance.

Even so, there was no simple clothing code or formula for dress in the lower Niger region. On the contrary, there were different conventional textiles for certain occasions, places, and individuals, all of which coexisted in society at large. Strictly for the purposes of historical analysis, however, the preceding chapters have emphasized two major modes of dress that developed before the colonial era. One of them was centered on the wrapper—cloth woven and sewn together into different-sized rectangles to be worn by either women or men. These were the earliest textiles produced, by an indigenous technology based on the vertical loom. Using at first the fibers that were locally available—leaves of raphia palm and processed tree bark, for example—weavers in the rainforests were making cloth in a variety of structural types by at least the ninth century. Sometime between then and the fifteenth century, certain special textile forms then became institutionalized as official costume in the Benin kingdom, Ijebu-Ode, and probably in other nearby kingdoms as well. Complex loom-patterned designs, dramatized with dyed threads, became the prerogative of individuals among the political and religious elite. These prestigious handwoven textiles, and the wrapper form itself, then held their own in the face of direct competition with international markets. When European trade opened up along the coast in the late fifteenth century, exotic articles of costume from abroad entered the wardrobes of high-placed officials as visible proof of their worldly contacts, but these exotic items did not displace the work of local weavers. Brightly embellished jackets, velvet capes, and impressive military caps and helmets were among the items displayed for foreign visitors, while elaborate textiles made in nearby workshops remained the proper dress to be worn in public on important ceremonial occasions. Meanwhile, long lengths of yardage from overseas—linens and woolens from Europe, cottons and silks from India—were welcomed as supplements to local production. Foreign-made fabrics were cut into shorter lengths and incorporated into the wrapper mode, with wealthy men cornering much of the market by adopting a showy, multilayered style of clothing.

The other major mode of dress was the tailored garment: fabric sewn into shirts, robes, and trousers to be worn primarily by men. Some of these garment forms may have preceded the adoption of Islam in sub-Saharan West Africa, but they surely became more common there as the number of Muslim believers and their influence grew in the thirteenth and fourteenth centuries. This mode arose by way of a very different textile technology, one that was based on a treadle-operated handloom that had originated in Asia. Weavers used it to produce narrow strips of cotton that were then sewn together edge-to-edge, sometimes to make turbans or women's wrappers and headcloths, but mostly to be fashioned for men into tunics and gowns or trousers that varied in size, style, and degree of elaboration. While tailored dress was not restricted entirely to Muslim males, it was they who were the most numerous and prominent consumers of it, especially the finest examples, whether that clothing was made abroad or closer to home. Narrow strip cloth proved to be quite versatile as various styles of shirt, tunic, robe, and trousers, some of them derived from foreign prototypes, were developed and standardized, each one with its own name in the vernacular languages of West Africa. The cloth itself tended to be rather severe in structure and design, and it was standardized most often as plain undyed or piece-dyed fabric, or as plain-weave strips patterned with many variations of stripes and checks. Embellishment was often added at the end of the production processes, as in the glazing or embroidering of finished garments. These visual qualities can be seen in part as reflections of pan-Islamic ideals of modesty, respectability, and correct behavioral practice. However, in this mode as well there were plenty of opportunities for conspicuous dress and exotic costume display. Sharp differences in taste arose, even among the most powerful elites, depending on the degree to which specific Muslim prescriptions about proper dress were known and followed.

Both the vertical-loom and treadle-loom technologies were well established in the lower Niger region before the era of Atlantic commerce, having been transferred to workshops in these new locales via networks of various overland and riverine trading systems. As communities grew ever more complex, cloth became increasingly a sign and conveyor of wealth and prosperity. During certain periods of economic expansion in the past, cloths produced on both types of loom circulated as commodity currencies, a phenomenon that must have quickened the pace and greatly extended the reach of textile technology transfer. The earliest such instance cannot be dated precisely, but may have started sometime around the fifteenth or sixteenth century in the northern savannas and Sahel, since there had been reports of a strip-cloth currency in Kanem as early as the fourteenth century. As the Hausa kingdoms began to prosper through direct connections with interregional and trans-Saharan trade, they were drawn into networks where cotton strips, woven to certain widths and bundled or wound in specified units of length, operated as a form of money. Similarly, widths of vertical loom cloth served as money in the coastal trade with Europeans, especially during the seventeenth and eighteenth centuries. Merchants bought them up in bulk, as wrapper-sized units of three or four cloths bundled together, in order to sell them elsewhere on the Guinea Coast. These same kinds of textiles became units of account in some of the ports along the Bight of Benin. Weavers, whether male or female, slave or free, thus had a hand in linking their workshops and local economies to wider regional and international networks.

Weaving nevertheless remained very much a labor-intensive process, the looms operating according to the same basic technical principles and production relying heavily on skilled labor. And before the era of factory-made yarns, no group was more important to textile manufacture than the spinners. Their history, and the history of their technology, developed gradually over hundreds of years, is still incompletely known. We have seen that it began before the ninth century, with experiments that revealed the advantages of twisting, spinning, and plying bast and other fibers into continuous lengths of thread, processes that were then vigorously exploited. This breakthrough meant that sturdier and longer cloths could be woven, cloths that had not only strong selvages but also finished dimensions that were greater than the individual lengths of raphia and other nonspun materials. More changes were set in motion with the introduction of cotton. New tools and techniques for cleaning and processing this fiber had to be developed, and spinning practice was revised. Cotton was spun in the z-direction, as it was in much of the Muslim world, and in contrast to the s-direction of the earlier bast threads. Over time, the work of spinning became much more specialized. A small spindle with a clay whorl, created specifically for the purpose of making cotton thread, appears to have made its way into the hands of many West African women, including some in the lower Niger region, via Muslim trade routes during the fifteenth and sixteenth centuries. It made possible the honing of spinning skills such that yarns could be produced according to clear specifications, from those that were spun very fine with a hard twist, to be used as warp threads, to ones that were thick and fluffy—just right for wefts or embroidery thread. Without these skills, the excellent quality of cloth and embroidered garments produced in the Sokoto Caliphate and its environs in the nineteenth century would never have been possible.

Other more-privileged and better-rewarded groups of workers developed various techniques and skills for embellishing textiles with imagery. The earliest examples we encountered for the region were shoulder cloths and wrappers woven on the vertical loom with elaborate brocaded patterning. Originally the prerogative of specific government officials, religious figures, and title holders in Ijebu-Ode, Benin, and other kingdoms, these precious textiles were manufactured in royal workshops. If we consider the ceremonial cloths of Ijebu-Ode as an example, the most significant motifs were religious ones—representations of supernatural beings and spiritual forces. Hence, wearing the imagery must have seemed to bestow the honor and blessing of religious sanction. A parallel development took place in a quite different historical context to the north, in Hausaland. The imagery was not the same and neither were the techniques, but there was a similar connection between embellished cloth and the world of politics. Embroidery—a highly respected skill through much of Muslim history—may well have been known to the rulers of the Hausa kingdoms from at least the fifteenth century onward, though direct evidence for this is lacking. What we do know is that by the time of the Sokoto Caliphate, particular kinds of embroidery stitches were being used conventionally to produce certain standard visual compositions and specific motifs. Among the articles of clothing that benefited from this use, embellished robes and trousers were special. They were produced by Quranic scholars and their young students, and the best of them were given as diplomatic gifts and signs of office or as a reward for unusual achievement. Here too, the motifs were endowed with supernatural significance and were meant to confer honor and protection upon the wearer. These revered textiles and their techniques of embellishment—brocading and embroidery—laid the groundwork for later generations of artisans to compete in twentieth-century markets by making fancy luxury clothing for wealthy Nigerian consumers.

Just as there had been, at times in the past, important political uses for certain textile products, there could also be considerable economic consequences to changes in the work of making cloth. One important avenue of change in textile production had to do with alterations in available materials and supplies and in the kinds of improvements they afforded. Several major examples have been noted and discussed in this book. The technological development of spinning outlined above, through which endogenous achievements were transformed by the arrival of new fibers from afar, was not the only such occurrence. And these kinds of events set off ripple effects that were felt in other economic domains. For example, all sorts of fibers available in the immediate rainforest and savanna environments were joined by cotton—Old World varieties first, and then varieties domesticated in the New

World—which then became crops that were grown locally, altering the way agriculture was practiced in the region. Similarly, the wild indigo that was native to much of West Africa was supplemented with Old and New World indigos of commerce via the Saharan and Atlantic trades. These introduced indigos too became integrated into lower Niger agricultural systems, to be replaced later, in the twentieth century, by synthetic indigo dye from Europe. Throughout the course of these changes, trade was shaped in part by textile workers seeking materials that they thought might be better or easier to work with. Such was the case when indigo dyers incorporated various types of mineral salts, some arriving from as far away as the Sahara, into their dye vats while the common but inconsistent vegetable salts continued to be used, especially in rural areas. Later on, during the colonial era, many new, less-skilled workers were able to enter the dyeing profession by taking up the much faster and easier soda-based vat process. Efforts at cost-cutting could also lead to wide repercussions. It may have been the importation of silk, from across the Sahara and through trade on the coast, that prompted experiments with using indigenous wild silk and the accompanying discovery of techniques for degumming and preparing the fiber for spinning. Later, bright rayons and knitting wools became the yarns of choice for weavers and embroiderers when the prices of these items dropped to affordable levels. These are only some of the most important examples of what could happen when textile workers initiated changes either in the quality of their products or in the reliability and efficacy of their production methods.

In short, textile technology was labor-intensive, but that did not mean that it was static, outmoded, or unprofitable. The various occupations involved with textile technology proved to be remarkably adaptable and flexible, and continued to attract new trainees over centuries of competition with products imported from overseas. African textile producers and consumers were linked to international trading systems long before the colonial era. During the heyday of Muslim commerce, robes, trousers, shirts, turbans, caps, and other garments made of narrow handwoven strip cloth were manufactured in workshops all over West Africa, even as a steady flow of foreign textiles came into sub-Saharan markets by caravan. The well-known Guinea cloth of Atlantic commerce—exported from India and then imitated by manufacturers in Europe—had to be made in the manner of plain handwoven African cottons in order to satisfy the tastes of choosy consumers along the Guinea Coast. Novelties—bright scarlet woolens from Europe—were incorporated into official costume in Benin, or unraveled so that the vibrantly colored yarns could be used by weavers of fancy cloth in the Yoruba kingdoms and Benin. What then happened in textile manufacture more recently was not the beginning of change but rather a quickening and intensification of it. Breakthroughs in transportation—first in international shipping, then in overland travel by railroad—had a major impact on price structures, eventually reversing the price position of overseas textiles in relation to those made in Africa. But even then, some groups of textile workers took advantage of this shift to engage in import replacement, as the example of "native chintz" shows. And resist dyeing, done originally on cloth that was handwoven in Africa, went through a boom in production when the cost of factory-made cotton yardage came down in the early years of colonial rule. These again are some of the many ways in which foreign trade and competition from overseas textiles could be a boon to textile producers, offering them new ideas and techniques to be absorbed, and market opportunities to be exploited.

This book has chronicled only a small fraction of the history of textile consumption and production in West Africa, a history going back over a millennium. It has focused on the lower Niger basin in particular, although some of the trends, events, and processes we have traced were interregional or international in scope. My aim has been to show how this history was given shape by countless textile workers across the continent. Through many of their own investments and initiatives, they built up and revised over time interconnected sets of skills and techniques and market strategies that contributed to textile technology and manufacture in the region. Different groups of such workers accomplished all of this while working in concert with others—merchants, farmers, government officials, religious leaders, and consumers across the social spectrum—thereby exercising influence at times on events, conditions, and practices well beyond the confines of their workplaces. They even generated change in the languages they spoke, by coining new names or borrowing words from other languages for the tools, techniques, and materials they used and for the imagery and products that they fashioned. The finest textiles that emerged from their many workshops can certainly be admired as art, but as the foregoing chapters have revealed, there is much more to them than their striking visual appeal. They are eloquent webs of time, and they stand as a testimony to the prominent and persistent role of textiles and textile makers in the history and culture of West Africa. And though it would be erroneous to consider textile manufacture to have been a deliberate and overt form of resistance to colonial policies, it is by now quite clear that Nigerians had their own ideas about what best to do with their cotton.

NOTES

1. John Picton, ed., *The Art of African Textiles: Technology, Tradition, and Lurex* (London: Barbican Art Gallery, 1995), 12.

2. Picton, *The Art of African Textiles*, 15; Judith Perani and Norma Wolff, *Cloth, Dress and Art Patronage in Africa* (Oxford: Berg Press, 1999), 179, 181.

3. Picton, *The Art of African Textiles*, 17.

4. Picton, *The Art of African Textiles*, 24–25.

5. For studies of dress and politics in the twentieth century, see Jean Allman, ed., *Fashioning Africa: Power and the Politics of Dress* (Bloomington: Indiana University Press, 2004); Leslie W. Rabine, *The Global Circulation of African Fashion* (Oxford: Berg Press, 2002); and Hildi Hendrickson, ed., *Clothing and Difference: Embodied Identities in Colonial and Post-colonial Africa* (Durham, N.C.: Duke University Press, 1996).

Glossary of Technical Terms

basket weave   A type of plain-weave structure using paired warps and paired wefts.

batik   A word derived from the Javanese root *tik*, which means "droplet." Batik originally referred to cloths made in central Java that were patterned with wax-resist techniques; it is used in English as a general term meaning wax resist.

batten (see also *reed*)   Long, flat, and smooth piece of wood used by weavers to beat in the weft when weaving on a simple loom such as the West African vertical loom or the Peruvian back-strap loom.

brocading   Method of creating patterns in a textile with the use of supplementary wefts, that is, weft threads that are supplementary to the threads that form the basic ground structure of the fabric.

carding   Process of combing or fluffing fibers before spinning them into thread.

chain stitch   Embroidery stitch that is often used to outline motifs or create linear patterns; individual stitches are sewn in a chain-like series of loops.

chintz   Europeanized version of the plural for *chint*, *chit*, or *chitta* (meaning "spotted cloth"), originally referring to an India-produced cotton cloth patterned in various ways by painting or printing with dyes, mordants, and resist materials.

compound weave/compound structure   Generally refers to a large group of textile structures that have two or more sets of warps and/or wefts, for example, a ground weave with brocading.

continuous weft   Refers to weft threads that pass the entire width of the textile, from selvage to selvage.

couching/self-couching   Method of embroidery that involves laying an element on the fabric surface and then securing it with small stitches at intervals. When the laid-down element and the stitching thread are one and the same, the method is called self-couching.

counterbalanced treadle loom   Loom used throughout West Africa, consisting of harnesses suspended from a pulley and foot pedals that raise and lower the harness frames. Beating in the weft is done with a reed.

damask   A method of patterning by reversing a weave structure so that both versions appear on the same side or face of the textile. Also a general term for textiles with richly woven patterns.

discontinuous weft   Weft threads that are woven back and forth to make individual motifs in only a portion or section of the fabric width, for example, as supplementary wefts in brocading or as the ground wefts in pictorial tapestry weaves.

dye (versus pigment)   A natural or synthetic substance that is used to transform the color of materials such as textiles, paper, or leather. In contrast to pigment, a dye penetrates the surface and bonds with the fibrous material.

embroidery   Embellishment of a fabric with stitches made by needle and thread.

encased seam/French seam   Type of seam made by folding the fabric edges each inside the other and sewing over the fold on both faces of the seam.

eyelet   Type of embroidery in which the edges of small openings are entirely bound and covered with thread, using overcast or buttonhole stitches. Some examples, by omitting the small openings, appear simply as small circles or "bird's eyes."

feather stitch   Type of embroidery in which looping or buttonhole stitches are placed on one side of a vertical axis and then the other, creating a pattern like a feather.

gauze   Textile structure in which adjacent warp elements are crossed over or under each other, secured by a weft thread, and then crossed back again, in contrast to a conventional flat and regular interlacing structure. Oftentimes this results in a delicate, lace-like textile.

gusset   An insert sewn into a garment to enlarge or strengthen it.

harness (see also *heddle, shed stick*)   A device that raises selected warp threads in order to make the shed opening. It consists of a frame with heddles, each one controlling a warp element.

heddle (see also *harness, shed stick*)   One of a series of looping cords or eyed-threads or wires that is used to repeatedly raise selected warp threads in order to make the shed opening. Heddles can be attached to a single rod (shed stick) or fixed within a frame (harness).

herringbone stitch   A type of "long-armed" cross stitch done in series, in which the stitches are sewn parallel to the axis of the series progression.

ikat   Indonesian word (meaning "to tie") for the technique of tie-dyeing threads before weaving them; also refers to the resulting design and to a textile made in this way.

loom   A device for making textiles by interlacing at least two independent sets of threads at right angles to each other. The lengthwise threads, the warps, are held under tension on the loom.

loom-patterning   Making patterns within the structure of the weaving process, for example, by using differently colored threads or by manipulating the arrangement and number of thread elements.

mordant   A chemical agent that serves to fix dye in textiles, leather, and the like.

openwork   General term for plain-weave structures that are made with slits or openings in the textile and for various types of gauze fabrics.

pigment (versus dye)   A natural or synthetic substance that is applied onto the surface of a material to color or coat it.

plain weave   Interlacing of single, alternating warp threads with single, alternating weft threads. When the warp and weft threads are equal in size and equally spaced, the plain weave is said to be "balanced."

plangi (see also *tie-dye*)   Indonesian word (meaning "rainbow") for the technique of tie-dyeing a textile.

plying   Process of twisting together two or more yarn elements in either a clockwise or counterclockwise direction.

reed/combed beater (see also *batten*)   Toothed frame through which warp threads are threaded on the treadle loom. It controls the warp threads and is used to beat in each shot of weft.

resist dyeing   Method of making patterns on cloth by preventing the dye from reaching and penetrating certain selected areas (e.g., by binding or sewing with threads, or by painting parts of the fabric surface with a waterproof substance).

selvage/selvedge The edge of a fabric, woven so that it will not unravel, and created by weft threads passing back across the warps in alternate sheds.

shed An opening created between two sets of warp threads so that the weft thread can be passed through it.

shed stick (see also *heddle, harness*) Simple mechanical device for repeatedly lifting up the same group of selected warp threads in order to make the shed opening.

shuttle A device used to hold and carry the weft threads back and forth in the weaving process.

spindle A thin stick, sometimes notched, for spinning fibers into thread by hand.

spindle whorl A disk or other circular form that is attached to a spindle, its weight thereby increasing the speed and momentum of the spinning process and also strengthening the yarn.

spinning The process of drawing out and twisting fiber into a continuous thread.

staple Fibers that are used for making textiles and are graded according to standards of length and fineness.

supplementary shed sticks/harnesses Additional shed sticks (on the vertical loom) or harnesses (on the treadle loom) that control selected groups of warp threads so that patterns such as gauze structures and brocading can be made mechanically.

supplementary weft Weft element that is supplementary to the wefts that make up the basic ground-weave structure of a textile.

textile Cloth woven on a loom, using at least two independent sets of thread elements interlacing each other at right angles.

tie-dye (see also *plangi*) Method of resist dyeing by sewing, wrapping, or binding areas of a fabric with thread.

treadle Foot-operated pedals that are used to raise and lower the harnesses of a loom so that the shed opening is created.

vat dye One of a large category of water-insoluble dyes (such as indigo) whose colors are created by oxidation of a soluble-reduced form that are prepared in a vat and are applied either by dipping or by direct application to a material.

vertical loom Loom used in the lower Niger region with a circular warp stretched between two cross-beams. Shedding is done with the hands, by raising shed sticks; the wefts are beaten with a batten.

warp   The longitudinal elements in a woven textile that intersect the weft threads at right angles. Warp threads are held under tension on a loom during the weaving process.

warp face   A type of plain weave in which there are more warp threads per inch than weft threads, so that the weft threads are either less visible or completely covered.

weaving   The process of making a textile, or woven fabric, on a loom with at least two sets of independent elements that cross each other at right angles.

weft/woof   The transverse elements in a woven textile that cross the warp elements at right angles. Weft threads are passed through the shed and beaten into place with a batten or reed.

weft face   A type of plain weave in which there are more weft threads per inch than warp threads, so that the warp threads are either less visible or completely covered.

worsted wool   Firm, strong, and smoothly twisted thread made from well-combed, long-staple wool.

Sources: Emery 1980; Geiger 1979; Gittinger 1982; Irwin and Hall 1971; Irwin and Schwartz 1966.

Bibliography

Adams, John. *Sketches Taken during Ten Voyages to Africa between the Years 1786 and 1800*. 1822. Reprint, New York: Johnson Reprint, 1970.

Adefuye, Ade, Babatunde Agiri, and Jide Osuntokun, eds. *History of the Peoples of Lagos State*. Lagos: Lantern Books, 1987.

Adenaike, Carolyn Keyes. "Putting the Color Back in the History." In *Paths toward the Past: African Historical Essays in Honor of Jan Vansina*, edited by Robert Harms et al., 415–25. Atlanta, Ga.: African Studies Association Press, 1994.

Africanus, Leo. *The History and Description of Africa and of the Notable Things therein Contained*. 1896. Reprint, New York: B. Franklin, 1963.

Ajayi, J. F. A. and Michael Crowder, eds. *History of West Africa*. Vol. 1. New York: Columbia University Press, 1976.

Akintoye, S. A. "The Economic Background of the Ekitiparapo, 1878–1893." *Odu* 4, no. 2 (1968): 30–52.

———. "The Northeastern Districts of the Yoruba Country and the Benin Kingdom." *Journal of the Historical Society of Nigeria* 4 (1969): 539–53.

Akpata, 'Bisi. "Comments on Adire in Western Nigeria," in Barbour and Simmonds, *Adire Cloths in Nigeria*, 95–98.

Alagoa, E. J. "The Niger Delta States and Their Neighbors, to 1800," in Ajayi and Crowder, *History of West Africa*, 1:331–72.

Alawode, Adebukola. "Akwete Weaving Complex in Ndoki Tribe of Ukwa Local Government, Aba, Imo State." *Humanitas: Man's Past and Present* 3 (1985/1986): 36–44.

Albers, Anni. *On Weaving*. Middletown, Conn.: Wesleyan University Press, 1965.

Allman, Jean, ed. *Fashioning Africa: Power and the Politics of Dress*. Bloomington: Indiana University Press, 2004.

Alpern, Stanley. "What Africans Got for Their Slaves: A Master List of European Trade Goods." *History in Africa* 22 (1995): 5–43.

Anderson, Martha and Philip Peek, eds. *Ways of the Rivers: Arts and Environment of the Niger Delta.* Los Angeles: UCLA Fowler Museum of Cultural History, 2002.

Anquandah, James. "Urbanization and State Formation in Ghana during the Iron Age," in Shaw et al., *The Archaeology of Africa,* 642–51.

Arèmú, P. S. O. "Yoruba Adire-Eleko Fabrics." *Nigerian Field* 44 (1979): 98–106.

———. "Yoruba Traditional Weaving: Kijipa Motifs, Colour, and Symbols." *Nigeria Magazine* 140 (1982): 3–10.

Aronson, Lisa. *Some Aspects of Women's Weaving among the Yoruba, Hausa, Nupe, and Igbirra Based on European Collections.* MA thesis, Indiana University, 1975.

———. "History of the Cloth Trade in the Niger Delta: A Study of Diffusion," in Idiens and Ponting, *Textiles of Africa,* 89–107.

———. *Akwete Weaving: A Study of Change in Response to the Palm Oil Trade in the Nineteenth Century.* PhD diss., Indiana University, 1982.

———. "Ijebu Yoruba Aso Olona: A Contextual and Historical Overview." *African Arts* 25, no. 3 (1992): 52–63, 101.

———. "Tricks of the Trade: A Study of Ikakibite (Cloth of the Tortoise) among the Eastern Ijo." In *Ways of the Rivers: Arts and Environment of the Niger Delta,* edited by Martha Anderson and Philip Peek, 251–67. Los Angeles: UCLA Fowler Museum of Cultural History, 2002.

Awe, Bolanle. "Militarism and Economic Development in Nineteenth Century Yoruba Country: The Ibadan Example." *Journal of African History* 14, no. 1 (1973): 65–77.

Ayandele, E. A. "Ijebuland 1800–1891: Era of Splendid Isolation." In *Studies in Yoruba History and Culture: Essays in Honour of Professor S. O. Biobaku,* edited by G. O. Olusanya, 88–107. Ibadan: University Press, 1983.

Banfield, A. W. *Dictionary of the Nupe Language.* 2 vols. 1914. Reprint, Farnborough, UK: Gregg International, 1969.

Barber, E. J. W. *Prehistoric Textiles: The Development of Cloth in the Neolithic and Bronze Ages.* Princeton, N.J.: Princeton University Press, 1991.

Barbour, Jane. "Nigerian 'adire' Cloths." *Baessler-Archiv,* N.F. 18 (1970): 363–426.

———. "The Origin of Some Adire Designs," in Barbour and Simmonds, *Adire Cloths in Nigeria,* 49–80.

Barbour, Jane and Doig Simmonds. *An Exhibition of Traditional Adire Cloth.* Exhibition catalogue, Trenchard Exhibition Gallery, University of Ibadan, Nigeria, 1969.

———, eds. *Adire Cloths in Nigeria.* Ibadan: Institute of African Studies, 1971.

Bargery, G. P. and Diedrich Westermann. *A Hausa-English Dictionary and English-Hausa Vocabulary.* London: Oxford University Press, 1934.

Barreteau, Daniel. "Les dénominations du coton dans le bassin du lac Tchad." In *L'homme et le milieu végétal dans le bassin du lac Tchad,* edited by D. Barreteau, R. Dognin, and Ch. Von Graffenried, 229–59. Paris: ORSTOM, 1997.

Barth, Heinrich. *Travels and Discoveries in North and Central Africa.* 3 vols. 1857. Reprint, London: Cass, 1965.

Bassani, Ezio and William B. Fagg. *Africa and the Renaissance: Art in Ivory.* New York: The Center for African Art, 1988.

Bassett, Thomas J. *The Peasant Cotton Revolution in West Africa: Côte d'Ivoire, 1880–1995.* Cambridge: Cambridge University Press, 2001.

Beauvois, Palisot de, AMFJ. *Flore d'Oware et de Benin, en Afrique.* Paris: Imprimerie de Fain Jeune et Compagnie, 1804–1807.

Bedaux, R. M. A. "Les plus anciens tissus retrouvés par les archéologues," in Musée National des Arts d'Afrique et d'Océanie, *Vallées du Niger*, 456–63.

———— and Rita Bolland. "Vêtements féminins médiévaux du Mali: Les cache-sexe de fibre des Tellem," in Engelbrecht and Gardi, *Man Does Not Go Naked*, 15–33.

Beier, Ulli. *Ein Meer aus Indigo*. Wuppertal, Germany: Peter Hammer, 1997.

————. "A Moment of Hope: Cultural Developments in Nigeria before the First Military Coup." In *The Short Century: Independence and Liberation Movements in Africa 1945–1994*, edited by Okwui Enwezor, 45–49. Munich: Prestel, 2001.

Ben-Amos, Paula. "Owina n'ido: Royal Weavers of Benin." *African Arts* 11 (1978): 48–53, 95–96.

————. *The Art of Benin*. London: Thames and Hudson, 1980.

————. "Who Is the Man in the Bowler Hat? Emblems of Identity in Benin Royal Art." *Baessler-Archiv*, N.F. 31 (1983): 161–83.

————. *Art, Innovation, and Politics in Eighteenth-century Benin*. Bloomington: Indiana University Press, 1999.

Bergman, Ingrid. *Late Nubian Textiles*. Stockholm: Scandinavian University Press, 1975.

Blench, Roger. "Ethnographic and Linguistic Evidence for the Prehistory of African Ruminant Livestock, Horses, and Ponies," in Shaw et al., *The Archaeology of Africa*, 71–103.

Bolland, Rita. *Tellem Textiles: Archaeological Finds from Burial Caves in Mali's Bandiagara Cliff*. Leiden: Rijksmuseum voor Volkenkunde, 1991.

Bonnell, Victoria E. and Lynn Hunt, eds. *Beyond the Cultural Turn*. Berkeley: University of California Press, 1999.

Borgatti, Jean. *Cloth as Metaphor: Nigerian Textiles from the Museum of Cultural History*. Los Angeles: UCLA Museum of Cultural History, 1983.

Boser-Sarivaxévanis, Renée. "Aperçus sur la teinture à l'indigo en Afrique Occidentale." *Verhandlungen der naturforschenden Gesellschaft in Basel* 80, no. 1 (1969): 151–208.

————. *Les tissus de l'Afrique Occidentale*. Basel: Pharos-Verlag, 1972.

————. *Textilhandwerk in Westafrika*. Basel: Museum für Völkerkunde, 1973.

————. "Recherche sur l'histoire des textiles traditionels tissées et teints de l'Afrique Occidentale." *Verhandlungen der naturforschenden Gesellschaft in Basel* 86, nos. 1 and 2 (1975): 301–41.

Bosman, William. *A New and Accurate Description of the Coast of Guinea*. New York: Barnes and Noble, 1967. Fourth edition of 1705 English translation, with notes by J. D. Fage and R. E. Bradbury.

Bowdich, T. Edward. *Mission from Cape Coast Castle to Ashantee*. 1819. Reprint, London: Frank Cass, 1966.

Bowen, T. J. *Grammar and Dictionary of the Yoruba Language*. Washington, D.C.: Smithsonian Institution, 1858.

Bradbury, R. E. *Benin Studies*. London: Oxford University Press, 1973.

Brennig, Joseph J. *The Textile Trade of Seventeenth Century Northern Coromandel: A Study of a Pre-modern Asian Export Industry*. PhD diss., University of Wisconsin, Madison, 1975.

————. "Textile Producers and Production in Late Seventeenth-century Coromandel," in Mazzaoui, *Textiles: Production, Trade, and Demand*, 153–74.

Brett, Michael and Elizabeth Fentress. *The Berbers*. Oxford: Blackwell, 1997.

Briggs, Lloyd Cabot. *Tribes of the Sahara.* Cambridge, Mass.: Harvard University Press, 1967.

Brommer, Bea, ed. *Katoendruk in Nederland.* Helmond: Gemeentemuseum, 1989.

———, ed. *Bontjes voor de Tropen: De Export van Imitatieweefsels naar de Tropen.* Helmond: Gemeentemuseum, 1991.

Brooks, George E. *Eurafricans in Western Africa: Commerce, Social Status, Gender, and Religious Observance from the Sixteenth to the Eighteenth Century.* Athens: Ohio University Press, 2003.

Bross, Michael and Hermann Jungraithmayr. "Hausa Cultural Vocabulary—Origin and Integration of Loanwords." In *West African Savannah: Culture, Language and Environment in an Historical Perspective,* edited by H. Jungraithmayr and G. Nagel. Frankfurt am Main: The Frankfurt-Maiduguri Joint Research Project, 1991.

Bross, Michael and Ahmad Tela Baba. *Dictionary of Hausa Crafts: A Dialectal Documentation.* Cologne: Köppe, 1996.

Bühler, Alfred. "Indigo Dyeing among the Primitive Races." *CIBA Review* 85 (1951): 3088–91.

———, Eberhard Fischer, and Marie-Louise Nabholz. *Indian Tie-Dyed Fabrics.* Ahmedabad: Calico Museum for Textiles, 1980.

Byfield, Judith. *The Bluest Hands: A Social and Economic History of Women Dyers in Abeokuta (Nigeria), 1890–1940.* Portsmouth, N.H.: Heinemann, 2002.

Carreira, António. *Panaria Cabo-Verdiano-Guineense.* Lisboa: Museu de Etnologia Ultramar, 1968.

Chaudhuri, K. N. *Trade and Civilisation in the Indian Ocean: An Economic History from the Rise of Islam to 1750.* Cambridge: Cambridge University Press, 1985.

Chavane, Bruno A. *Villages de l'ancien Tekrour: Recherches archéologiques dans la moyenne vallée du fleuve Sénégal.* Paris: Karthala, 1985.

Chogudo, Aliyu Sule Ododo. *Traditional Textile Industry among the Ebira Tao since 1920s: A Case Study of Okene Local Government Area, in Kwara State, Nigeria.* BA thesis, University of Ilorin, Nigeria, 1987.

Christaller, J. G. *A Dictionary of the Asante and Fante Language Called Tshi (Twi).* Basel: Basel Evangelical Missionary Society, 1881.

Clapperton, Hugh. *Journal of a Second Expedition into the Interior of Africa.* 1829. Reprint, London: Cass, 1966.

Clarke, Duncan. "Colonial Intervention and Indigenous Responses: The Introduction of European Broad Loom Weaving in Oyo Town." *Kurio Africana* (1996): 14–27.

Clarke, J. D. "Ilorin Weaving." *Nigeria Magazine* 14 (1938): 121–24.

Clutton-Brock, Juliet. "The Spread of Domestic Animals in Africa," in Shaw et al., *The Archaeology of Africa,* 61–70.

Connah, Graham. *The Archaeology of Benin.* Oxford: Oxford University Press, 1975.

———. *Three Thousand Years in Africa: Man and His Environment in the Lake Chad Region of Nigeria.* Cambridge: Cambridge University Press, 1981.

———, ed. *Transformations in Africa: Essays on Africa's Later Past.* London: Leicester University Press, 1998.

———. *African Civilizations: An Archaeological Perspective.* 2nd ed. Cambridge: Cambridge University Press, 2001.

Cooper, Barbara. *Marriage in Maradi: Gender and Culture in a Hausa Society in Niger, 1900–1989.* Portsmouth, N.H.: Heinemann, 1997.

Cordwell, Justine and Ronald Schwarz, eds. *The Fabrics of Culture: The Anthropology of Clothing and Adornment.* The Hague: Mouton, 1979.

Crossland, Leonard B. "Traditional Textile Industry in North West Brong Ahafo, Ghana—the Archaeological and Contemporary Evidence." *Sankofa* 1 (1975): 69–73.

Crowfoot, Grace. "Spinning and Weaving in the Sudan." *Sudan Notes and Records* 4 (1921). 20–39.

———. *Methods of Handspinning in Egypt and the Sudan.* Bankfield Museum Notes. 2nd series, no. 12. Halifax: King and Sons, 1931.

Crowther, Samuel. *A Vocabulary of the Yoruba Language.* London: Seeleys, 1852.

———. *A Grammar and Vocabulary of the Nupe Language.* London: Church Missionary House, 1864.

——— and James F. Schön. *Vocabulary of the Ibo Language.* London: Society for Promoting Christian Knowledge, 1882–1883.

——— and E. J. Sowande. *A Dictionary of the Yoruba Language.* 1937. Reprint, London: Oxford University Press, 1950.

Curtin, Philip, ed. *Africa Remembered.* Madison: University of Wisconsin Press, 1967.

———. *Economic Change in Precolonial Africa: Senegambia in the Era of the Slave Trade.* Madison: University of Wisconsin Press, 1975.

Dalziel, J. M. *The Useful Plants of Western Tropical Africa.* London: Crown Agents, 1937.

Daniel, F. "Yoruba Pattern Dyeing." *Nigeria Magazine* 14 (1938): 125–29.

Dark, Philip. *An Introduction to Benin Art and Technology.* Oxford: Clarendon Press, 1973.

———. *An Illustrated Catalogue of Benin Art.* Boston: G.K. Hall, 1982.

de Lestrange, Monique. "Les Sarankole de Badyar." *Etudes Guinéennes* (Conakry) 6 (1950): 17–26.

de Miré, Ph. Bruneau and H. Gillet. "Contribution à l'étude de la flore du massif de l'Aïr." *Journal d'Agriculture Tropicale et de Botanique Appliquée* 3, nos. 5–12 (1956): 221–47, 422–38, 701–60, 857–86.

De Negri, Eve. "Nigerian Textile Industry before Independence." *Nigeria Magazine* 89 (1966): 95–101.

Denham, Dixon, Hugh Clapperton, and Walter Oudney. *Narrative of Travels and Discoveries in Northern and Central Africa in the Years 1822, 1823, and 1824.* 2 vols. 1828. Reprint, London: Darf, 1985.

Dewey, Clive and A. G. Hopkins, eds. *The Imperial Impact: Studies in the Economic History of Africa and India.* London: Athlone Press, 1978.

de Zeltner, Fr. "Tissus Africains à dessins réservés ou décolorés." *Bulletins et Mémoires de la Société d'Anthropologie de Paris,* sér. 6, n. 1 (1910): 224–27.

Dozy, R. P. A. *Dictionnaire détaillée des noms des vêtements chez les Arabes.* Amsterdam: Jean Müller, 1845.

Drewal, Henry John, John Pemberton III, and Rowland Abiodun. *Yoruba: Nine Centuries of African Art and Thought.* New York: The Center for African Art, 1989.

Duncan, T. Bentley. *Atlantic Islands: Madeira, the Azores, and the Cape Verdes in Seventeenth-century Commerce and Navigation.* Chicago: University of Chicago Press, 1972.

du Plessis, Antoinette. "Adinkra Cloth of Ntonso, Ghana." *De Arte* [Pretoria] 50 (1994): 21–28.

Effah-Gyamfi, K. *Bono Manso: An Archaeological Investigation into Early Akan Urbanism.* Calgary: University of Calgary Press, 1985.

Eicher, Joanne. *African Dress: A Select and Annotated Bibliography of Subsaharan Countries.* East Lansing: Michigan State University, African Studies Center, 1970.

———. *Nigerian Handcrafted Textiles.* Ile-Ife, Nigeria: University of Ife Press, 1976.

——— and Tonye Erekosima. "Kalabari Cut Thread and Pulled Thread Cloth: An Example of Cultural Authentication." *African Arts* 14, no. 2 (1981): 48–51, 87.

———, Sandra Lee Evenson, and Hazel A. Lutz, eds. *The Visible Self: Global Perspectives on Dress, Culture, and Society.* New York: Fairchild, 2000.

Elbl, Ivana. *The Portuguese Trade with West Africa, 1440–1521.* PhD diss., University of Toronto, 1986.

Emery, Irene. *The Primary Structures of Fabrics.* Washington, D.C.: The Textile Museum, 1980.

Ene, J. C. "Indigenous Silk Weaving in Nigeria." *Nigeria Magazine* 81 (1964): 127–36.

Engelbrecht, Beate and Bernhard Gardi, eds. *Man Does Not Go Naked: Textilien und handwerk aus afrikanischen und anderen Ländern.* Basel: Museum für Völkerkunde, 1989.

Enwezor, Okwui, ed. *The Short Century: Independence and Liberation Movements in Africa 1945–1994.* Munich: Prestel, 2001.

Esposito, John, ed. *The Oxford History of Islam.* Oxford: Oxford University Press, 1999.

es-Sadi. *Tarikh es-Soudan.* Translated by O. Houdas. Paris: Maisonneuve, 1964.

Euba, Titilola. "Dress and Status in 19th Century Lagos," in Adefuye, Agiri, and Osuntokun, *History of the Peoples of Lagos,* 142–63.

Eyo, Ekpo and Frank Willett. *Treasures of Ancient Nigeria.* New York: Alfred A. Knopf, 1980.

Ezra, Kate. *Royal Art of Benin: The Perls Collection in the Metropolitan Museum of Art.* New York: Metropolitan Museum of Art, 1992.

Falola, Toyin. "Warfare and Trade Relations between Ibadan and the Ijebu in the Nineteenth Century," in Falola and Law, *Warfare and Diplomacy in Precolonial Nigeria,* 26–30.

———, ed. *African Historiography: Essays in Honour of Jacob Ade Ajayi.* Harlow: Longman, 1993.

——— and Robin Law, eds. *Warfare and Diplomacy in Precolonial Nigeria.* Madison: University of Wisconsin, Madison, African Studies Program, 1992.

Ferguson, Douglas. *Nineteenth-century Hausaland, Being a Description by Imam Imoru of the Land, Economy, and Society of His People.* PhD diss., University of California, Los Angeles, 1973.

Fletcher, R. S. *Hausa Sayings and Folklore.* Oxford: Oxford University Press, 1912.

Folorunso, C. A. "The Archaeology and Ethnoarchaeology of Soap and Dye-Making at Ijaye, Yorubaland." *African Archaeological Review* 19, no. 3 (2002): 127–45.

Fosu, Kojo. *Emblems of Royalty (Kayan Sarauta).* Zaria, Nigeria: Fine Arts Gallery, Ahmadu Bello University, 1982.

Garba, Abubakr, ed. *State, City, and Society: Processes of Urbanization.* Maiduguri, Nigeria: Centre for Trans-Sahara Studies, 2002.

Gardi, Bernhard. *Boubou, c'est chic: Gewänder aus Mali und anderen Ländern west-afrikas.* Basel: C. Merian, 2000.

Geijer, Agnes. *A History of Textile Art.* London: Pasold Research Fund, 1979.

Gervers, Michael. "Cotton and Cotton Weaving in Meroitic Nubia and Medieval Ethiopia." *Textile History* 21, no. 1 (1990): 13–30.

Gervers, Veronika, ed. *Studies in Textile History: In Memory of Harold B. Burnham.* Toronto: Royal Ontario Museum, 1977.

Gilfoy, Peggy Stoltz. *Patterns of Life: West African Strip-Weaving Traditions.* Washington, D.C.: National Museum of African Art, 1987.

Gittinger, Mattiebelle. *Master Dyers to the World: Technique and Trade in Early Indian Dyed Cotton Textiles.* Washington, D.C.: The Textile Museum, 1982.

Golding, F. D. "The Wild Silkworms of Nigeria." *Farm and Forest* 3 (1942): 35–40.

———. "The Wild Silkworms of the Northern Provinces of Nigeria." *Farm and Forest* 3 (1942): 147–50.

Goody, Esther, ed. *From Craft to Industry.* Cambridge: Cambridge University Press, 1982.

———. "Daboya Weavers: Relations of Production, Dependence, and Reciprocity," in Goody, *From Craft to Industry,* 50–84.

——— and Jack Goody. "The Naked and the Clothed." In *The Cloth of Many Colored Silks: Papers on History and Society Ghanaian and Islamic in Honor of Ivor Wilks,* edited by John Hunwick and Nancy Lawler, 67–89. Evanston, Ill.: Northwestern University Press, 1996.

Gordon, Stewart. *Robes and Honor: The Medieval World of Investiture.* New York: Palgrave, 2001.

Greenberg, Joseph. *The Influence of Islam on a Sudanese Religion.* New York: Augustin, 1946.

———. "Linguistic Evidence for the Influence of the Kanuri on the Hausa." *Journal of African History* 1, no. 2 (1960): 205–12.

———. *Languages of Africa.* Bloomington: Indiana University Press, 1966.

Griffith, F. L. and G. M. Crowfoot. "On the Early Use of Cotton in the Nile Valley." *Journal of Egyptian Archaeology* 20 (1934): 5–12.

Hair, P. E. H. "An Ethnolinguistic Inventory of the Lower Guinea Coast, Part II." *African Language Review* 8 (1969): 225–56.

Hall, Rosalind. *Egyptian Textiles.* Princes Risborough, UK: Shire, 2001.

Haller, R. "Production of Indigo." *CIBA Review* 85 (1951): 3072–75.

———. "The History of Indigo Dyeing." *CIBA Review* 85 (1951): 3077–81.

Hamani, Djibo. "Proto-Hausa et Hausa," in Musée National des Arts d'Afrique et d'Océanie, *Vallées du Niger,* 192–202.

Harms, Robert W., Joseph Miller, David Newbury, and Michele Wagner, eds. *Paths toward the Past: African Historical Essays in Honor of Jan Vansina.* Atlanta, Ga.: African Studies Association Press, 1994.

Harunah, Hakeem B. "Lagos-Abeokuta Relations in 19th Century Yorubaland," in Adefuye, Agiri, and Osuntokun, *History of the Peoples of Lagos,* 195–203.

Heathcote, David. "Some Hausa Lizard Designs." *Embroidery* 23, no. 4 (1972): 114–16.

———. "A Hausa Embroiderer of Katsina." *The Nigerian Field* 37, no. 3 (1972): 123–31.

————. "Hausa Embroidered Dress." *African Arts* 5, no. 2 (1972): 12–19, 82, 84.

————. "Hausa Embroidery Stitches." *The Nigerian Field* 39, no. 4 (1974): 163–69.

————. "Aspects of Style in Hausa Embroidery." *Savanna* 3, no. 1 (1974): 15–40.

————. *Arts of the Hausa*. London: World of Islam Festival Ltd., 1976.

Hendrickson, Hildi, ed. *Clothing and Difference: Embodied Identities in Colonial and Post-colonial Africa*. Durham, N.C.: Duke University Press, 1996.

Henige, David and T. C. McCaskie, eds. *West African Economic and Social History: Studies in Memory of Marion Johnson*. Madison: University of Wisconsin, Madison, African Studies Program, 1990.

Hill, Sarah H. *Weaving New Worlds: Southeastern Cherokee Women and Their Basketry*. Chapel Hill: University of North Carolina Press, 1997.

Hodder, B. W. "The Markets of Ibadan." In *The City of Ibadan*, edited by P. C. Lloyd, A. L. Mabogunje, and B. Awe, 173–90. Cambridge: Cambridge University Press, 1967.

Hodgkin, Thomas, ed. *Nigerian Perspectives*. 2nd ed. Oxford: Oxford University Press, 1975.

Hogendorn, J. S. and H. A. Gemery. "The Hidden Half of the Anglo-African Trade in the Eighteenth Century: The Significance of Marion Johnson's Statistical Research," in Henige and McCaskie, *West African Economic and Social History*, 81–91.

Holy Ghost Fathers. *English, Ibo, and French Dictionary*. Salzburg: Missionary Printing Office of the Sodality of St. Peter Claver, 1904.

Hunwick, John O., trans. and ed. *Timbuktu and the Songhay Empire: Al-Sa'di's Ta'rikh al-Sudan down to 1613, and Other Contemporary Documents*. Leiden: Brill, 1999.

Hutchinson, T. J. *Narrative of the Niger, Tshadda, and Binue Exploration*. London: Longman, Brown, Green, and Longman, 1855.

Idiens, Dale and K. G. Ponting, eds. *Textiles of Africa*. Bath, UK: Pasold Research Fund, 1980.

Ikegwuonu, Richard Nwewueze. *Akwete Traditional Weaving*. BA thesis, University of Nigeria, Nsukka, 1971.

Index Kewensis and supplements. Oxford: Clarendon Press, 1895.

Inikori, Joseph. "Slavery and the Revolution in Cotton Textile Production in England." In *The Atlantic Slave Trade: Effects on Economies, Societies, and Peoples in Africa, the Americas, and Europe*, edited by J. E. Inikori and S. L. Engerman, 145–81. Durham, N.C.: Duke University Press, 1992.

Insoll, Timothy. *The Archaeology of Islam*. Oxford: Blackwell, 1999.

Irwin, John and Margaret Hall. *Indian Painted and Printed Fabrics*. Ahmedabad: Calico Museum for Textiles, 1971.

Irwin, John and P. R. Schwartz. *Studies in Indo-European Textile History*. Ahmedabad: Calico Museum of Textiles, 1966.

Isaacman, Allen and Richard Roberts, eds. *Cotton, Colonialism, and Social History in Sub-Saharan Africa*. Portsmouth, N.H.: Heinemann, 1995.

————. *Cotton Is the Mother of Poverty: Peasants, Work, and Rural Struggle in Colonial Mozambique, 1938–1961*. Portsmouth, N.H.: Heinemann, 1996.

Jackson, George. "The Devolution of the Jubilee Design," in Barbour and Simmonds, *Adire Cloths in Nigeria*, 82–93.

Johnson, Marion. "Calico Caravans: The Tripoli-Kano Trade after 1880." *Journal of African History* 17, no. 1 (1970): 95–117.

———. "Cotton Imperialism in West Africa." *African Affairs* 73 (1974): 178–87.

———. "Cloth Strips and History." *West African Journal of Archaeology* 7 (1977): 169–78.

———. "Technology, Competition and African Crafts." In *The Imperial Impact· Studies in the Economic History of Africa and India*, edited by C. Dewey and A. G. Hopkins, 529–69. London: Athlone Press, 1978.

———. "Cloth as Money: The Cloth Strip Currencies of Africa." *Textile History* 11 (1980): 193–202.

——— (T. J. Lindblad, and Robert Ross, eds.). *Anglo-African Trade in the Eighteenth Century: English Statistics on African Trade 1699–1808*. Leiden: Centre for the History of European Expansion, 1990.

Jones, Adam, trans. and ed. *German Sources for West African History, 1599–1669*. Wiesbaden: Franz Steiner, 1983.

———. "A Collection of African Art in Seventeenth-century Germany." *African Arts* 27, no. 2 (1994): 28–43, 92–94.

———. "Drink Deep, or Taste Not: Thoughts on the Use of Early European Records in the Study of African Material Culture." *History in Africa* 21 (1994): 349–70.

———, trans. and ed. *West Africa in the Mid-Seventeenth Century: An Anonymous Dutch Manuscript*. Atlanta, Ga.: African Studies Association Press, 1995.

———, trans. and ed. *Olfert Dapper's Description of Benin*. Atlanta, Ga.: African Studies Association Press, 1998.

Kamalu, A. E. *Akwete Cloth*. BA thesis, Ahmadu Bello University, Zaria, 1965.

Kati, M. et l'un de ses petit fils. *Tarikh el-fettach*. Translated by O. Houdas and M. Delafosse. Paris: Maisonneuve, 1981.

Kea, Ray. *Settlement, Trade, and Polities in the Seventeenth Century Gold Coast*. Baltimore: Johns Hopkins Press, 1982.

Kent, Kate. *Introducing West African Cloth*. Denver, Colo.: Denver Museum of Natural History, 1971.

Keyes, Carolyn. *Adire: Cloth, Gender, and Social Change in Southwestern Nigeria, 1841–1991*. PhD diss., University of Wisconsin, Madison, 1993.

Koelle, Sigismund W. *African Native Literature: Or, Proverbs, Tales, Fables, and Historical Fragments in the Kanuri or Bornu Language*. 1854. Reprint, Freeport, N.Y.: Books for Libraries Press, 1970.

Kriger, Colleen. *Garments of the Sokoto Caliphate: A Case Study from the Banfield Collection, Royal Ontario Museum, Toronto*. MA thesis, York University, Canada, 1985.

———. "Nineteenth Century Textiles from the Niger Basin Region." Paper, York University Department of History, 1986.

———. "Robes of the Sokoto Caliphate." *African Arts* 21 (1988): 52–57, 78–79, 85–86.

———. "Textile Production in the Lower Niger Basin: New Evidence from the 1841 Niger Expedition Collection." *Textile History* 21, no. 1 (1990): 31–56.

———. "Textile Production and Gender in the Sokoto Caliphate." *Journal of African History* 34 (1993): 361–401.

————. Review of *African Material Culture*, in *Technology and Culture* (January 1998): 142–44.

Kroese, W. T. *De oorsprong van de wasdruk textiel op de kust van West Afrika.* Enschede: Stichting Textielgeschiedenis, 1976.

————. *The Origin of the Wax Block Prints on the Coast of West Africa.* Hengelo: NV Uitgeverij Smit van 1876, 1976.

Küller, Paul. *Wilde Seiden Afrikas.* Berlin: Radetzki, 1913.

Labat, J. B. *Nouvelle relation de l'Afrique Occidentale.* 5 vols. Paris: G. Cavelier, 1728.

Lamb, Venice. *West African Weaving.* London: Duckworth Press, 1975.

———— and Alastair Lamb. "The Classification and Distribution of Horizontal Treadle Looms in Sub-Saharan Africa," in Idiens and Ponting, *Textiles of Africa,* 22–62.

———— and Judy Holmes. *Nigerian Weaving.* Hertingfordbury, UK: Roxford Books, 1980.

Lamm, Carl Johan. *Cotton in Medieval Textiles of the Near East.* Paris: Librairie Orientaliste Paul Geuthner, 1937.

Lander, Richard and John Lander. *Journal of an Expedition to Explore the Course and Termination of the Niger.* 2 vols. New York: J. and J. Harper, 1832.

Landeroin, M. and J. Tilho. *Dictionnaire Haoussa.* Paris: Imprimerie Nationale, 1910.

Landolphe, J. F. *Mémoires du Capitaine Landolphe contenant l'histoire de ses voyages pendant 36 ans, au côtes d'Afrique et aux deux Amériques.* 2 vols. Paris: J.S. Quesne, 1823.

Larymore, Constance. *A Resident's Wife in Nigeria.* London: Routledge, 1911.

Last, Murray. *The Sokoto Caliphate.* New York: Humanities Press, 1967.

Law, Robin. *The Horse in West African History.* Oxford: Oxford University Press, 1980.

————. "Trade and Politics behind the Slave Coast: The Lagoon Traffic and the Rise of Lagos, 1500–1800." *Journal of African History* 24 (1983): 321–48.

————. "King Agaja of Dahomey, the Slave Trade, and the Question of West African Plantations: The Embassy of Bulfinch Lambe and Adomo Tomo to England, 1726–32." *Journal of Imperial and Commonwealth History* 19 (1991): 137–63.

————. *The Slave Coast of West Africa, 1550–1750: The Impact of the Atlantic Slave Trade on an African Society.* Oxford: Clarendon, 1991.

————, ed. *Correspondence of the Royal African Company's Chief Merchants at Cabo Corso Castle with William's Fort, Whydah, and the Little Popo Factory, 1727–1728.* Madison: University of Wisconsin, Madison, African Studies Program, 1991.

————, ed. *Further Correspondence of the Royal African Company of England Relating to the "Slave Coast," 1681–1699.* Madison: University of Wisconsin, Madison, African Studies Program, 1992.

————. *From Slave Trade to "Legitimate" Commerce: The Commercial Transition in Nineteenth-century West Africa.* Cambridge: Cambridge University Press, 1995.

————, ed. *The English in West Africa, 1681–1683: The Local Correspondence of the Royal African Company of England, 1681–1699, Part I.* Oxford: Oxford University Press, 1997.

Levtzion, Nehemia and J. F. P. Hopkins, eds. *Corpus of Early Arabic Sources for West African History.* Cambridge: Cambridge University Press, 1981.

————. "Islam in Africa to 1800." In *The Oxford History of Islam,* edited by John Esposito, 475–507. Oxford: Oxford University Press, 1999.

Likaka, Osumaka. *Rural Society and Cotton in Colonial Zaire.* Madison: University of Wisconsin Press, 1997.

Lloyd, P. C., A. L. Mabogunje, and B. Awe, eds. *The City of Ibadan.* Cambridge: Cambridge University Press, 1967.

Losi, John B., trans. and ed. *History of Lagos.* 1914. Lagos: African Education Press, 1967.

Lovejoy, Paul. "Plantations in the Economy of the Sokoto Caliphate." *Journal of African History* 19, no. 3 (1978): 341–68.

———. *Caravans of Kola: The Hausa Kola Trade, 1700–1900.* Zaria, Nigeria: Ahmadu Bello University Press, 1980.

———. *Salt of the Desert Sun: A History of Salt Production and Trade in the Central Sudan.* Cambridge: Cambridge University Press, 1986.

———, ed. *Identity in the Shadow of Slavery.* London: Continuum, 2000.

Lynn, Martin. *Commerce and Economic Change in West Africa. The Palm Oil Trade in the Nineteenth Century.* Cambridge: Cambridge University Press, 1997.

MacDonald, Kevin C. "More Forgotten Tells of Mali: An Archaeologist's Journey from Here to Timbuktu." *Archaeology International* 1 (1997–1998): 40–42.

Magnavita, S., M. Hallier, C. Pelzer, S. Kahlheber, and V. Linseele. "Nobles, guerriers, paysans: Une nécropole de l'Age de Fer et son emplacement dans l'Oudalan pré- et protohistorique." *Beiträge zur Allgemeinen und Vergleichenden Archäologie* 22 (2002): 21–64.

Maier, Donna J. E. "Persistence of Precolonial Patterns of Production: Cotton in German Togoland, 1800–1914." In *Cotton, Colonialism, and Social History in Sub-Saharan Africa,* edited by A. Isaacman and R. Roberts. Portsmouth, N.H.: Heinemann, 1995.

Makepeace, Margaret, ed. *Trade on the Guinea Coast, 1657–1666.* Madison: University of Wisconsin Press, 1991.

Manning, Patrick. *Slavery and African Life: Occidental, Oriental, and African Slave Trades.* Cambridge: Cambridge University Press, 1990.

Martin, Phyllis. "Power, Cloth, and Currency on the Loango Coast." *African Economic History* 15 (1986): 1–12.

Martin, Susan. *Palm Oil and Protest: An Economic History of the Ngwaa Region, Southeastern Nigeria, 1800–1980.* Cambridge: Cambridge University Press, 1988.

———. "Slaves, Igbo Women and Palm Oil in the Nineteenth Century." In *From Slave Trade to "Legitimate Commerce,"* edited by R. Law, 172–94. Cambridge: Cambridge University Press, 1995.

Mason, Michael. *Foundations of the Bida Kingdom.* Zaria, Nigeria: Ahmadu Bello University Press, 1981.

Masquelier, Adeline. "Mediating Threads: Clothing and the Texture of Spirit/Medium Relations in Bori (Southern Niger)." In *Clothing and Difference: Embodied Identities in Colonial and Post-colonial Africa,* edited by Hildi Hendrickson, 66–93. Durham, N.C.: Duke University Press, 1996.

Mato, Daniel. *Clothed in Symbol: The Art of Adinkra among the Akan of Ghana.* PhD diss., Indiana University, 1986.

Mazzaoui, Maureen. *The Italian Cotton Industry in the Later Middle Ages, 1100–1600.* Cambridge: Cambridge University Press, 1981.

————, ed. *Textiles: Production, Trade and Demand.* Aldershot, UK: Ashgate, 1998.

McCusker, John and Kenneth Morgan, eds. *The Early Modern Atlantic Economy.* Cambridge: Cambridge University Press, 2000.

McIntosh, Susan Keech and Roderick J. McIntosh. "Cities without Citadels: Understanding Urban Origins along the Middle Niger," in Shaw et al., *The Archaeology of Africa*, 622–41.

————, ed. *Excavations at Jenné-Jeno, Hambarketolo, and Kaniana (Inland Niger Delta, Mali): The 1981 Season.* Berkeley: University of California Press, 1995.

Melzian, Hans. *A Concise Dictionary of the Bini Language of Southern Nigeria.* London: Kegan Paul, 1937.

Menzel, Brigitte. *Textilien aus Westafrika.* 3 vols. Berlin: Museum für Völkerkunde, 1972–1974.

Metcalf, George. "A Microcosm of Why Africans Sold Slaves: Akan Consumption Patterns in the 1770s." *Journal of African History* 28, no. 3 (1987): 377–94.

Mischlich, Adam. *Wörterbuch der Hausasprache.* Berlin: Georg Reimer, 1906.

————. *Uber die Kulturen im mittel-Sudan.* Berlin: Dietrich Reimer, 1942.

Monteil, Charles. *Le coton chez les Noirs.* Paris: Librairie Emile Larose, 1927.

Moraes Farias, P. F. de, and Karin Barber, eds. *Self-Assertion and Brokerage: Early Cultural Nationalism in West Africa.* Birmingham, UK: Centre of West African Studies, Birmingham University, 1990.

Morgan, Kenneth, ed. *The British Trans-Atlantic Slave Trade.* 4 vols. London: Pickering and Chatto, 2003.

Murphy, Veronica and Rosemary Crill. *Tie-Dyed Textiles of India: Tradition and Trade.* New York: Rizzoli, 1991.

Murray, K. C. "Women's Weaving among the Yorubas at Omu-aran in Ilorin Province." *Nigerian Field* 5 (1936): 182–91.

————. "Tiv Pattern Dyeing." *Nigeria Magazine* 32 (1949): 41–46.

Murray, Shawn S. "Medieval Cotton and Wheat Finds in the Middle Niger Delta (Mali)." Poster presented at the Fourth International Workshop of African Archaeobotany, Groningen, NL, 30 June–2 July 2003.

————. "The Archaeobotanical Research." In *Recherches Archéologiques à Dia dans le delta intérieur du Niger, Mali: Bilan des saisons de fouilles 1998–2003,* edited by R. M. A. Bedaux, J. Polet, K. Sanogo, and A. Schmidt. Leiden, NL: Rijksmuseum voor Volkenkunde, forthcoming.

Musée National des Arts d'Afrique et d'Océanie. *Vallées du Niger.* Paris: Réunion des Musées Nationaux, 1993.

Musée Royal de l'Afrique Centrale. *Des fils de l'émir de Gombe* (Nigeria). Postcard, M.R.A.C., Tervuren, Belgium, 1972.

Museum voor Land- en Volkenkunde, Rotterdam. *Een Adinkra doek van de Goudkust in het Museum voor Land en Volkenkunde te Rotterdam.* Rotterdam: Gemeente-Drukkerij, 1954.

Nachtigal, Gustav. *Sahara and Sudan.* 1879. Translated and edited by Allan G. B. Fisher and Humphrey J. Fisher, with Rex S. O'Fahey, 4 vols. New York: Barnes and Noble, 1971–1984.

Nadel, S. *A Black Byzantium: The Kingdom of Nupe in Nigeria.* London: Oxford University Press, 1951.

National Museum of African Art. *History, Design, and Craft in West African Strip-Woven Cloth*. Washington, D.C., 1992.

———. *Adire: Resist-Dyed Cloths of the Yoruba*. Washington, D.C., 1997.

Nicolaisen, Johannes and Ida Nicolaisen. *The Pastoral Tuareg: Ecology, Culture, and Society*. 2 vols. London: Thames and Hudson, 1997.

Norris, Robert. *Memoirs of the Reign of Bossa Ahadee*. 1789. Reprint, London: Frank Cass, 1968.

Obayemi, Ade. "The Evolution of the Culture and Institutions of the Northern Yoruba, the Nupe and the Igala, before A.D. 1800." *Image: Quarterly Journal of the Kwara State Council for Arts and Culture* 1, no. 2 (1974): 5–9.

———. "Cultural Evolution of Northern Yoruba, Nupe and Igala. Part II, before A.D. 1800." *Image: Quarterly Journal of the Kwara State Council for Arts and Culture* 2, no. 1 (1976): 24–37.

———. "The Yoruba and Edo-Speaking Peoples and Their Neighbors before 1600," in Ajayi and Crowder, *History of West Africa*, 1:196–263.

———. "Archaeology and the History of Western Hausaland: An Introductory Contribution." *Fourth Interim Report, Northern History Research Scheme*, 72–82. Zaria, Nigeria: Ahmadu Bello University, 1977.

———. "An Archaeological Mission to Akpaa." *Confluence* 1, no. 1 (1978): 60–67.

———. "Cultural Dynamics and History of the Niger-Benue Confluence Area before 1900." *Kiabàrà* 4, no. 2 (1981): 41–50.

———. "History, Culture, Yoruba and Northern Factors." In *Studies in Yoruba History and Culture: Essays in Honour of Professor S. O. Biobaku*, edited by G. O. Olusanya, 72–87. Ibadan: University Press, 1983.

Ogundiran, Akinwumi. "Filling a Gap in the Ife-Benin Interaction Field." *African Archaeological Review* 19, no. 1 (2002): 27–60.

O'Hear, Ann. *The Economic History of Ilorin in the Nineteenth and Twentieth Centuries: The Rise and Decline of a Middleman Society*. PhD diss., University of Birmingham, 1983.

———. "The Introduction of Weft Float Motifs to Strip Weaving in Ilorin," in Henige and McCaskie, *West African Economic and Social History*, 175–88.

———. "The Yoruba and the Peoples of the Niger-Benue Confluence." In *Yoruba Frontiers*, edited by F. Afolayan and T. Falola, forthcoming.

Ohiare, J. A. "Textile Production in the Ebira-Speaking Region: An Aspect of its Technological Development from the 19th Century to Date." In *Archaeology and Society: Proceedings of the 8th Annual Conference of the Archaeological Association of Nigeria*, Minna, June 25–July 1, 1989, edited by J. F. Jemkur and A. D. Igirgi, 50–60. Zaria, Nigeria: Archaeological Association of Nigeria, 1989.

Olukoju, Ayodeji. "The Politics of Free Trade between Lagos and the Hinterland 1861–1907," in Adefuye, Agiri, and Osuntokun, *History of the Peoples of Lagos State*: 85–103.

Oyelaran, Philip. "Early Settlement and Archaeological Sequence of Northeast Yorubaland." *African Archaeological Review* 15, no. 1 (1998): 65–71.

Pacheco Pereira, Duarte. *Esmeraldo de situ orbis*. Translated and edited by George H. T. Kimble. London: Hakluyt Society, 1937.

Paris, François. "Les sépultures monumentales d'Iwelen (Niger)." *Journal des Africanistes* 60, no. 1 (1990): 47–74.

Park, Mungo. *Travels in the Interior Districts of Africa*. Durham, N.C.: Duke University Press, 2000.

Perani, Judith. *Nupe Crafts: The Dynamics of Change in Nineteenth and Twentieth Century Weaving and Brasscasting*. PhD diss., Indiana University, 1988.

———. "Northern Nigerian Prestige Textiles: Production, Trade, Patronage, and Use," in Engelbrecht and Gardi, *Man Does Not Go Naked*, 65–80.

Perani, Judith and Norma Wolff. "Embroidered Gown and Equestrian Ensembles of the Kano Aristocracy." *African Arts* 25, no. 3 (1992): 70–81, 102–4.

———. *Cloth, Dress and Art Patronage in Africa*. Oxford: Berg Press, 1999.

Petrie, Carl. "Robing Ceremonials in Late Mamluk Egypt: Hallowed Traditions, Shifting Protocols." In *Robes and Honor: The Medieval World of Investiture*, edited by Stewart Gordon, 353–77. New York: Palgrave, 2001.

Pettit, Florence H. *America's Indigo Blues: Resist-Printed and Dyed Textiles of the Eighteenth Century*. New York: Hastings House, 1974.

Pfister, R. *Les toiles imprimées de Fostat et l'Hindoustan* Paris: Les Editions d'Art et d'Histoire, 1938.

Picton, John. "Women's Weaving: The Manufacture and Use of Textiles among the Igbirra People of Nigeria." *Textile History* 11 (1980): 63–88.

———, ed. *The Art of African Textiles: Technology, Tradition, and Lurex*. London: Barbican Art Gallery, 1995.

Picton, John and John Mack. *African Textiles*. London: British Museum, 1979.

Pitt-Rivers, Augustus. *Antique Works of Art From Benin*. New York: Dover Publications, 1976.

Pitts, Delia Carol. *An Economic and Social History of Cloth Production in Senegambia*. PhD diss., University of Chicago, 1978.

Porcher, Michel et al. *Sorting Gossypium Names: Multilingual Multiscript Plant Name Database—A Work in Progress*. Melbourne: University of Melbourne Institute for Land and Food Resources, 2004. www.plantnames.unimelb.edu.au/Sorting/Gossypium.html (last accessed 24 September 2005).

Posnansky, Merrick and Christopher Ehret, eds. *The Archaeological and Linguistic Reconstruction of African History*. Berkeley: University of California Press, 1982.

Poynor, Robin. "Traditional Textiles in Owo, Nigeria." *African Arts* 14, no. 1 (1980): 48–51, 88.

Prussin, Labelle. *Hatumere: Islamic Design in West Africa*. Berkeley: University of California Press, 1986.

Quarcoo, A. K. *The Language of Adinkra Patterns*. Legon: Institute of African Studies, University of Ghana, 1972.

Rabine, Leslie W. *The Global Circulation of African Fashion*. Oxford: Berg Press, 2002.

Ramaswamy, Vijaya. *Textiles and Weavers in Medieval South India*. Delhi: Oxford University Press, 1985.

Rattray, R. S. *Religion and Art in Ashanti*. Oxford: Clarendon, 1927.

Reikat, Andrea. *Handelstoffe: Grundzüge des Europäisch-Westafrikanischen Handels vor der industriellen Revolution am Beispiel der Textilien*. Cologne: Köppe, 1997.

Renne, Elisha. "The Decline of Women's Weaving among the Northeast Yoruba." Paper presented at the annual meeting of the African Studies Association, Chicago, 28–31 October 1988.

————. "Aso Ipo, Red Cloth from Bunu." *African Arts* 25, no. 3 (1992): 64–69, 102.

————. *Cloth That Does Not Die: The Meaning of Cloth in Bùnú Social Life.* Seattle: University of Washington Press, 1995.

Richardson, David. "West African Consumption Patterns and Their Influence on the Eighteenth-century English Slave Trade." In *The Uncommon Market: Essays in the Economic History of the Atlantic Slave Trade*, edited by Henry Gemery and Jan Hogendorn, 303–30. New York: Academic Press, 1979.

Roberts, Richard. "Guinée Cloth: Linked Transformations within France's Empire in the Nineteenth Century." *Cahiers d'Etudes Africaines* 32, no. 4 (1992): 597–627.

————. *Two Worlds of Cotton: Colonialism and the Regional Economy in the French Soudan, 1800–1946.* Stanford, Calif.: Stanford University Press, 1996.

Robertson, G. A. *Notes on Africa, Particularly Those Parts Which Are Situated between Cape Verd and the River Congo.* London: Sherwood, Neely, and Jones, 1819.

Robinson, Charles. *Dictionary of the Hausa Language.* Cambridge: Cambridge University Press, 1913.

Robinson, Stuart. *A History of Printed Textiles.* Cambridge, Mass.: Massachusetts Institute of Technology Press, 1969.

Rodney, Walter. *A History of the Upper Guinea Coast 1545–1800.* Oxford: Clarendon Press, 1970.

Rømer, Ludewig Ferdinand. *A Reliable Account of the Coast of Guinea (1760).* Translated and edited by Selena A. Winsnes. Oxford: Oxford University Press, 2000.

Ryder, A. F. C. *Benin and the Europeans, 1485–1897.* New York: Humanities Press, 1969.

Schaedler, Karl-Ferdinand. *Weaving in Africa South of the Sahara.* Munich: Panterra Verlag, 1987.

Schneider, Jane. "Rumpelstiltskin's Bargain: Folklore and Merchant Capitalist Intensification of Linen Manufacture in Early Modern Europe." In *Cloth and Human Experience*, edited by Annette Weiner and Jane Schneider, 177–213. Washington, D.C.: Smithsonian Institution, 1991.

Schön, James F. *Dictionary of the Hausa Language.* 1876. Reprint, Farnborough: Gregg, 1968.

Serjeant, R. B. *Islamic Textiles.* Beirut: Librairie du Liban, 1972.

Shaw, Thurstan. *Igbo-Ukwu. An Account of Archaeological Discoveries in Eastern Nigeria.* 2 vols. Evanston, Ill.: Northwestern University Press, 1970.

————. *Nigeria: Its Archaeology and Early History.* London: Thames and Hudson, 1978.

————. "The Nok Sculptures of Nigeria." *Scientific American* 244 (1981): 154–66.

————, Paul Sinclair, Bassey Andah, and Alex Okpoko, eds. *The Archaeology of Africa: Food, Metals, and Towns.* London: Routledge, 1993.

Shea, Philip. *Collection of Notes on Interviews Concerned with the History of Production of Indigo Dyed Cloth in Kano Emirate, Nigeria.* Manuscript, 1970–1971.

————. *The Development of an Export-Oriented Dyed Cloth Industry in Kano Emirate in the Nineteenth Century.* PhD diss., University of Wisconsin, Madison, 1975.

————. "Kano and the Silk Trade." *Kano Studies* 2, no. 1 (1980): 96–112.

Shinnie, Peter. *Meroë: A Civilization of the Sudan.* New York: Praeger, 1967.

Sieber, Roy. *African Textiles and Decorative Arts*. New York: Museum of Modern Art, 1972.

Smith, Abdullahi. "The Early States of the Central Sudan," in Ajayi and Crowder, *History of West Africa*, 1:152–95.

Southern, A. E. "Cloth Making in Nigeria." *Nigeria Magazine* 32 (1949): 35–40.

Staatliches Museum für Völkerkunde, Munich. Accession documentation and photographs, Leo Frobenius Collection, 1915.

Stanfield, Nancy. "Dyeing Methods in Western Nigeria," in Barbour and Simmonds, *Adire Cloths in Nigeria*, 7–42.

Steiner, Christopher. "Another Image of Africa: Toward an Ethnohistory of European Cloth Marketed in West Africa, 1873–1960." *Ethnohistory* 32, no. 2 (1985): 91–110.

Stillman, Yedida Kalfon. *Arab Dress: A Short History, from the Dawn of Islam to Modern Times*. Leiden: Brill, 2000.

Sundström, Lars. *The Exchange Economy of Pre-colonial Tropical Africa*. New York: St. Martin's Press, 1974. Reprint of *The Trade of Guinea*, 1965.

Suny, Ronald Grigor et al. "Review Essays on *Beyond the Cultural Turn*." *American Historical Review* 107, no. 5 (December 2002): 1475–520.

Thomas, Northcote Whitridge. *Anthropological Report on the Ibo-speaking Peoples of Nigeria*. 1913. Reprint, New York: Negro Universities Press, 1969.

Thurman, Christa C. M. and Bruce Williams. *Ancient Textiles from Nubia*. Chicago: Art Institute of Chicago, 1979.

Trigger, Bruce. "The Myth of Meroë and the African Iron Age." *African Historical Studies* 2, no. 1 (1969): 23–50.

———. *A History of Archaeological Thought*. Cambridge: Cambridge University Press, 1989.

Ukeje, L. O. "Weaving in Akwete." *Nigeria Magazine* 74 (1962): 32–41.

Ulrich, Laurel Thatcher. *The Age of Homespun: Objects and Stories in the Creation of an American Myth*. New York: Knopf, 2001.

University of Minnesota. *West African Textiles and Garments*. Minneapolis, 1980.

Usher, George. *A Dictionary of Plants Used by Man*. London: Constable, 1974.

Usman, Aribidesi Adisa. *Cloth-Weaving Technology in Ilorin*. BA thesis, University of Ibadan, Nigeria, 1985.

———. *State-Periphery Relations and Sociopolitical Development in Igbominaland, North-Central Yoruba, Nigeria: Oral-Ethnohistorical and Archaeological Perspectives*. Oxford: Archaeopress, 2001.

Van Danzig, Albert. *The Dutch and the Guinea Coast 1674–1742: A Collection of Documents from the General State Archive at The Hague*. Accra: Ghana Academy of Arts and Sciences, 1978.

van Nyendael, David. "A Description of Rio Formosa, or, the River of Benin," in Bosman, *A New and Accurate Description*.

Vansina, Jan. *Oral Tradition as History*. Madison: University of Wisconsin Press, 1985.

———. "Raffia Cloth in West Central Africa, 1500–1800," in Mazzaoui, *Textiles: Production, Trade, and Demand*, 263–81.

Vetterli, W. A. "The History of Indigo." *CIBA Review* 15 (1951): 3066–71.

Wakeman, C. W. *Dictionary of Yoruba Language*. Lagos: Church Missionary Society, 1913.

Walz, Terence. *Trade between Egypt and Bilad as-Sudan.* Cairo: Institut Français d'Archéologie Orientale, 1978.

Washburn, Dorothy and Donald Crowe. *Symmetries of Culture: Theory and Practice of Plane Pattern Analysis.* Seattle: University of Washington Press, 1988.

———, eds. *Symmetry Comes of Age: The Role of Pattern in Culture.* Seattle: University of Washington Press, 2004.

Wass, Betty. *Yoruba Dress: A Systematic Case Study of Five Generations of a Lagos Family.* PhD diss., Michigan State University, 1975.

———. "Yoruba Dress in Five Generations of a Lagos Family." In *The Fabrics of Culture*, edited by Justine Cordwell and Ronald Schwarz, 331–48. The Hague: Mouton, 1979.

Watson, Andrew. "The Rise and Spread of Old World Cotton." In *Studies in Textile History: In Memory of Harold B. Burnham*, edited by Veronika Gervers, 355–68. Toronto: Royal Ontario Museum, 1977.

———. *Agricultural Innovation in the Early Islamic World: The Diffusion of Crops and Farming Techniques, 700–1100.* Cambridge: Cambridge University Press, 1983.

Weiner, Annette and Jane Schneider, eds. *Cloth and Human Experience.* Washington, D.C.: Smithsonian Institution, 1989.

Wenger, S. and H. Ulli Beier. "Adire-Yoruba Pattern Dyeing." *Nigeria Magazine* 54 (1957): 208–55.

Willett, Frank. *Ife in the History of West African Sculpture.* New York: Thames and Hudson, 1967.

Zaslavsky, Claudia. *Africa Counts: Number and Pattern in African Culture.* 1973. Reprint, Westport, Conn.: Lawrence Hill, 1979.

TEXTILE COLLECTIONS

Baikie Collection, Kew Museum, Royal Botanic Garden at Kew, England.

Banfield Collection, Royal Ontario Museum, Toronto, Canada.

Dallimore Collection, Kew Museum, Royal Botanic Garden at Kew, England.

Di Cardi Collection, Museum for Textiles, Toronto, Canada.

Dundas Collection, Royal Museum of Scotland, Edinburgh, Scotland.

Frobenius Collection, Staatliches Museum für Völkerkunde, Munich, Germany.

Kriger Collection, UCLA Fowler Museum of Cultural History, Los Angeles, California, USA.

Murphy Collection, Phoebe A. Hearst Museum of Anthropology, Berkeley, California, USA.

Niger Expedition (1841) Collection, Ethnology, British Museum, London, England.

Ross Collection, Kew Museum, Royal Botanic Garden at Kew, England.

Stanger Collection, Wisbech and Fenland Museum, Wisbech, England.

Weickmann Collection, Ulmer Museum, Ulm, Germany.

Index

Note: Page numbers referring to figures, tables, or maps are italicized.

Abeokuta, *xxii*; founding of, 134; resist dyeing, 148–49, 151, 162–64
Accra, *xx*, 141, 142
adinkra cloth, 158–60, *160*
Air, *xxi*, 79–80
Akoko, *xx*, 42
Akwete, *xxii*. *See also* textile products, lower Niger region: Akwete cloth
Allada, *xx*; dress, 37; dyeing, 133, 144; prices of Allada cloth, *41*; robes collected in, 135–39, *136*, 143; textile production, 40, 41, 133
animal fiber, 9, 11, 74. *See also* silk; wool
Arabic written accounts, 4, 79; description of cloth strip currency, 26, 74–75, 82, 83; description of West African dress, 74–75, 92–93
Arbo, *xx*, 41
archaeological evidence, xiv–xvi, 3, 6, 7, 16n3, 17n16, 120; brocading, 31, *31*; cotton, 74, 75–76; cotton textiles, 74, 76–77, *77*, 131; dress, 31–32, 71; embroidery, 73; spinning, 11, 28–29, 75–76, 78; tailored garments, 73, 77,

77, 93; weaving, 28–29, 30–31, *32*, 73; wool, 73, 74, 77, *77*
archaeological sites, *xix*; Begho, 76; Benin City, xiv–xv, 28, 31, *32*, 54, 79; Bono Manso, 76; Bura, 167n48; Daima, 75; Dia, 76; Fostat (old Cairo), 90; Igbo-Ukwu, 28, 30–31, 54, 62n16, 62n24; Iwelen, 73; Kissi (in Burkina Faso), xvi, 73; Nok, 71; Ogo, 75; Sanga, 76
archaeology, historical, 7
artisans, 4–15; Quranic scholars as, 26, 86, 95, 97
artisans, specialization, 137; in dyeing, 119, 140, 150–51; in embroidery, 97, 99–100, 104–5; in potash production, 127–28; in resist patterning, 119, 150–51, 158; in spinning, 9–10, 69, 90–92; in tailoring, 97–99; in weaving, 33–34, 40, 51, 58, 87–88
artisans' occupations. *See* dyeing; embroidery; spinning; tailoring; weaving
artisans' strategies, 4–5, 14; in embroidery, 105; in men's dyeing, 130; in men's resist patterning,

About the Author

Colleen E. Kriger has studied handcrafted textiles and textile technology for many years as both a practitioner and a scholar. She earned her BA in Fine Art at the School of Fine and Performance Art at Portland State University, Portland, Oregon, and worked as a textile consultant and weaver on a project to restore Timberline Lodge, a National Historic Landmark, in the 1970s. During that time she also showed her artwork in museum and gallery exhibitions in the northwest and was a member of Blackfish Gallery in Portland.

She began her graduate studies in 1982 at York University where she completed her MA in 1984 and her PhD in African history in 1992. She then spent a year of postdoctoral study with Jan Vansina at the University of Wisconsin, Madison. Her scholarship centers on artisans and their labor in precolonial Africa, and specifically, on textile production in the Sokoto Caliphate (now Nigeria) and ironworking in the Congo basin. These case studies have spelled out more precisely the ways in which indigenous manufacturing has over the centuries been crucial to the economies and societies of Africa. Her first book, *Pride of Men: Ironworking in Nineteenth Century West Central Africa*, was published in 1999 as part of the Social History of Africa Series. She has also published articles in the *Journal of African History*, *African Arts*, *Textile History*, the *Encyclopedia of Fashion and Clothing*, and the *Oxford Encyclopedia of Economic History*. She is currently associate professor of history at the University of North Carolina, Greensboro, and was the 2005 recipient of the UNC Board of Governors Teaching Excellence Award.

Dr. Kriger has received a number of prestigious grants for her research, including a Fulbright-Hays Fellowship, and she has enjoyed support from the Pasold Research Fund, the Social Science Research Council, Fondation Dapper (Paris), the American Philosophical Society, the Queen Elizabeth II Ontario Scholarship, the Social Sciences and Humanities Research Council of Canada, and the Zdenka Volavka Postdoctoral Research Fellowship.